Masterworks of God

Essays in Liturgical Theory and Practice

M. Francis Mannion

HillenbrandBooks

Chicago / Mundelein, Illinois

MASTERWORKS OF GOD: ESSAYS IN LITURGICAL THEORY AND PRACTICE
© 2004 Archdiocese of Chicago: Liturgy Training Publications, 1800 North Hermitage Avenue, Chicago IL 60622-1101; 1-800-933-1800, fax 1-800-933-7094, e-mail orders@ltp.org. All rights reserved. See our website at www.ltp.org.

Hillenbrand Books is an imprint of Liturgy Training Publications (LTP) and the Liturgical Institute / University of St. Mary of the Lake. The Hillenbrand Series is focused on contemporary theological thought concerning the liturgy of the Catholic Church. Further information about **Hillenbrand Books** is available from LTP or from www.usml.edu/liturgical institute; phone: 847-837-4542. University of St. Mary of the Lake/Mundelein Seminary, 1000 East Maple, Mundelein IL 60060.

Cover photograph: Dennis Mecham Photography

Printed in the United States of America.

Library of Congress Control Number: 2003113216

ISBN: 1-56854-511-8

HMOG

Contents

Preface v

Introduction
The Masterworks of God: The Liturgical Theology
of the Catechism of the Catholic Church 1

Part I: Liturgical Systems
   Chapter 1: Penance and Reconciliation: A Systemic Analysis 22
   Chapter 2: Mass Stipends and Eucharistic Praxis 42
   Chapter 3: Catholic Worship and the Dynamics
         of Congregationalism 65

Part II: Liturgy and Culture
   Chapter 4: Liturgy and the Present Crisis of Culture 76
   Chapter 5: Sunday in Modern America: A Cultural Perspective 102

Part III: The Arts and Liturgy
   Chapter 6: Paradigms in American Catholic Liturgical Music 116
   Chapter 7: Toward a New Era in Liturgical Architecture 144
   Chapter 8: The "Musification" of the Word: Cardinal Ratzinger's
         Theology of Liturgical Music 176

Part IV: The Liturgical Future
   Chapter 9: The Catholicity of the Liturgy:
         Shaping a New Agenda 202
   Chapter 10: Rejoice, Heavenly Powers! The Renewal
         of Liturgical Doxology 236

Acknowledgments 264

Msgr. Reynold Hillenbrand
1904-1979

Monsignor Reynold Hillenbrand, ordained a priest by Cardinal George Mundelein in 1929, was Rector of St. Mary of the Lake Seminary from 1936 to 1944.

He was a leading figure in the liturgical and social action movement in the United States during the 1930s and worked to promote active, intelligent, and informed participation in the Church's liturgy.

He believed that a reconstruction of society would occur as a result of the renewal of the Christian spirit, whose source and center is the liturgy.

Hillenbrand taught that, since the ultimate purpose of Catholic action is to Christianize society, the renewal of the liturgy must undoubtedly play the key role in achieving this goal.

Hillenbrand Books strives to reflect the spirit of Monsignor Reynold Hillenbrand's pioneering work by making available innovative and scholarly resources that advance the liturgical and sacramental life of the Church.

Preface

This book brings together a collection of essays written and published over nearly two decades, which some have found useful in undergraduate, graduate, and continuing education courses. While the essays originated in different contexts and were addressed to diverse audiences, it is hoped that together they will exhibit an acceptable degree of consistency. Though they have been edited somewhat for style as well as corrected for earlier errors, only a limited attempt has been made to avoid the repetition that inevitably accompanies a project of this kind.

Attempting to impose a single theme on this collection would produce an artificial result. It is more realistic to recognize that there are four thematic clusters in the book. "The Masterworks of God: The Liturgical Theology of the Catechism of the Catholic Church" serves both as a title essay and introduction to the book. While many are critical of the liturgical theology of the Catechism, I take the view that the section of the Catechism that deals with the worship life of the church is rich in content and serves well the task of bringing together and synthesizing the best of Catholic tradition and the most valuable insights and concerns of the Second Vatican Council.

The first thematic cluster, entitled Liturgical Systems, expresses the conviction that many problems in liturgical theory and practice are fundamentally systemic. By this I mean that when one or more of the elements that make up a liturgical structure become displaced, then the whole system malfunctions. The solution to such problems is found not only in analysis of the particular structure, but also in the manner in which all the elements cooperate and interact synergistically.

The essay entitled "Penance and Reconciliation: A Systemic Analysis" examines the church's baptismal theology and practice as the basis for a differentiated and stable understanding of the church's postbaptismal rites of penance and reconciliation. The essay proposes that penance and reconciliation represent two quite distinct processes in the church's postbaptismal life and practice. Particular issues surveyed in this context include the crisis in sacramental confession, the first penance of children, and general absolution.

The next essay, "Mass Stipends and Eucharistic Praxis," seeks to analyze the evolution in the church's use of monetary transactions within the eucharist from an early New Testament praxis of inclusion to the later medieval praxis based on ecclesial privilege. The essay does not suggest, nevertheless, that the Mass stipend system be abolished, but that it be renewed. At the heart of a renewed theology and practice of Mass stipends is the Pauline model in which gifts and money are brought to the eucharist, collected ritually, and distributed out of the bounty of the church.

The fundamental and irreducible elements that go to make up the church's eucharist are reviewed in "Catholic Worship and the Dynamics of Congregationalism." Within Catholicism in recent decades there has been considerable discussion of the questions, Who celebrates the eucharist? What does it mean to say that the priest presides over the eucharist? What does it mean to say that the eucharist is a celebration? This essay proposes that in order to be faithful to Catholic orthodoxy, three irreducible elements must cooperate synergistically: the liturgical rite, the congregation, and the ordained ministry.

The second thematic cluster is entitled Liturgy and Culture. The relationship between liturgy and culture continues to be one of the most complex and challenging issues for the church as it seeks to advance the program of reform established by the Second Vatican Council. Most writing on this subject deals with the matter of the necessity of the reconfiguration of the church's liturgical rites in multicultural context. The two essays on this topic here look in a more limited way at the impediments to liturgy offered by modern North American culture.

The essay titled "Liturgy and the Present Crisis of Culture" is concerned with two related aspects of the liturgy/culture relationship: first, the degree of success of the modern liturgy in generating social and cultural transformation; and, second, the impact of modern culture on the perception and practice of the liturgy. The foci of attention are three dynamics proposed as having a negative impact on the reformed liturgy: the subjectification of reality, the intimization of society, and the politicization of culture.

The tension that exists between the Catholic celebration of Sunday and modern American culture is treated in "Sunday in Modern America: A Cultural Perspective." In this essay, I suggest the existence of a number of conditions that make Sunday observance problematic in modern culture. Five of these have their origin in the larger culture, and seven within the church's own life. It will be evident that there is considerable overlap in these elements, as well as significant complexity in the relationship between the ecclesial and the cultural contexts of their origin.

The third thematic cluster is The Arts and Liturgy. This area of liturgical renewal continues to be one of the most underdeveloped both in theory and practice. While there exists a great deal of writing on liturgical music, art, and architecture, most does little to advance an adequate theory of the arts in Catholic worship. This is signified by the scarcity in this area of material — either in book or essay form — useful for graduate education in the liturgical arts.

"Paradigms in American Catholic Liturgical Music" attempts to bring some conceptual organization to the diverse attitudes and practices that exist in the area of Catholic liturgical music in the United States. Toward this end, the essay suggests the coexistence of six principal paradigms in musical theories and style: the neo-Caecilian, the folk/popular, the ethnic, the ritual-functional, the modern classical, and the ecumenical/eclectic. The diversity of paradigms and their failure to engage each other adequately suggests the need for the formation of more adequate theoretical bases for mutual understanding.

The essay "Toward a New Era in Liturgical Architecture" is undergirded by the conviction that, at both conceptual and practical levels, Catholic liturgical architecture is today beset by critical problems that require substantive solutions. The fundamental conviction, set forth in ten theses, is that the modernist era in church architecture, which reigned during the twentieth century, is rapidly giving way to a more adequate paradigm influenced by postmodernism and new classicism.

Outside a limited audience, Cardinal Joseph Ratzinger is not associated with the field of liturgical music. "The 'Musification' of the Word: Cardinal Ratzinger's Theology of Liturgical Music" serves as a summary and synthesis of the relatively small but highly important corpus of writings by the Cardinal Prefect of the Congregation for the

Doctrine of the Faith. In my view, the cardinal's writing in this area constitutes the most sophisticated and substantive contribution to a theory of liturgical music in theological and anthropological context.

Two essays under the heading The Liturgical Future complete this collection. The essay, "The Catholicity of the Liturgy: Shaping a New Agenda," suggests that there are five major agendas at work today in the area of liturgical renewal: advancing official reform, restoring the preconciliar, reforming the reform, inculturating the reform, and recatholicizing the reform. The essay proposes the need for a significant paradigm shift toward the *recatholicizing* agenda. The word recatholicizing in this context signifies new attention to the rich and expansive Catholic culture within which the liturgy operates.

The final essay, "Rejoice, Heavenly Powers! The Renewal of Liturgical Doxology," suggests that three important themes that were prominent in the early liturgical movement—eschatology, cosmology, and doxology—be renewed for the future. The renewal of liturgical eschatology will mean a new focus in worship on the kingdom of God; the advancement of liturgical cosmology will require that the liturgy be situated anew within the whole order of divine creation; renewing liturgical doxology will require a new elaboration of the praise-filled ethos of worship, restoring to the latter the glory that has its origin in the Holy Trinity.

Introduction

The Masterworks of God: The Liturgical Theology of the Catechism of the Catholic Church

In this essay, I shall focus attention on those affirmations and emphases in the general treatment of the sacraments in the Catechism of the Catholic Church that, in my view, need to be underscored today and which serve as correctives to some problematic trends in popular Catholic understanding.[1] This need not be a defensive or reactionary posture. Few would dismiss modern catechesis or, more generally, pastoral theology as simple failures. But they do have lacunae, in relation to which the Catechism is a counter-statement, bringing back to Catholic consciousness rich and valuable elements of the liturgical and sacramental tradition. Part Two of the Catechism draws to our attention those elements of Catholic tradition that must be present in any adequate sacramental theology and practice. The Catechism both affirms and incorporates the genuine gains of modern renewal and restores elements that are crucial to authentic Catholic life. What I have to say will be set out under the rubric of "critical affirmations." The word *critical* underscores my conviction that the affirmations in question are crucial to the life of the church and need to be rescued from a post-conciliar history of neglect or rejection.

Church, Liturgy, and Life

Before I proceed, I want to offer two general comments. The first concerns the relationship between the theological and practical aspects of the liturgy. Part Two of the Catechism is called "The Celebration of the Christian Mystery." This part has two sections: Section One deals with the whole Christian sacramental economy, what in sacramental theology has traditionally been dealt with under the heading *de sacramentis in genere,* sacraments in general. Section One offers a detailed and comprehensive statement of the liturgy as the salvific work of the Holy Trinity within the church, the living body of Christ in history. Section Two deals with the seven particular sacraments of the church. These two sections of the Catechism should be read in close correlation. We can never adequately understand the particular sacraments of the church except against the background of what the church holds regarding its sacramental life in general at a theological level. By the same token, a sacramental theology that is not closely informed by the concrete rites and symbols of the liturgy tends to lose its bearings. The separation of sacramental theology and liturgical practice into different areas of study has not produced good results in the church's liturgical history. I want to suggest at the outset, then, the closest possible integration of sacramental doctrine and liturgical practice. Thus, while what I say in this essay will focus on Section One, both sections need to be constantly cross-referenced and interrelated.

My second general comment has to do with the relationship between the liturgy and the whole life of the church. Section Two on the sacraments needs to be read in the context of the whole Catechism. The reason for this is that the sacramental life of the church does not exist in isolation from the credal, the moral, and the spiritual. How could it? The proper integration of these various facets of the church's life is evident from the fact that the liturgical life of the church is, in fact, invoked all through the Catechism. A cursory glance at the footnotes in all sections reveals a profusion of liturgical sources. We might even say that the whole Catechism has a liturgical frame of reference. The liturgical profession of faith provides the framework for Part One, which deals with the dogmatic elements of faith. The Lord's Prayer forms an important part of the basis of Part Four on prayer and spirituality, and Part Three on Christian morality is shot through with an ethos of praise and glory.

My point is not that Part Two has some sort of priority over the other parts of the Catechism. My intent is to say how crucial the liturgical life of the church is to Catholic belief and practice. The *lex orandi lex credendi* axiom associated with Prosper of Aquitaine in the fifth century offers an important insight here. The axiom states that the law of worship is the law of belief. How we pray shapes our belief. What this implies is that deformities in the way the church prays leads to deformities in Catholic belief and practice. If the church's liturgy is distorted or severed from some of its key elements, the church's doctrine and belief system suffers.

Given this truth, it is not surprising that controversies in the church today often crystallize around worship, around the rites of ordination, the orientation of the altar, styles of architecture and music, God-language and liturgical texts. Controversial issues in liturgy are not as benign as is often thought. They are not merely aesthetic; they are theological. They enter deeply into the very integrity and authenticity of Catholic faith. The increasing recognition of this point probably stands behind the greater degree of attention the church's liturgy is receiving among the American Catholic bishops today, both individually and corporately. If the insight of Prosper of Aquitaine is correct, the future of the church is being forged in its liturgical life. Article 10 of the Constitution on the Sacred Liturgy of Vatican II (hereafter noted as SC) pointed out that the liturgy is both the fount and summit of Christian life. We wisely look to the liturgy, then, for some indication of the direction in which the church is moving theologically, pastorally, morally, and spiritually. Good stewardship of the church's liturgical life is good stewardship of the whole life of the church.

Let me go on now to identify what I call the critical affirmations of the Catechism in the area of sacramental theology. I will identify seven such affirmations. The term "critical affirmation" does not, of course, appear in the Catechism, but it is, I think, a useful way of highlighting the contents of the material on the sacraments.

Trinitarian Structure

The first critical affirmation concerns the Trinitarian structure of the liturgy. The liturgy is declared in the Catechism to be the "work of the Holy Trinity." The Father is the source and goal of all Christian worship. The liturgy has the form of a dialogue between the Father and humankind (cf. CCC, 1083). In this dialogue, God unceasingly blesses creation, human activity, and history. This process of blessing "is a divine and life-giving action, the source of which is the Father" (#1078). Paragraph 1079 provides a magnificent statement of God's act of blessing: "From the beginning until the end of time the whole of God's work is a *blessing*. From the liturgical poem of the first creation to the songs of the heavenly Jerusalem, the inspired authors proclaim the plan of salvation as one vast divine blessing."[2] In the liturgy of the church, "the divine blessing is fully revealed and communicated. The Father is acknowledged and adored as the source and the end of all the blessings of creation and salvation" (#1082). The blessings of God are coextensive with biblical history, stretching from creation, through Noah, Abraham, the exodus, the history of Israel, the exile, the return. In the liturgy of the Chosen People, in the Law, the Prophets, and the Psalms we are given the magnificent record of God's blessings (#1080–81).

The Father's blessing in history has at its core the roles of the Word and the Spirit. At the heart of the Father's creating and saving action in history—and at the heart of the liturgy—is "the 'economy of the Word incarnate'" (CCC, 1066). In his "Word who became incarnate, died and rose for us," the Father fills us with his blessings (#1082). In turn, "Through his Word, he pours into our hearts the Gift that contains all gifts, the Holy Spirit" (#1082). The liturgy is not only the generalized locus of the person of Christ but is the very action of Christ in his paschal mystery. In turn, the grace of the liturgy is the gift of the Holy Spirit himself.

According to the Catechism, the dynamics of the liturgy are profoundly trinitarian. Remove the Trinity and the liturgy has no reality, no existence. The relations between the Father, Son, and Spirit are the very relations of the liturgy itself. Paragraph 1083 states this as follows:

> On the one hand, the Church, united with her Lord and "in the Holy Spirit" [Luke 10:21], blesses the Father "for his inexpressible gift" [2 Corinthians 9:15] in her adoration, praise and thanksgiving. On the other hand, until the consummation of God's plan, the Church never ceases to present to the Father the offering of his own gifts and to beg him to send the Holy Spirit upon that offering, upon herself, upon the faithful, and upon the whole world, so that through communion in the death and resurrection of Christ the Priest, and by the power

of the Spirit, these divine blessings will bring forth the fruits of life "to the praise of his glorious grace" [Ephesians 1:6].

There is much more to the trinitarian structure of the liturgy in Part Two than I am able to summarize here. Let me suggest now why this statement of the trinitarian structure of the liturgy is critical. Not since the early centuries has the trinitarian faith of the church been as controversial as it is today. One of the great achievements of the modern liturgical movement was the renewal of the church's understanding of the trinitarian framework of Christian worship. Yet in the last two decades or so, liturgical theology has begun to let this gain recede, not least because the more radical types of feminist theology and interreligious dialogue have begun to relativize traditional Christian God-language and take recourse in a kind of deism, a diffuse and nondefinable approach to God. This generalized deism prefers to speak of God in tentative images, models, and metaphors. God is separated from the biblical language about Him. The language of Father, Son, and Spirit are not uncommonly recast in modern worship as Creator, Redeemer, and Sanctifier. This process of relativizing trinitarian language has been further compounded by some new directions in christology and by idealistic theories of the Spirit. The general effect has been a loosening of commitment to biblical salvation history as the framework for Christian worship.

Against all this, the Catechism implicitly offers the critical affirmation that the liturgy is integrally and profoundly trinitarian and that the celebration of the liturgy can have no other foundation or frame of reference than the biblical self-revelation of God as Father, Son, and Holy Spirit. Liturgical history is biblical salvation history. This history and its narrative expression cannot be ignored, replaced, or reconstructed.

Christological Foundation

The second critical affirmation I want to propose concerns the christological foundation of the liturgy. This affirmation clearly flows from what I have just said. Considerable attention was accorded the matter of the personal role of Christ in the liturgy in the early modern liturgical movement, not because post-Tridentine theology had denied the christological foundation of the liturgy (not at all!), but because this truth needed to be stated and highlighted anew. In view of the modern movement of liturgical and christological renewal, it is surprising how much liturgical theology, especially of the more popular kind, is today constructed without an adequate foundational reference to Christ. One may think I am exaggerating, but for reassurance I went back to some popular texts on the liturgy and found serious justification for concern in this matter. While the values of Christ, the example of Christ, and the memory of Christ are habitually invoked in texts about the way the liturgy works, there is often lacking a sense that the liturgy is in its very foundation the personal, living action of Christ. This lack is evident in popular affirmations about the liturgy which take the symbolic self-expression of the worshiping community as the starting point of liturgical action. To question this starting point is not to deny the importance of the community in worship; not at all. The community is integral to liturgical action. But it is Christ who is the fundamental source of the community itself and the foundation of its very being. The principal actor in the liturgy is Christ; Christ is the head of the worshiping church. It is only in Christ that the worshiping community knows how to render true and fitting praise to God.

The affirmation of Christ as foundational agent of the liturgy is made in numerous ways throughout Part Two. We read: "For it was from the side of Christ as he slept the sleep of death upon the cross that there came forth 'the wondrous sacrament of the whole Church' [SC 5, 2]" (CCC, 1067). What the liturgy primarily celebrates is "the Paschal mystery by which Christ accomplished the work of our salvation" (#1067). Through the action of the liturgy, "Christ, our redeemer and high priest, continues the work of our redemption in, with, and through his Church" (#1069; cf. #1076, 1084). The liturgy is inseparable from Christ: " 'Seated at the right hand of the Father' and pouring out the Holy Spirit on his body which is the Church, Christ now acts through the sacraments he instituted to communicate his grace" (#1084). The Catechism emphasizes that the presence of Christ in the liturgy is a real and living presence (#1085–89). Christ acts in the liturgy not in *absentia*, but by a powerful and marvelous presence that is intrinsically personal.

The traditional Catholic affirmation of the institution of the sacraments by Christ, which is repeated in the Catechism, has its most profound meaning in relation to the church's conviction that the sacraments are the personal actions of Christ. This matter is dealt with in paragraph 1114, which takes up the affirmation of the Council of Trent: "'Adhering to the teaching of the Holy Scriptures, to the apostolic traditions, and to the consensus . . . of the Fathers,' we profess that 'the sacraments of the new law . . . were all instituted by Jesus Christ our Lord' [DS, 1600–01]." Modern scholars can continue to tease out and refine this teaching, but little room is left for the kind of affirmation so often popularly heard that what we call sacraments today were not providentially ordained, or that the sacraments are no more than the products of early Christian symbolic self-expression.

The Catechism strongly reaffirms the inner and divinely ordained continuity between the person and ministry of Christ and the sacramental life of the church (cf. CCC, 1117). This inner connection has never been more beautifully expressed than in the affirmation of Saint Leo the Great, quoted in paragraph 1115: " 'What was visible in our Savior has passed over into his mysteries' [*Sermo.* 74, 2]." This is the reason that the Christian sacraments are sacraments of salvation, as paragraphs 1127 to 1129 point out. The sacraments 'are *efficacious* because in them Christ himself is at work: it is he who baptizes; he who acts in his sacraments in order to communicate the grace that each sacrament signifies" (#1127). The efficacy of the sacraments occurs "by virtue of the saving work of Christ, accomplished once for all" (#1128). Indeed, so strongly has the church understood the agency of Christ that she affirms with St. Thomas that " 'the sacrament is not wrought by the righteousness of either the celebrant or the recipient, but by the power of God' " (#1128; cf. St. Thomas Aquinas, STh III, 68, 8). Indeed, Christ's action is independent of the minister's personal holiness.

The liturgy, then, has Christ as its theological foundation, as its principal actor and agent. It is he who gives the liturgy its very reality. This critical affirmation suggests a more doctrinally sound way of speaking about the foundational agency of Christian liturgy and a more adequate way of speaking about the role of the Christian community in the celebration of the church's worship.

Pneumatological Dynamism

The third critical affirmation of the Catechism concerns the pneumatological dynamism of the liturgy, or simply the role of the Spirit in the liturgy. One of the more distinctive aspects of the Catechism is the high attention it gives to the theology and spirituality of Eastern

Christianity, especially in the area of pneumatology. In this regard, it is significant that the present patriarch of Constantinople has given strong praise to the Catechism, despite his reservations along the lines of the usual East–West controversies.[3] The strong pneumatological emphasis is particularly notable in Part Two. The Spirit's role is set forth in an especially strong way in paragraphs 1091 to 1109. In paragraph 1076, for example, we read: "The Church was made manifest to the world on the day of Pentecost by the outpouring of the Holy Spirit. The gift of the Spirit ushers in a new era in the 'dispensation of the mystery'—the age of the Church, during which Christ manifests, makes present, and communicates his work of salvation through the liturgy of his Church, 'until he comes' [1Corinthians 11:26]." The Spirit is intrinsic to the very being and operation of the church and its liturgical life.

Most noteworthy is the way the role of the Spirit is said to be directed toward the manifestation of the mysteries of Christ. "The desire and work of the Spirit in the heart of the Church is that we might live from the life of the risen Christ' (CCC, 1091). The role of the Spirit is spelled out as follows in paragraph 1092: "The Spirit 'prepares the Church to encounter her Lord; he recalls and makes Christ manifest to the faith of the assembly. By his transforming power, he makes the mystery of Christ present here and now. Finally the Spirit of communion unites the Church to the life and mission of Christ."

The Spirit calls forth conversion and commitment (CCC, 1098). The Spirit is "the Church's living memory" (#1099). The Spirit gives "life to the Word of God" (#1100). The Spirit "puts both the faithful and the ministers into a living relationship with Christ" (#1101). The Spirit who "awakens the memory of the Church" inspires thanksgiving and praise *(doxology)* (#1103). In every liturgical celebration "there is an outpouring of the Holy Spirit that makes the unique mystery present" (#1104). By the power of the Spirit, the eucharistic gifts become the body and blood of Christ (#1105, 1106). "The Spirit's transforming power in the liturgy hastens the coming of the kingdom and the consummation of the mystery of salvation" (#1107). The Spirit who "gives life to those who accept him is, even now, the 'guarantee' of their inheritance" (#1107). The Spirit "is sent in order to bring us into communion with Christ and so to form his Body" (#1108). The Spirit "is like the sap of the Father's vine which bears fruit on its branches" (#1108).

Why does this emphatic statement of the Spirit's role in the liturgy constitute a critical affirmation? Because it underlines the truth that the Spirit, who is the Spirit of Christ, has no other role than the manifestation in the church of the mystery of Christ; has no other arena of operation than the arena of Christ, which is the church; has no career or agenda, so to speak, than that of Christ; and has no self-expression that is not the revelation of Christ in his saving ministry. This affirmation is critical because it is inadequately affirmed and poorly understood today. Under the influence of modern Enlightenment philosophy and theology, the Spirit is often regarded as another name for human subjectivity, imagination, or creativity. The Spirit is sometimes understood today as simply the self. In liberal theological perspectives, the Spirit is no longer thought of as the Spirit of Christ. Not surprisingly, some modern theologies emphasize the Spirit more than Christ or the Father. The Spirit is invoked to inspire new names for God and to generate new agendas in the church and in the world at large. Indeed, the Spirit is often invoked in a manner that relativizes Christ and the church.

In view of all this, the church needs to renew in its pastoral and liturgical consciousness the sense (so strong in the New Testament) that the Spirit allows us to imagine only Christ; to encounter only Christ; to express only Christ. The Spirit is indeed the source of human subjectivity, but only such subjectivity as has been baptized and conformed to Christ. The agenda of the Spirit is profoundly ecclesial and christocentric. The liturgy is not merely one of many arenas of the Spirit. The liturgy is the great work of the Spirit in the life of the church (cf. CCC, 1091).

Ecclesial Character

The fourth critical affirmation follows directly from what I have just said. It concerns the ecclesial character of the sacraments. If the Spirit is directed toward the manifestation of Christ, then the Spirit's arena *par excellence* is Christ's body on earth: the church. Here we return to the matter of the ongoing presence and ministry of Christ in the world through the church and to the affirmation of Saint Leo the Great that what was visible in Christ has passed over into the sacramental mysteries. It is an axiom, since the Second Vatican Council, that the sacraments are sacraments of the church. According to paragraph 1118, the sacraments are sacraments of the church in two ways: "by her" and "for her": The sacraments "are 'by the Church,' for she is the sacrament of Christ's action at work in her through the mission of the Holy Spirit. They are 'for the Church' in the sense that 'the sacraments make the Church' [St. Augustine, *De civ. Dei* 22, 17], since they manifest and communicate to men, above all in the Eucharist, the mystery of communion with the God who is love, One in three persons." In the popular axiom, the church makes the sacraments and the sacraments make the church. The sacramental activity of Christians is profoundly and integrally ecclesial. The sacramentality of the church's worship arises out of, flows from, and leads back to the sacramentality of the church.

This understanding might be contrasted with mainstream American views of worship and the church inspired by liberal Protestantism. As studies like those of Robert Wuthnow, Wade Clark Roof, and Robert Bellah show, the typical modern American does not see worship in integrally ecclesial terms.[4] Participation in public worship for Americans today does not necessarily mean commitment to the church. Indeed, church life is often seen to serve only a purely functional purpose: to help Christians get in touch with God or Christ or the Spirit within the self. The extent to which American Catholics have absorbed this cultural point of view about worship and ecclesial life is troubling. Some pastoral theology on small Christian communities is expressive of precisely this perspective. Such theology does not generate commitment to the rich ecclesial tradition of Catholic Christianity. In its perspective, worship is often detached from ecclesial commitment. In this light, it becomes clear that a renewed commitment to teaching and forming people in the dignity, vocation, and identity of the church as the framework for worship constitutes today a crucial challenge for pastors and catechists.

The fundamental point here may be elaborated by the recognition that the sacraments do not constitute the whole life of the church. There are crucial dimensions of Christian life that go beyond worship. Quoting the Constitution on the Sacred Liturgy of Vatican II, paragraph 1072 states: " 'The sacred liturgy does not exhaust the entire activity of the Church' [SC, 9]: it must be preceded by evangelization, faith, and conversion. It can then produce its fruits in the lives of the faithful: new life in the Spirit, involvement in the mission of the Church, and service of her unity." Paragraph 1074, restating the Constitution on the Liturgy, puts this another way: "The liturgy is the summit toward which the activity of the Church is directed; it is also the font from which all her power flows [SC, 10]." This means, in the words of Pope John Paul II, for instance, that "Catechesis is intrinsically linked with the whole of liturgical and sacramental activity, for it is in the sacraments, especially in the Eucharist, that Christ Jesus works in fullness for the transformation of men" (cf. *Catechesi Tradendae*, 23). In the same way, the liturgy both generates and expresses a whole life of prayer and spirituality that goes beyond itself. "In the liturgy, all Christian prayer finds its source and goal. Through the liturgy the inner man is rooted and grounded in "the great love with which [the Father] loved us" in his beloved Son [Ephesians 2:4; 3:16–17]. It is the same "marvelous work of God" that is lived and internalized by all prayer, 'at all times in the Spirit' [Ephesians 6:18]" (CCC, 1073).

Quoting the Constitution on the Sacred Liturgy, the relationship between worship, ecclesial life, and mission is set out well at the beginning of Part Two:

> It is this mystery of Christ that the Church proclaims and celebrates in her liturgy so that the faithful might live from it and bear witness to it in the world: "For it is in the liturgy, especially in the divine sacrifice of the Eucharist, that the work of our redemption is accomplished [SC, 2]," and it is through the liturgy especially that the faithful are enabled to express in their lives and manifest to others the mystery of Christ and the real nature of the true Church (CCC, 1068).

Indeed, the word *liturgy* itself, the Catechism reminds us, has this wider ecclesial reference: "The word 'liturgy' originally meant a 'public work' or a 'service in the name of/on behalf of the people.' In Christian tradition, it means the participation of the People of God in 'the work of God' [cf. John 17:4]. Through the liturgy Christ, our redeemer and high priest, continues the work of our redemption in, with, and through his Church' (#1069). Paragraph 1070 states:

> In the New Testament the word "liturgy" refers not only to the celebration of divine worship but also to the proclamation of the Gospel and to active charity. In all of these situations it is a question of the service of God and neighbor. In a liturgical celebration the Church is servant in the image of her Lord, the one *"leitourgos"*; she shares in Christ's priesthood (worship), which is both prophetic (proclamation) and kingly (service of charity).

Quoting the Constitution on the Sacred Liturgy, the ecclesial dimension of the liturgy is summed up expressively in paragraph 1089: The

Church is Christ's " 'beloved Bride who calls to her Lord and through him offers worship to the eternal Father' [SC, 7]."

HIERARCHICAL ORDER

The fifth critical affirmation concerns the hierarchical order of worship. In liturgical theory and practice today, considerable attention is accorded the Christian assembly, and rightly so. The role of the liturgical assembly is well underlined in the Catechism. The liturgical assembly has the dignity of being a fellowship of the Holy Spirit. In its liturgical life, the church is " 'one mystical person' " with Christ as its head (CCC, 1119). The dignity of the worshiping assembly is a well-affirmed feature of modern catechesis and liturgical theology and needs no critical emphasis here. What does need critical emphasis is the qualifying principle stated in paragraph 1119: "The Church acts in the sacraments as 'an organically structured priestly community' [LG, 11]." Thus Christ is present and active in the liturgical assembly in diverse modes according to a hierarchical structure (CCC, 1088). The liturgical assembly is not a simple body; it is a complex, differentiated body in which special duties are variously assigned. Among such duties are those given to the ordained. These duties are not merely incidental, but are designed to guarantee that it is Christ who is acting in the Church: "The ordained minister is the sacramental bond that ties the liturgical action to what the apostles said and did and, through them, to the words and actions of Christ, the source and foundation of the sacraments" (#1120; cf. #1087).

This matter receives notable treatment at the beginning of Chapter Two under the question: "Who Celebrates?" The answer, quoting the Constitution on the Sacred Liturgy, is the following: "It is the whole *community,* the Body of Christ united with its Head, that celebrates. 'Liturgical services are not private functions, but are celebrations of the Church, which is "the sacrament of unity," namely, the holy people united and organized under the authority of the bishops. Therefore liturgical services pertain to the whole Body of the Church' [SC, 27]" (CCC, 1140). Again we read: "The celebrating assembly is the community of the baptized who, 'by regeneration and anointing of the Holy Spirit, are consecrated to be a spiritual household and a holy priesthood, so that . . . they may offer spiritual sacrifices' [LG, 10].

This 'common priesthood' is that of Christ the sole priest, in which all his members participate" (CCC, 1141).

However, in the liturgical assembly, " 'the members do not all have the same function' [SC, 14]. Certain members are called by God, in and through the Church, to a special service of the community. These servants are chosen and consecrated by the sacrament of Holy Orders, by which the Holy Spirit enables them to act in the person of Christ the head, for the service of all the members of the Church" (CCC, 1142). Among the nonordained in the assembly, various roles are also distributed: "Other *particular ministries* also exist, not consecrated by the sacrament of Holy Orders; their functions are determined by the bishops, in accord with liturgical traditions and pastoral needs. 'Servers, readers, commentators, and members of the choir also exercise a genuine liturgical function'" (#1143; cf. SC, 29).

The roles of the ordained and nonordained, however, come together in the action of the liturgical assembly in an integrated and cooperative way. "In the celebration of the sacraments it is thus the whole assembly that is *leitourgos,* each according to his function, but 'in the unity of the Spirit' who acts in all" (CCC, 1144). Thus, in liturgical celebrations "each person, minister or layman, who has an office to perform, should carry out *all* and *only* those parts which pertain to his office by the nature of the rite and the norms of the liturgy" (#1144, cf. SC, 28).

This principle of differentiation in the liturgical assembly needs critical attention today in light of what some perceive as a congregationalist tendency in Catholic liturgical theology and practice. By a congregationalist tendency, I mean one that collapses the role of the ordained into the general ministry of the baptized. This phenomenon represents an understandable overreaction to clericalism, which I would describe as the collapsing of the priestly role of the laity into that of the ordained. But it is an overreaction, nevertheless, and it denies an essential principle of Catholic doctrine. While it is true that the whole assembly *does* celebrate the liturgy, it celebrates as an organically structured and hierarchically ordered body. The celebrating role of the assembly is never appropriately understood or promoted in a congregationalist manner.[5]

Cosmic and Eschatological Orientation

The question of who celebrates the liturgy leads to another critical affirmation of the Catechism: this concerns the cosmic and eschatological orientation of the liturgy. Indeed, the first answer in the Catechism to the question "who celebrates" is: the whole church on earth and in heaven. We read in paragraph 1136: "Liturgy is an 'action' of the *whole Christ (Christus totus)*. Those who even now celebrate it without signs are already in the heavenly liturgy, where celebration is wholly a communion and feast." This is amplified further in paragraph 1137:

> The Book of *Revelation* of St. John, read in the Church's liturgy, first reveals to us, "A throne stood in heaven, with one seated on the throne: 'the Lord God' [Revelation 4:2]." It then shows the Lamb, "standing, as though it had been slain" Christ crucified and risen, the one high priest of the true sanctuary, the same one "who offers and is offered, who gives and is given" [Revelation 5:6]. Finally, it presents "the river of the water of life . . . flowing from the throne of God and of the Lamb" [Revelation 22:1], one of the most beautiful symbols of the Holy Spirit.

The following are said to take part in the service of God's praise and the fulfillment of his plan:

> the heavenly powers, all creation (the four living beings), the servants of the old and New Covenants (the twenty-four elders), the new People of God (the one hundred and forty-four thousand) [cf. Revelation 4:5; 7:1–8]—especially the martyrs "slain for the Word of God," and the all-holy Mother of God (the Woman), the Bride of the Lamb [Revelation 6:9–11], and finally "a great multitude which no one could number, from every nation, from all tribes, and peoples and tongues" [Revelation 7:9] (CCC, 1138).

In the liturgy of earth, we are told, the church already enjoys a " 'foretaste of that heavenly liturgy which is celebrated in the Holy City of Jerusalem toward which we journey as pilgrims' " (CCC, 1090; cf. SC 8). This is why the sacraments are called the sacraments of eternal life. Paragraph 1130 declares:

> The Church celebrates the mystery of her Lord "until he comes," when God will be "everything to everyone" [1 Corinthians 11:26; 15:18]. Since the apostolic age the liturgy has been drawn toward its goal by the Spirit's groaning in the Church: *Marana tha!* [1 Corinthians 16:22]. The liturgy thus shares in Jesus' desire: "I have earnestly desired to eat this Passover with you . . . until it is fulfilled in the kingdom of God" [Luke 22:15].

> In the sacraments of Christ the Church already receives the guarantee of her inheritance and even now shares in everlasting life, while "awaiting our blessed hope, the appearing of the glory of our great God and Saviour Christ Jesus" [Titus 2:13]. The "Spirit and the Bride say: 'Come . . . Come, Lord Jesus!' [Revelation 27:17, 20]."

All this is summed up in the statement of Saint Thomas quoted in the same paragraph: " 'Therefore a sacrament is a sign that commemorates what precedes it—Christ's passion; demonstrate what is accomplished in us through Christ's passion—grace; and prefigures what the Passion pledges to us—future glory' " (STh III, 60, 3).

The cosmic and eschatological orientation of the liturgy is, in the opinion of some commentators, not adequately to the fore of modern Catholic consciousness. The privatization of the liturgy, which reduces worship to a small group activity detached from the universal church and from the church of heaven, is partly to blame here. So, too, is the secularization of the liturgy, which goes hand in hand with a decrease of belief in heaven and eternal life, and a reorientation of liturgy both toward the immediate social and psychological needs of the community and the political needs of the larger society. From the side of liturgical celebration, this problem is generated by styles and forms of liturgical architecture, music, and ritual that simply do not invoke the liturgy of heaven adequately or at all. Without liturgical art and images that evoke the heavenly, the cosmic and the eschatological, those features of the Christian faith, remain unexpressed and unencountered (CCC, 1159–62) and they evaporate from Christian consciousness. If I were to point to the one area of modern liturgical celebration that is the most troublesome, it would be this one.

The manner in which the Catechism both states and evokes the cosmic and eschatological character of the liturgy is one of the most remarkable and important aspects of the document. In this regard, one of the original and strongest intents of the modern liturgical movement—which for complex reasons was derailed—finds magnificent expression here.

Divine Artistry

Finally, the Catechism critically affirms the divine artistry of the liturgy. By this I mean the diverse, ordered, and multifaceted liturgical and sacramental system of Catholicism that has emerged from the activity of God in creation and history. The protocol for speaking of the divine artistry of the liturgy is found in paragraph 1091, which speaks of the sacraments as "God's masterpieces." Paragraph 1116 describes the sacraments as the "masterworks of God." This artistic language aptly points to all the interactive and cooperative variety of signs and symbols, words and actions, music and imagery, times and seasons, and persons and places that constitute Christian worship. The sacraments are woven together from signs and symbols whose meaning "is rooted in the work of creation and in human culture" (CCC, 1145). They are part of the fabric of the natural necessity to communicate (#1146). They emerge out of the materiality of creation which contains in itself "traces of its Creator" (#1147). The sacraments take up signs and symbols from human social life: washing and anointing, breaking bread and sharing the cup (#1148). These are integrated into the church's liturgy, becoming signs of the new creation in Jesus Christ (#1149). These social symbols, taken up into the church's liturgy, encounter the Word of God that unifies and gives life to them (#1153; cf. #1154–55).[6]

The divine artistry of the sacramental system incorporates the elements of times and seasons. The natural passage of time, the hours and days, the movement from darkness to light, are invoked to unfold the mystery of Christ. This artistry of time is elaborated ritually in the Lord's Day, the liturgical year and the liturgy of the hours. Every time-focused liturgical event is an event of eternity in time—*now*.[7] "There is a word that marks her [the Church's] prayer: 'Today!'—a word echoing the prayer her Lord taught her and the call of the Holy Spirit. This 'today' of the living God which man is called to enter is 'the hour' of Jesus' passover, which reaches across and underlies all history" (CCC, 1165). Paragraph 1085 states: "The Paschal mystery of Christ, by contrast [with other historical events], cannot remain only in the past." All that Christ is or did "participates in the divine eternity, and so transcends all times while being made present in them all." At the heart of eternity in time is the Lord's Day—Sunday—which is the foundation and core of the whole liturgical year (#1167; cf. #1166). The mystery of Christ is unfolded through the whole liturgical year, the "year of the Lord's favor" [Luke 4:19] (#1168). Through it, the kingdom of God enters into time and time itself reaches toward its final culmination. Within this framework, the liturgy of the hours allows the permeation and transfiguration of every day and every hour with the mystery of Christ, so that day and night are made holy and the church prays without ceasing (#1174–77). The church in its worship lives "between the passover of Christ, already accomplished once for all, and its consummation in the kingdom of God" (#1164).

The divine artistry of the sacraments includes holy persons and holy places. In Mary, the saints, and the martyrs, we venerate those who are our models and in whom the paschal mystery has been completed (CCC, 1172–73). God's artistry raises up holy places in which the worship of God takes place. While it is true that "the whole earth is sacred" (#1179), the places of Christian worship signify and reveal the living church on earth and "the dwelling of God with men reconciled and united in Christ" (#1180). The church building "is a symbol of the Father's house towards which the People of God is journeying" (#1186). The liturgical house of God is part of the economy of images (#1159) that has followed the incarnation of the Son of God and reveals God's glory in the world (cf. #1160–62; also #1181–85). Music, too, is a privileged and crucial part of the divine artistry of the Christian liturgy (cf. #1156–58).

Toward the end of the book on the sacraments, there is a fine statement (taken from CELAM, Third General Conference, 1979) that expresses well this sense of the divine artistry of God extending into the most ordinary aspects of human life. The statement concerns popular religiosity:

> At its core the piety of the people is a storehouse of values that offers answers of Christian wisdom to the great questions of life. The Catholic wisdom of the people is capable of fashioning a vital synthesis. . . . It creatively combines the divine and the human, Christ and Mary, spirit and body, communion and institution, person and community, faith and homeland, intelligence and emotion. This wisdom is a Christian humanism that radically affirms the dignity of every person as a child of God, establishes a basic fraternity, teaches people how to encounter nature and understand work, and provides reasons for joy and humor even in the midst of a very hard life (#1676).

The truth that the liturgy is a cooperative divine-human act of creativity is signified by the fact that the marvelous system of God's praise is made up of immutable elements divinely constituted and human elements subject to change (CCC, 1205). The latter are adapted to cultures without being submerged by them. This process is verified in the rich tradition of rites within the Catholic Church and is the basis for ongoing liturgical development, including the process of inculturation (#1200–06).

The affirmation of the divine artistry of the liturgy underscores something often missing in our thinking about the liturgy today: the truth that the liturgy of the church is not arbitrarily constructed and may not be changed or manipulated at will. The liturgy has its roots in nature and the rhythms of nature—themselves created by God. It has its roots in history, in the order of the human soul, in the deepest impulses of the mind and heart. The liturgy draws together immense patterns of symbolism and expression that touch every area of human existence. It is made up of an arrangement of symbolic and thematic elements that are integrally interconnected. When we shear some of these off, then the liturgy suffers; it loses power, and God's rich outreach to humankind is thwarted. The sacramental system of the church is made up of providentially chosen elements from which we cannot pick and choose and yet expect them to be salvific for us. We accept and yield to the liturgy as a whole, as a system, as a rich and magnificent tapestry of divine creativity.

We live in a culture that disposes us to regard the liturgy as man-made, functional, therapeutic, and dispensable. This is a culture that is given to subjectivism, privatization, and politicization. Christian attitudes formed in this culture tend to be anti-incarnational (and therefore anti-sacramental); to be closed to the possibility of divine revelation. Against all this, the Catechism emphasizes the liturgy as the great and magnificent work of God in history. The liturgy is God's poetry, the great doxology, the divine act of blessing that reaches across history, transforming the cosmos in the process.

Conclusion

There are many excellent things that may be said about the Catechism of the Catholic Church. The most unexpected is that it should be beautiful. Book Three on the liturgy and sacraments is often beautiful and inspiring. It has moments of great poetry. That is indeed providential. I encourage all who serve in pastoral ministry to discover its treasures for themselves and to use the Catechism as a basic and worthy guide in the ongoing development of the church's pastoral liturgy.

1. *Catechism of the Catholic Church,* second ed. (Rome: Libreria Editrice Vaticana, 1997).

2. For the sake of simplicity, footnote numbers within quotations are not indicated in this text. The reader is referred to the Catechism itself for source information. The source of more significant quotations is indicated in brackets.

3. See Gianni Valente, "The Essential that Unites," *30 Days* No. 4 (1993) 16–20.

4. See Wade Clark Roof, *A Generation of Seekers: The Spiritual Journey of the Baby Boom Generation* (San Francisco: Harper, 1993); Robert N. Bellah et al., *Habits of the Heart: Individualism and Commitment in American Life* (New York: Harper and Row, 1986); Robert Wuthnow, *Sharing the Journey: Support Groups and America's New Quest for Community* (New York: The Free Press, 1994).

5. On this matter, see M. Francis Mannion, "Priestless Parishes: What Is at Stake? *The Priest* 49:2 (1993) 31–33; 49:3 (1993) 29–34.

6. The Catechism is careful to state the dynamic relationship between the orders of creation and redemption in the area of the sacraments. The pre-Christian history of liturgy in human religiosity is affirmed (CCC, 1149), as are the roots of liturgy in the Old Testament dispensation (#1150). It is clear that "the sacraments of the Church do not abolish but purify and integrate all the richness of the signs and symbols of the cosmos and social life" (#1152).

7. The Catechism's theology of liturgical time is refined and well stated. There is the recognition that every day is the day of salvation and every action of Christ is *now.* "There is a word that marks her [the Church's] prayer: 'Today!' —a word echoing the prayer her Lord taught her and the call of the Holy Spirit. This 'today' of the living God which man is called to enter is 'the hour' of Jesus' passover, which reaches across and underlies all history" (CCC, 1165). Paragraph 1085 states: "The Paschal mystery of Christ, by contrast [with other historical events], cannot remain only in the past." All that Christ is or did "participates in the divine eternity, and so transcends all times while being made present in them all." At the heart of eternity in time is the Lord's Day— Sunday—which is the foundation and core of the whole liturgical year (#1167; cf. #1166). They mystery of Christ is unfolded through the whole liturgical year, the "year of the Lord's favor" [Luke 4:19] (#1168). Through it, the Kingdom of God enters into time and time itself reaches toward its final culmination. Within this framework, the Liturgy of the Hours allows the permeation and transfiguration of every day and every hour with the mystery of Christ, so that day and night are made holy and the church prays without ceasing (#1174–77).

Part I

Liturgical Systems

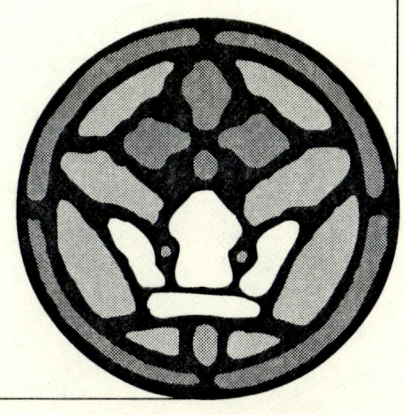

Chapter 1

Penance and Reconciliation: A Systemic Analysis

The ongoing malaise affecting penance and reconciliation in the Church's life is, to a great extent, due to systemic disorders in the theology of penance and reconciliation, in the liturgical rites themselves, and in the Church's use of the rites. This essay proposes that the solutions to the problems identified be consequently systemic.

The fundamental systemic problem regarding penance and reconciliation may be stated both theologically and practically. At the theological level, we may point to an inadequate differentiation between penance and reconciliation, accounted for, in part, by lack of stability in the terms themselves and, in part, by the tendency to found these terms almost exclusively in biblical theology rather than in baptismal theology and ecclesiology.

At the practical level, we can say that the Church's ritual system of penance and reconciliation demonstrates the same lack of differentiation and that the problem is further intensified by the unharmonious coexistence within the rites of processes and elements directed both to penance and reconciliation. The problem is further compounded by the fact that the ritual system of penance and reconciliation is not adequately correlated with the Church's baptismal order.

The systemic analysis proposed in this essay will proceed in three stages. First, I shall examine baptism and its theology in order to indicate that they provide the only proper source for a statement of the theological and ecclesiological elements that must found an adequate theology of *penance* and *reconciliation*. Second, on the basis of baptismal theology, I will propose a differentiated and stable ecclesiological scheme for penance and reconciliation. I shall propose, for instance, that *penance* and *reconciliation* represent quite distinct processes in the Church's liturgy and practice. Third, I shall examine the systemic problems inherent in the rites of penance and reconciliation, showing how the problems identified stand at the root of some contemporary difficulties surrounding sacramental confession, the first penance of children, and the practice of general absolution.

Baptism: The Systemic Foundation

One of the prominent features of modern liturgical renewal is the identification of the sacraments of initiation as the foundation of the whole theological and soteriological reality of Christian existence. An examination of the Church's official documents amply demonstrates this point. The General Introduction which serves the 1972 Rite of Christian Initiation of Adults, as well as the 1969 Rite of Baptism of Children, declares the efficacy of Christian initiation as follows: "Through the sacraments of Christian initiation men and women are freed from the power of darkness. With Christ they die, are buried and rise again. They receive the Spirit of adoption which makes them God's sons and daughters."[1] The Introduction goes on to say that "through baptism men and women are incorporated into Christ. They are formed into God's people, and they obtain forgiveness of all their sins. They are raised from their natural human condition to the dignity of adopted children. They become a new creation through water and the Spirit."[2] In the eucharist, in which initiation is completed, "the entire community of the redeemed is offered to God by the high priest."[3]

In this light, it is significant that the Introduction to the 1974 Rite of Penance begins by setting forth in a baptismal focus the whole sweep of God's saving activity in Christ before it goes on to consider penance and reconciliation explicitly. Jesus, it declares, proclaimed the coming of the kingdom, exhorting people to repentance and reconciliation with the Father. He healed the sick, forgave sins, finally died and rose for our justification and poured out the Spirit upon his people.[4] Then in Pauline language it states that Christ's victory over sin "is first brought into light in baptism where our fallen nature is crucified with Christ so that the body of sin may be destroyed and we may no longer be slaves to sin but rise with Christ and live for God."[5]

All this is completed in the eucharist where "the passion of Christ is made present; his body given for us and his blood shed for the forgiveness of sins are offered to God again by the Church for the salvation of the world."[6] For in the eucharist, "Christ is present and is offered as 'the sacrifice which has made our peace' with God and in order that 'we may be brought together in unity' by his Holy Spirit.' "[7]

A similarly foundational statement of the efficacy of Christian initiation appears in Pope John Paul II's 1984 Apostolic Exhortation on Reconciliation and Penance.[8] According to the pope, baptism has its significance as an act of "conversion and of reintegration into the right order of relationships with God, of reconciliation with God, with the elimination of the original stain and the consequent introduction into the great family of the reconciled."[9] This process, ratified in confirmation, finds its completion in the eucharist, which effects personal sanctification and reconciliation, which "derive from the very essence of the eucharistic mystery as an unbloody renewal of the sacrifice of the cross, the source of salvation and of reconciliation for all people."[10]

What is underscored in these questions is the significance of sacramental initiation in effecting repentance, the forgiveness of sin, the reconciliation with God, and in bringing men and women into the community of the redeemed. The appearance of these assertions either in official church documents or in theology in general does not of itself, however, ensure their systemic significance. These assertions often appear more as edifying introductions than as means of establishing foundations and trajectories to be rigorously respected.

This is evident by the fact that what is commonly asserted about baptism is often later, and with equal weight, affirmed in the church's postbaptismal rites of penance and reconciliation. These latter rites are often conceived of more as structures of personal grace parallel to baptism, then, as elements within a ritual and ecclesial system founded upon baptism. This confusion is also apparent in the fact that theological writing on the rites of penance and reconciliation often invokes precisely the same New Testament theology as is invoked for baptism.

The fundamental disorder here derives from a failure to relate in a systemic manner the postbaptismal rites of penance and reconciliation to baptism, and to see the total complex of rites, in turn, as elements within an ecclesial order which is itself the bearer of grace and reconciliation.

Before we proceed to an examination of penance and reconciliation, we need, then, to secure the foundational systemic importance of baptism and its theology. Here we make reference to a highly significant work by Jerome Theisen, which offers a valuable analysis of the ecclesial nature of sin, redemption and grace.[11]

According to Theisen, human beings are born into a condition of disunity, a condition that they confirm "in various ways by a life that is devoted, at least partially, to disjunctive self-centeredness."[12] Disunity, he suggests, is a symbol of "the multiple aspects of conflict and dividedness in the human situation."[13] Consequently, "disunity is the human condition that calls out for redemption, a reaching for community."[14]

Theisen goes on to propose "community" as a symbol of the grace of reconciliation, the forgiveness of sin, and the overcoming of estrangement. Thus the church, which is the gathering of those who adhere to the person and work of Christ, "exists to provide humans the effective sacraments of reconciliation, both with God and with one another."[15] Christian community, he says, "offers a place of meeting the Lord, a place of healing and freedom. In short, it exists to overcome the loneliness of isolation and to effect a community of persons."[16] By entering Christian community, "the sinner moves away from the condition of hostility and estrangement and is restored to peaceful relationship with God."[17] The Christian fellowship, then, "becomes a community of salvation, the place where there is forgiveness of sins, healing of spirits, and reconciliation with the Father."[18]

While Theisen does not present anything in the way of an extended analysis of Christian baptism, he does open the way to an appreciation of that sacrament's profoundly ecclesial significance. His ecclesiological presentation of fundamental Christian themes translates easily into a baptismal theology of the forgiveness of sin, repentance, and reconciliation with God. We are thus allowed to see the efficacy of baptism in initiating believers into what Saint Augustine calls a "reconciled world."[19] In this perspective, it will be seen that the forgiveness of sin, repentance, and reconciliation with God are all qualities of entrance into this reconciled world, into the church as the ecclesial sacrament of salvation and reconciliation.[20] Neither repentance nor reconciliation is an individual achievement available without the mediation of the church, nor do they have any reality except as qualities of actual reconciled ecclesial existence. This is the proper sense in the affirmation of Monika Hellwig that "the basic sacrament of repentance, conversion, and reconciliation is baptism, the entrance into the Church, because the essence of the Church is reconciliation."[21]

This sort of consciousness about baptism presses us, then, with all due caution about improper adulation of the church, to take seriously the salvific nature of ecclesial existence. It promotes, in turn, a necessary sense of contrast between ecclesial existence and the alienated, scattered social systems out of which men and women are called.

If we are to take seriously the full implications of this ecclesiological and soteriological scheme, then Christian baptism will be recognized as the primary and fundamental sacrament of penance and reconciliation. Baptism becomes, furthermore, the point of reference for all subsequent considerations regarding the postbaptismal rites of penance and reconciliation. These rites will be seen to be qualified and defined by reference to baptism and to have their efficacy in relation to the ecclesial system founded on baptism. As a consequence, the application of the New Testament theology of reconciliation and the forgiveness of sin to these postbaptismal rites can be made only by reference to baptism and can be applied to these rites only in a manner that recognizes the salvific and reconciliatory achievements of baptism.[22] Consequently, any direct application of the great "reconciliation" passages of Paul to postbaptismal penance and reconciliation rites must be considered theologically improper.[23]

The first element of systemic differentiation that we propose to establish here, then, is between baptismal reconciliation and postbaptismal reconciliation. The first has to do with the universal work of God in Christ and with the manner in which the Christian is initiated into the realm of reconciliation by virtue of being initiated into the community of the redeemed. The second has to do with the process of restoring a baptized Christian to the communion of the church after serious postbaptismal sin. Each involves different ecclesial dynamics and theological components. The great sweep of the biblical theology of reconciliation may be unrestrictedly invoked for the first, but it may be invoked for the second only in a manner that recognizes that what is involved there is not reconciliation in the primary theological sense, but an ecclesial crisis of a specific kind.

This is not to assert that reconciliation in the Pauline sense is complete with baptism. Reconciliation does, of course, continue in the church, especially in the celebration of the eucharist and the sacraments and will not be complete until the final advent of the kingdom. As we shall point out later, however, this involves a concept of reconciliation of a kind distinct from that already elaborated above. Our fundamental point here is only to assert that Christian baptism is the first and original sacrament of reconciliation and the forgiveness of sin, not only in a temporal sense, but in a primordial and paradigmatic one, and that all other forms and concepts of reconciliation are subservient to and derivative of what is said about baptism.

Penance and Reconciliation in Postbaptismal Context

Having offered a theoretical and practical differentiation between baptismal reconciliation and postbaptismal reconciliation as systemic elements related to a baptismal ecclesiology, we move next to establishing an adequate differentiation between penance and reconciliation in postbaptismal context. We shall thus seek to indicate for each a stable ecclesial field of reference.

The difficulty of this task is at once apparent in that there is little stability in the usage of the words *penance* and *reconciliation* either in official ecclesiastical parlance or in theology in general. In an examination of the language of the 1974 Rite of Penance, Paul De Clerck identified five meanings for the word *reconciliation* and six meanings for the word *penance*.[24] De Clerck found no real logic in the manner of choice of these terms and concluded that, as a result, the rite itself betrays an overall lack of coherence.[25] A further dimension of the problem is that the words penance and reconciliation are often used interchangeably in official documents, as well as in theological use generally. What I shall define as penance, for instance, is often referred to as reconciliation, and what I shall call reconciliation is often referred to as penance. This is the case even in instances where some sort of distinction is being offered. For example, the 1984 Papal Exhortation at one point suggests a distinction between penance and reconciliation along the lines espoused in this essay, yet later reverts to interchangeable usage.[26] (Accordingly, the reader is warned that in what follows I shall be quoting from sources that use penance and reconciliation interchangeably. The reader is invited to make the necessary translations as the terms arise.)

In order to suggest some terminological stability, we shall look first at the proper ecclesial reference of postbaptismal reconciliation. I have already pointed out that by postbaptismal reconciliation, I mean the reconciliation of serious sinners to the communion of the church.

The use of the term *reconciliation* precisely for this purpose is, of course, quite traditional and was identifiably used in this way in early Christianity. This usage is reflected also in the later developed tradition, from which we have more adequate textual data. For instance, the prayers for the public restoration of a sinner found in the eighth-century Gelasian Sacramentary (itself a compilation of much earlier materials) bear a clear reconciliation motif.[27] The prayers represented there are profoundly ecclesial in character, indicating a definite conception of the church as the community of reconciliation.

Up to the beginning of the Middle Ages, at least, the rites of reconciliation were markedly public, procedural in character, and clearly restricted to cases of serious sin. Typically they involved some form of excommunication, a period of intense ascetical reparation and finally a liturgical act of reconciliation by the bishop. When this tradition eventually merged with the private form of penance developed in the Celtic Church, the reconciliation motif remained dominant and survived in all subsequent developments of the rite. Thus there is clear precedent for continuing to speak of "the sacrament of reconciliation" in reference to the rite that performs the task of restoring sinners to the Church.

It is precisely this sense of reconciliation that is underlined in the Decree prefacing the 1974 Rite of Penance, in which we read: "Because of human weakness, Christians 'turn aside from [their] early love' (see Revelation 2:4) and even break off their friendship with God by sinning. The Lord, therefore, instituted a special sacrament of penance for the pardon of sins committed after baptism (see John 20:21–23), and the Church has faithfully celebrated the sacrament through the centuries—in various ways, but retaining its essential elements."[28] It goes on to say that in this sacrament "the faithful 'obtain from the mercy of God pardon for their sins against him; at the same time they are reconciled with the Church which they wounded by their sins and which works for their conversion by charity, example, and prayer'."[29] Again it is asserted that by the Church's reconciling ministry in the sacrament, "those who by grave sin have withdrawn from the communion of love of God are called back"[30] to the life they have lost. The choreography of return and reconciliation is dramatized in the document in a set of biblical images: "the Father receives the repentant son who comes back to him"; "Christ places the lost sheep on his shoulders and brings it back to the sheepfold"; "there is great joy at the banquet of God's Church over the sinner who has returned from afar."[31]

With this brief sketch we shall leave postbaptismal reconciliation aside for a moment and turn, by way of contrast, to the concept and practice of penance in postbaptismal context, identifying the ecclesial processes to which it refers. It may be said that penance differs from reconciliation in that the former appears to have in biblical tradition a less dramatic meaning than does reconciliation. The closest biblical equivalent to penance is *metanoia,* which has to do with profound, interior conversion of life.

Characteristically, the "Jewish background of *metanoia* focuses attention on the deeply interior quality of repentance."[32] Latin Christianity came to translate *metanoia* as *paenitentia,* a word suggesting conversion of life or moral transformation. To good effect, Saint Augustine devised a scheme in which he identified penance as an aspect of the whole ecclesial process of sanctification. Baptism he identified as first penance; the act of sacramental reconciliation after grave sin he called second penance. Finally, Augustine identified the whole range of ascetical and sanctifying acts performed by Christians as yet a third kind of penance.[33]

Augustine's scheme is helpful in allowing us to see that penance is the interior aspect of reconciliation, whether baptismal or postbaptismal. Doubtless, there is considerable justification in using reconciliation language in speaking of the whole complex of ecclesial acts and processes that Augustine identified as penance in a third sense. Such a usage would underscore the fact that those who continue to strive for perfection and sanctification and who sin without placing themselves outside the communion of the church still stand, as does the whole church, in need of that final eschatological reconciliation of all things in Christ. Indeed, it is precisely in this principle that we find the protocol for speaking of all the sacraments, especially the eucharist, as sacraments of reconciliation.[34] However, there is good systemic reason for favoring the primacy of the language of penance rather than reconciliation here. Even traditionally, while reconciliation had the more limited reference to the restoration of sinners to ecclesial communion, the word *penance* came to be used to refer to the comprehensive range of ascetical and sanctifying activities to which every faithful Christian is obliged. Indeed, the 1974 revisions of the sacrament, despite the inherent terminological instability, seem to conceive of penance in this more comprehensive sense. Thus on the question of the name of the revised rite, the United States Bishops' Commission on the Liturgy had this explanation: "The rite does not contain only the sacramental rites of reconciliation but also presents a variety of non-sacramental celebrations which, while penitential in character, are not sacramental celebrations. The broader title of the Rite of Penance also embraces these celebrations."[35]

This leads us, then, to define penance as inclusive of all those actions and processes that facilitate the sanctification, moral transformation and ongoing conversion of the Church and its members at every level of corporate and individual Christian life. It is precisely this comprehensive and progressive sense of penance that is underlined by Pope John Paul in his 1984 exhortation when he says, "If we link penance with the *metanoia* which the synoptics refer to, it means the inmost change of heart under the influence of the word of God and in the perspective of the kingdom."[36] Thus, in the pope's words, "it is one's whole existence that becomes penitential, that is to say, directed toward a continuous striving for what is better."[37] Penance means, then, "in the Christian theological and spiritual vocabulary, asceticism, that is to say, the concrete daily effort of a person, supported by God's grace, to lose his or her own life for Christ as the only means of gaining it."[38] It refers to the "effort to put off the old man and put on the new; an effort to overcome in oneself what is of the flesh in order that what is spiritual may prevail; a continual effort to rise from the things of here below to the things of above, where Christ is."[39] Penance is "a conversion that passes from the heart to deeds and then to the Christian's whole life."[40]

From what we have been indicating so far, it will be evident that the ecclesial dynamics and processes of postbaptismal penance and reconciliation, as we have defined them, are quite distinct. Penance refers to the comprehensive dynamic that involves the whole Church, as well as the individual believer, in building up and ennobling corporate existence in Christ. It has to do with continual growth within the body of the Church. It deals typically with ongoing conversion and moral transformation. This fundamental sense of penance is expressively captured by liturgist Regis Duffy when he says, "Penance is the continuing process of conversion that helps us 'walk' in the Gospel way of life, as credible disciples of a Risen Lord."[41] In this sense penance is never absent from the life of any faithful believer, nor from any element in the Church's ministry or liturgical self-expression.

Reconciliation, by contrast, is the overcoming of the radical break with the community of believers, and with God, that takes place through a falling away from baptismal grace. It is the return to the communion of the church after a virtual withdrawal from it by what is traditionally and still properly called mortal sin.

This is not for a moment to suggest a complete disjunction between penance and reconciliation. As already stated, penance has an element of incompleteness in that it involves a vigilance for the final reconciliation with God in the consummation of the kingdom, just as reconciliation to baptismal grace always involves penance because it is a return to the penitential life of true discipleship. No clear compartmentalization is possible or desirable.

It will be seen, finally, that the distinction between postbaptismal penance and reconciliation has its ultimate grounding in the social dynamics of ecclesial existence, as well as in a theology of sin and morality that is radically communal in concept. As David Power has pointed out, the imposition of penance and rituals of forgiveness always concern more than the individual sinner and the need to make personal expiation for sin: "They would seem to be better understood in the way they affect and reflect social structures and community ideal."[42] In the case of rites of penance and reconciliation, then, "the question at issue is how to maintain community holiness, upholding common standards, without being unduly severe on the individual sinner."[43] On the one hand, the church itself is called to "probe her own life and seek always to live as a sign of reconciliation."[44] Each individual, in turn, is called "to scrutinize his own conscience and progress on the path of conversion."[45] Power also points out that this has traditionally been achieved through the complex of penitential acts, in which "the whole Church places itself in a 'liminal' situation, as the community of the redeemed which lives out its life and witness in expectation of the *eschaton*."[46]

Given this ecclesial framework, the tradition that not all sins and deviations are ecclesially intolerable makes sense. In the case of less serious transgressions in the early tradition, sinners submitted themselves to penitential discipline without the necessity of formal excommunication and reconciliation. Certain sins, however, were thought to cause a severe disruption in the church's life and so were regarded as intolerable. Thus, in an effort to maintain community holiness, a process of excommunication, reparation and reconciliation was imposed upon the sinner. Significantly, in the ecclesial manner of handling serious sin, "it is the offense against public order which is uppermost in the rulings, not the extent of the individual's malice."[47] Indeed, as Nathan Mitchell points out, in the determination of seriousness among the fathers, "those sins were 'deadly' which directly tore at the social fabric of the community itself."[48] They demanded exclusion from the eucharist precisely "because these sins were like an acid that ate away the very bonds which united believers around the table."[49]

Our concern, so far, has been with theological and ecclesiological definitions of penance and reconciliation. Our next task is to relate these definitions to the actual postbaptismal rites of penance and reconciliation and to identify some of the systemic problems in these rites.

AN ANALYSIS OF THE RITES

The rites of reconciliation to which we are referring are, of course, those represented in the 1974 Rite of Penance. These include a Rite for the Reconciliation of Individual Penitents, a Rite for Reconciliation of Several Penitents with Individual Confession and Absolution, and a Rite for Reconciliation of Penitents with General Confession and Absolution. In both traditional and modern understanding, as already pointed out, these rites have as their primary purpose the reconciliation of serious sinners. This is clear from the fact that only those conscious of mortal sin are canonically and doctrinally subject to them.[50]

On the other hand, as we saw already, penance finds expression in much more diverse ways and is not limited to any particular rite or process. Accordingly, the Introduction to the 1974 revisions states that the people of God accomplishes penance and renewal "in many different ways."[51] It does this when "it shares in the suffering of Christ by enduring its own difficulties, carries out works of mercy and charity, and adopts ever more fully the outlook of the Gospel message."[52] In this way, the church becomes a sign of conversion. This penitential dimension of the church's life is expressed and celebrated "in the liturgy when the faithful confess that they are sinners and ask pardon of God and of their brothers and sisters. This happens in the penitential services, in the proclamation of the word of God, in prayer, and in the penitential aspects of the eucharistic celebration."[53] To this list the 1984 Papal Exhortation added pilgrimages, fasting and works of charity.[54] In the circumstances of the modern church, we would add the increasingly popular practice of spiritual direction.

Traditionally, however, sacramental confession, though principally a rite of reconciliation, has also been commended as a privileged mode of penance. The protocol for this has been found in the concept of "confession of devotion." This use of the sacrament is promoted in the Introduction to the 1974 revisions, when it is said that "frequent and careful celebration of this sacrament is also very useful as a remedy for venial sin."[55] This penitential and devotional use of the rite represents "a serious striving to perfect the grace of baptism so that, as we bear in our body the death of Jesus Christ, his life may be seen in us ever more clearly."[56] In this way, Christians "should try to conform more closely to Christ and to follow the voice of the Spirit more attentively."[57]

A major systemic problem becomes immediately apparent, however, when we recognize that the same rite is being used for the two quite distinct purposes of penance and reconciliation. This problem is adverted to by De Clerck who recognizes that "what we have at present is one sacramental process with two different objectives."[58] There is, on the one hand, the objective of reconciliation after grave sin and, on the other, the objective of ongoing penitential transformation.

Indeed, even a third purpose is noted by liturgist Peter Fink when he says that

> the sacrament of penance has over the centuries taken on two other functions in addition to the original reconciliation of serious sinners: the process of spiritual purification and growth once accomplished through intercession and other acts of the eucharistic assembly, and, in the case of children prior to their first eucharist, characteristics more akin to initiation than to reconciliation.[59]

That it is possible for a single ritual form to perform these various functions is reasonably doubtful. Indeed, this very problem was the subject of some of the more interesting interventions at the 1983 Synod of Bishops, which was devoted to the topic of penance and reconciliation. Archbishop Decourtray of Lyons and Bishop Favreau of Nanterre asked whether the church is not expecting too much from a single rite. What is called the rite of reconciliation, they pointed out, is designed specifically for the confession of serious sin. In their opinion, a new form should be drawn up which would be adapted specifically to penitential confession of devotion.[60]

Cardinal Pappalardo of Palermo also expressed the view at the synod that one of the reasons for the lessening of the popularity of confession is that the same rite is required to handle both serious sins, which destroy communion with God, and less serious sins. To remedy the problem, the cardinal suggested that the Church "consider creating other forms of celebration, with sacramental characteristics, for minor sins, not linked with the confession of sins, but expressing repentance and the purpose of amendment."[61]

As these synodal interventions imply, two systemic solutions to this problem are possible. (In my view, the second is the more desirable.) Either sacramental confession should become more exclusively identified with the purpose of reconciling those in serious sin, while the many other forms are promoted for ongoing penitential conversion, or a second rite of confession more adapted to penitential usage should be created. Minimally, this second solution would require the provision of two forms of ministerial declaration at the end of the rite of confession as it presently exists: one for the reconciliation of those in serious sin (absolution), and a second for the blessing of persons engaged in ongoing penitential conversion of life.[62]

Beyond that, a new or adapted rite would find its formal focus in a renewed spirituality of confession of devotion,[63] as well as in a renewal of appreciation of the powerful dynamics of the act of confession within the larger context of spiritual direction.[64] The perspectives on the phenomenon of conversion set forth in recent theological reflection would be greatly relevant in this process.

The second systemic issue that we want to take up here relates directly to the one just mentioned. It involves a changing attitude to penance and reconciliation on the part of believers brought about by the successful reemergence of the baptismal ecclesiology already outlined. While there seems to be no insurmountable loss of confidence in the pastoral efficacy of the rite of reconciliation in its function of restoring to the communion of the church those persons seeking to repent of their serious state of sin, there are serious problems with its penitential purpose.

As already mentioned, in regard to this second purpose, the rite has inherent problems, one of which is the requirement it makes on believers to translate all issues into terms of sin and absolution. However, the changing self-image of Catholic Christians (which is certainly not without its negative dimensions) severely limits their ability to translate every dynamic of conversion and sanctification into terms of sin and reconciliation (an ability generally assumed in the older spirituality of devotional confession). This inability is occasioned by the emergence in the postconciliar period of an attitude that does not incline people to view themselves easily as sinners holding a more or less habitual status of "outsiderhood" in the church.[65] While this process could be accompanied by a loss of the sense of sin, this changing self-image represents, perhaps, the most profound transition which characterizes the postconciliar church and, indeed, is a feature of modern Christianity in general. This is verified in Protestantism in what Wolfhart Pannenberg has described as a movement from a piety of guilt consciousness, with its intense sense of separation from God, to a eucharistic piety which promotes a profound sense of participation within the communion of Christ's body.[66]

The dynamics of liturgical and ministerial inclusion promoted by the Second Vatican Council, by contrast with the dynamics of exclusion operative in some aspects of church life before the council, is bound to have attitudinal consequences in relation to the rite which effectively controls and handles issues of inclusion and exclusion. What is operative here is what Gerald Lardner calls a restructured symbol-to-user relationship in changing social situations.[67] In effect, there is occurring a progressive alienation from the given rites because of a shift in ecclesial sensibility. Thus, the promotion of alienation/reconciliation language within processes that are really penitential generates conflict with and disaffection from the rites themselves.

What this underlines fundamentally, then, is the necessity, from yet another perspective, of a systemic reordering of the ecclesial processes of penance and reconciliation and of ritually and pastorally advancing the theoretical and practical differentiation already proposed.

The third systemic issue that I want to take up here is one that I can examine only briefly. It concerns the confession of children before first communion. Peter Fink rightly points out that "it is almost impossible to make reconciliation sense out of penance for children before their first communion.[68] It is, in my opinion, however, possible to make *penitential* sense out of confession before first communion. While it cannot be assumed that children, even at the age of reason, are serious sinners needing reconciliation with the church, the rite of confession can be seen as an appropriate way for children to recall, renew, and grow in their baptismal faith as they prepare for the completion of initiation into the church's life through the eucharist. In this penitential conception of first penance before first communion, there is less of a disruption of the baptism–eucharist initiation process. This will be the case especially if first confession has the context of an ongoing exposure to penitential practices and celebrations going back to the very beginning of religious formation, both in the home and in church or school education programs. What this opens up is the question of whether or not there should be devised a special form of penance for children who have not yet been initiated into eucharistic communion. Minimally, some modifications in the existent rite could be a move in the right direction.

The practical and theological reconceptualization of the first confession of children not yet brought to the eucharist as penance rather than reconciliation would also go a long way toward clarifying the official requirement of first confession before first communion with the doctrines and canons which clearly require the sacrament of reconciliation only for those conscious of mortal sin.[69]

We turn now to the final systemic issue in our analysis, which concerns the ecclesial dynamics operative in the use of reconciliation by general absolution. The subject of general absolution has been extensively studied from doctrinal and canonical perspectives, but hardly, if at all, from a systemic perspective.[70] While theological and pastoral perspectives generally favor a liberal and normative use of the rite of reconciliation with general absolution, a systemic approach can raise serious doubts about the wisdom of such a trend. Systemically, it can be argued that the normalization of the rite of general absolution would, in fact, bring about shifts of ecclesial processes and dynamics of the proportion capable of modifying negatively the powerful baptismal ecclesiology promoted in the postconciliar church.

It also seems naive, from a systemic perspective, to imagine that the normative use of a rite of general absolution alongside the ritual forms involving individual confession and absolution can be harmonized by appeal to the desirability of a variety of expressions of reconciliation. Nor again does it seem adequate to argue that the rite of general absolution is necessary to articulate the communal dimensions of reconciliation. It can be argued that an element of community presence is not verified only by the actual participation of the community in a public service of reconciliation, but, even more fundamentally, by the presence of the community to the sinner in search of reconciliation at the level of effective ministry and pastoral support systems.[71]

The fundamental problem with the normative use of a general absolution mode of reconciliation is that too much would remain undramatized and unsymbolized. Rosemary Haughton's assertion that the great mysteries of faith become saving statements only when enacted and dramatized is very much to the point here. The dynamics of dramatic presentation, she points out, provide not merely an image of the way in which salvation works, but "more importantly, are an example of the way in which the spiritual energy—the stuff of salvation—has to work, according to its own inherent nature, as something happening in, to, and between people."[72]

It is arguable, then, that in reconciliation by general absolution there would be a loss of the sense of the boundaries between ecclesial existence and the kind of alienated existence caused by serious sin. It is probable that there would be an inadequate consciousness of the communal criteria by which serious sin is distinguished from less serious sin. The absence of the experience of being critically engaged in a personal manner by the church's minister would generate an individualism that envisages the issues of sin and reconciliation in an overly privatized and introspective manner. Not least, from the perspective of the present analysis, the distinction between penance and reconciliation would be inadequately apprehended. In short, it seems that the strong and participatory baptismal ecclesiology promoted in the modern church implies not an "easier" or less critical theology and practice of postbaptismal reconciliation, but rather one that is grounded in a radical appreciation of the profound social dynamics of ecclesial existence and articulated in an adequately differentiated liturgical system.

In this essay, I have sought to identify some systemic problems with regard to the church's theology and practice of penance and reconciliation. Fundamental to these problems, I contend, is an inadequate differentiation between baptismal reconciliation, postbaptismal reconciliation, and the penitential dimensions of Christian life. This inadequate differentiation is evident at both theological and liturgical levels. On the basis of a baptismal ecclesiology, I have sought to establish adequate systemic differentiation between the church's practice of penance and reconciliation. I suggest that it is precisely this lack of differentiation that lies at the root of some practical difficulties in the specific areas of the use of confession, the first penance of children, and the practice of general absolution. Within these contexts, I have offered some suggestions which, I believe, could provide a way forward in this critically important area in the life of the postconciliar church.

---

1. General Introduction, no. 1, Rite of Christian Initiation of Adults, *The Rites of the Catholic Church as Revised by the Second Vatican Ecumenical Council*, vol. 1, second ed. (New York: Pueblo, 1983), 3. Hereafter referred to as The Rites.

2. ___.

3. ___.

4. Introduction, no. 1, Rite of Penance, *The Rites,* 361.

5. ___, 362.

6. ___.

7. ___.

8. Apostolic Exhortation on Reconciliation and Penance, published in *Origins* 14:27 (20 December 1984) 432–58 (hereafter referred to as Apostolic Exhortation with pagination referring to the Origins edition).

9. Apostolic Exhortation, no. 27, 449.

10. ___.

11. Jerome Theisen, *Community and Disunity: Symbols of Grace and Sin* (Collegeville, MN: St. John's University Press, 1975).

12. ___, 83.

13. ___, 82.

14. ___, 83.

15. ___, 127.

16. ___.

17. ___, 107.

18. ___, 108.

19. Sermon, 96, 7.

20. The theme of the church as the sacrament of reconciliation is developed at length by Pope John Paul II in his Apostolic Exhortation, esp. nos. 8–12, 25–26; 437–39; 446–48.

21. Monika K. Helwig, *The Meaning of the Sacraments* (Dayton: Pflaum/Standard, 1972) 80. See also her essay, "Christian Initiation: Gate to Salvation," *Chicago Studies* 22 (1983) 227–37.

22. It will be recognized, for instance, that New Testament references to the forgiveness of sin are primarily baptismal. See Raymond E. Brown, "We Profess One Baptism for the Forgiveness of Sins" *Worship* 40 (1966) 260–71.

23. Among such frequently cited texts are Romans 5:6–11; 2 Corinthians 5:17–21; Ephesians 2:12–22; Colossians 1:13–20.

24. See Paul De Clerck, "Celebrating Penance or Reconciliation?" *The Clergy Review* 68 (1983) 313–14.

25. On the choice of the terms *reconciliation* and *penance* in the revised rites, see F. Sottocornola, *A Look at the New Rite of Penance*, trans. Thomas A. Krosnicki (Washington, DC: United States Catholic Conference, 1975) 4–5; Bishops' Committee on the Liturgy, *Commentary on the Rite of Penance.* Study Text 4 (Washington, DC: United States Catholic Conference, 1975) 9–12; Pierre Jounel, "La liturgie de la réconciliation," *La Maison-Dieu* 117 (1974) 7–37.

26. See Apostolic Exhortation, no. 4, 434–36.

27. See *Liber sacramentorum romanae ecclesiae ordinis anni circuli*, ed. L. Mohlbert (Rome: Herder, 1960) esp. 356, 357, 363, 367.

28. Decree, Rite of Penance, *The Rites*, 359.

29. Introduction, Rite of Penance, no. 4, *The Rites*, 364, quoting the Dogmatic Constitution on the Church of the Second Vatican Council, no. 11.

30. Introduction, no. 7, Rite of Penance, *The Rites*, 366.

31. See Introduction, no. 6, *The Rites*, 366.

32. Carrol Stuhlmueller, "The Gospel According to Luke," *The Jerome Biblical Commentary*, ed. Raymond E. Brown et al. (Englewood Cliffs, NJ: Prentice-Hall, 1968), vol. 2, no. 46, 127.

33. Sermon 351:3, 6.

34. This point is developed by Pope John Paul II in his Apostolic Exhortation, esp. no. 27, 448–49. See also Nathan Mitchell, "The Table of the Eucharist: Christian Fellowship and Christian Forgiveness," in *The Rite of Penance: Commentaries*, vol. 3: *Background and Directions* (Washington, DC: The Liturgical Conference, 1978) 62–81; John Quinn, "The Lord's Supper and Forgiveness of Sin," in R. Kevin Seasoltz, ed., *Living Bread, Saving Cup: Readings on the Eucharist* (Collegeville, Minn.: Liturgical Press, 1987) 231–59; Jean-Marie Tillard, "The Bread and Cup of Reconciliation," in *Sacramental Reconciliation.* Concilium 61, ed. Edward Schillebeeckx (New York: Herder and Herder, 1971) 38–54.

35. *Commentary on the Rite of Penance*, 10.

36. Apostolic Exhortation, no. 4, 435.

37. ___.

38. ___.

39. ___.

40. ___.

41. Regis A. Duffy, *Real Presence: Worship, Sacraments, and Commitment* (San Francisco: Harper and Row, 1982) 161.

42. David N. Power, "The Sacramentalization of Penance," *The Heythrop Journal* 18 (1977) 10.

43. ___.

44. ___, 21.

45. ___.

46. ___, 9.

47. ___, 12.

48. Nathan Mitchell, "The Table of the Eucharist," 72. Typically, three kinds of sins were classed in this category: murder, apostasy and adultery. See, for example, Augustine, *De Fide et Operibus,* 19. A social analysis of these sins is provided in Power, "The Sacramentalization of Penance," 10–14.

49. Mitchell, "The Table of the Eucharist," 73.

50. See *Code of Canon Law,* canons 960, 988, 989; Introduction, nos. 7a, 31, 34, The Rite of Penance, *The Rites,* 366–67, 375, 376; Apostolic Exhortation, 31, 451; 28, 449.

51. Introduction, no. 4, *The Rites,* 363.

52. ___.

53. ___.

54. Apostolic Exhortation, nos. 28, 449; 32, 453. On the penitential dimensions of dialogue, catechesis, and the sacraments (though here the language of reconciliation, rather than of penance, is used), see nos. 25–27, 446–49.

55. Introduction, no. 7b, *The Rites,* 367.

56. ___.

57. ___. See also Apostolic Exhortation, no. 32, 453; *Code of Canon Law,* canon 998, 2.

58. De Clerck, "Celebrating Penance or Reconciliation?" 319.

59. Peter E. Fink, "Investigating the Sacrament of Penance: An Experiment in Sacramental Theology," *Worship* 54 (1980) 209.

60. Archbishop Derek Worlock, *Repent and Believe: The Sixth Synod of Bishops in Rome 1983* (London: Catholic Truth Society, 1984) 7.

61. Report published in *L'Osservatore Romano* (English weekly edition), 31 October 1983, 4.

62. This possibility was apparently considered out of the question by the editors of the 1974 rite. See Pierre Jounel, "La liturgie de la réconciliation," *La Maison-Dieu* 117 (1974) 14.

63. For a survey of modern approaches to devotional confession, see John F. Dedek, "The Theology of Devotional Confession," *Proceedings of the Catholic Theological Society of America* 22 (1967) 215–22. See also Karl Rahner, "The Meaning of Frequent Confession of Devotion," Theological Investigations, vol. 3 (Baltimore: Helicon, 1967) 117–89.

64. See David N. Power, "Confession as Ongoing Conversion," The *Heythrop Journal* 18 (1977) 180–90; Jean Leclercq, "Confession and Praise of God," *Worship* 42 (1968) 169–76; "Confession," in Xavier Leon-Dufour, *Dictionary of Biblical Theology* (New York: Seabury, 1973) 87–88.

65. On the concept of "outsiderhood" in social systems, see Victor Turner, *Dramas, Fields, and Metaphors: Symbolic Action in Human Society* (Ithaca, NY: Cornell University), 231ff.

66. See Wolfhart Pannenberg, *Christian Spirituality* (Philadelphia: Westminster, 1983) 13–49.

67. See Gerald V. Lardner, "Communication Theory and Liturgical Research," *Worship* 51 (1977) esp. 303ff.

68. Peter E. Fink, "Investigating the Sacrament of Penance," 220.

69. See *Code of Canon Law*, canons 913, 914, 916, 989.

70. A useful summary of some of the theological, historical, and canonical issues involved in general absolution are found in Ladislaus Orsy, "General Absolution: New Law, Old Tradition, Some Questions," *Theological Studies* 45 (1984) 676–89.

71. In any case, the second official form of reconciliation (Rite for Reconciliation of Penitents with Individual Confession and Absolution), though a hybrid and internally unsatisfactory, along with the category of rites called "penitential celebrations," is effective in giving occasional liturgical expression to communal presence.

72. Rosemary Haughton, *The Drama of Salvation* (New York: Seabury, 1975) viii.

Chapter 2

Mass Stipends and Eucharistic Praxis

The analysis of the monetary transactions represented in the Mass stipend system as eucharistic praxis involves the assertion that these transactions are highly consequential and that they have played and continue to play a highly generative role in the formation of attitudes and ideas about the church, eucharist, and ministry. Without prejudice to the contemporary debates about the nature of praxis, I understand praxis as the dynamic by which action generates and shapes theoretical formulations and is in turn modified by theory. Attention to Mass stipends as eucharistic praxis, then, means attention to the origin and evolution of monetary transactions in the eucharist with a view to ascertaining theological effects and consequences.

    It is not possible, of course, to isolate the practice of money in the eucharist from the larger complex of eucharistic transactions represented by the presentation, blessing and sharing of gifts to bread and wine. The use of the language of "transaction" here represents an approach that seeks to highlight the relationship between the parts in a ritual complex as well as the manner in which modifications and changes in one part of the ritual system affect and modify the whole, and consequently the activity and role of the participants.

    This essay then, seeks to situate the question of Mass stipends within two related perspectives: that of the generative relationship between liturgical practice and theological reflection; and that of the ecological relationship between money offerings and the whole complex of acts that go to make up the Christian eucharist. It will be suggested that these two contexts provide the only adequate criteria for a prospective evaluation of the Mass stipend system.

The Pauline Model and Its Development

Edward Kilmartin has pointed out that "the meaning attached to the presentation of gifts at the Eucharist is determined by the basic idea that governs the understanding of the Eucharist in any given period."[1] The same may be said for all eucharistic transactions. At the risk of oversimplification, it may be suggested that the early church had one eucharistic praxis, that is, one set of eucharistic transactions involving bread, wine, and money, with an attendant theology and ecclesiology, that stands in marked contrast to that of the medieval church. An analysis of the performance of bread, wine and money in these transactions, and of the movement from the one praxis to the other is the first task of this essay.

The fundamental economy of Christian eucharistic transactions is set forth in the New Testament texts that give accounts of the Last Supper and the Christian eucharist. Attention is focused at once on a bread action and a wine action presented as ordinances for continuing discipleship in memory of Jesus. The fundamental structure of these actions has been reduced to four in the classical analysis of Gregory Dix: taking, giving thanks, breaking, and giving.[2] It is Paul who provides an elaboration of the broader ecclesial dynamics of these eucharistic actions. In his First Letter to the Corinthians, we are given the fundamental outlines of an ecclesial act of eucharistic sharing in which bread and wine are taken, blessed and shared, and the poor are fed. It is clear that for Paul, sharing in the eucharist and service to the poor are intimately related. In the transaction of the bread and the cup, there is established a *koinonia* in the body and blood of Christ. Eucharistic incorporation represents the fundamental definition of the church. Eating together at the common table actualizes the church and represents the fundamental paradigm for all transactions in the community, transactions essentially of *diakonia* and service: the sharing of food and drink, especially between those who are well-to-do and those who have nothing, is fundamental to the celebration of the Christian eucharist. For Paul, these eucharistic transactions are made in the Spirit who is the life principle of the body (1 Corinthians 12:13; Romans 12: 9–11), and they embody the church as a doxological sacrifice (Romans 12:1–12). A code of conduct is symbolized in the eucharist. A charge to share food and drink is intrinsic to the full reality of the eucharistic gathering. This explains why Paul rails against selfishness and factionalism in the assembly (1 Corinthians 11:17–34). Failure to share bread with the needy is an assault upon the eucharistic community and upon the Lord's body.

The most remarkable thing that emerges from a study of the Pauline assemblies is their profoundly inclusive ethos, that is, their deep sense of participation in the body of Christ. Every eucharistic act intensifies and radicalizes this communion in Christ, not least those acts expressive of care and concern for the poor and needy. This fundamental character of the Pauline eucharist is continued in the practice of the eucharist in the post-apostolic and patristic periods. Gifts of bread, wine, and money are transacted in eucharistic communities deeply attentive to the charge of charity and *diakonia*. In the eucharist of Justin Martyr in the second century, the inclusive activity of the assembly in the various transactions of the gifts is clearly in evidence, and care for the poor is integral to the meaning of Christian assembly: "The wealthy who are willing to make contributions, each as he pleases, and the collection is deposited with the president, who aids orphans and widows, those who are in want because of sickness or some other reason, those in prison, and visiting strangers—in short, he takes care of all in need."[3] In the baptismal eucharist of Hyppolytus some generations later, the one who received gifts to bring to a widow or a sick person is exhorted to do so at once, or at least the next day, "adding something of his own, because the bread of the poor has stayed in his possession."[4] In the Syrian *Didascalia Apostolorum* from the early part of the third century, charity is placed so completely at the heart of the liturgical assembly that the bishop is exhorted to sit on the floor and give up his throne to a poor man when he welcomes him into the gathering.[5] The Pauline ideal is eloquently expressed when Cyprian of Carthage chides a wealthy member of his congregation for offending against the ethics of the eucharist: "You should blush to come to the Lord's assembly without a sacrifice and to partake of the sacrifice offered by some poor person."[6]

An important aspect of the eucharistic *koinonia* of the early centuries was the offering of gifts in the name of the dead. In the words of Edward Kilmartin, "Since the dead were regarded as members of the Church, it was natural that they should be drawn into the fellowship of the earthly worshipers by gifts offered 'in their name.'"[7] The earliest references to this practice occur in the writings of Tertullian, where we learn of the custom of anniversary offerings for the deceased.[8]

In Augustine's time, communion between the living and the dead was still practiced by means of memorial meals at tombs, at which the poor were often fed.[9] These eucharists and agapes represented acts of communion deepened and solidified because the poor members of the community were fed by the offerings made in the name of the dead.

Was there anything akin to the Mass stipend as we know it today in the early centuries? The answer is yes. For one thing, the eucharist celebrated in small groups and involving special concerns seems to have been a feature of Christianity from the beginning.[10] Those involved in such eucharists provided the material elements for the occasion, and donations were often made to the one who presided.[11] We find figures such as Jerome preaching of the obligation to support the church's ministers who live from the altar in terms derived from the Old Testament: "The tithes and first fruits, which were once given by the people to the priests and levites, apply also to the people of the church."[12] Jerome is quick to follow up this appeal, however, with the important qualification that the Christian obligation to charity extends to all goods and properties, not just to the tithe.

It is this qualification, more than anything else, however, that warns against an easy appeal to the practice of the early centuries in support of the full-fledged Mass stipend system. The Mass stipend does appear, on the surface, to have some precedent in the practice of early Christianity, but the similarities amount only to evidence of special prayers sought by individuals, gifts provided by the people, and the support of the church's ministers derived from these gifts. The difference between the early practice and that of the developed Mass stipend system is the difference between the eucharistic praxis of early Christianity and that of the medieval and post-medieval periods.

In the Pauline eucharistic model and its practical and theological elaboration in the post-apostolic and patristic periods, the eucharistic transactions of bread, wine, and money took place *out of the fullness* of the church's communion in Christ and gave expression to the bounty of the church. Eucharistic *koinonia* involved the care of the poor and the dead; offerings of food and money found their radical identity in this involvement. In the dynamics of the eucharist in this early period, there was operative what might be called a *principle of inclusion,* by which Christians acted not *in order to* gain access to sacred realities, but rather *on the basis of* their inclusion through the Holy Spirit in the communion of Christ. Gifts and money were transacted in the fullness of communion and flowed from this communion as its embodiment and expression.

The early Christian eucharist differed essentially from the manner in which pagan sacrifices and offerings were made in order to gain divine favor. Christian eucharistic transactions were not envisaged within the categories of pre-Christian sacrifice; neither was the *sacrum commercium,* the holy exchange, interpreted in any way that suggested contingency upon ritual priesthood and temple cult. The Christian eucharist was a radically different affair; the act of a transformed people embodying a living cult in its common life.

We cannot go into the question here of the relationship between the Old Testament practice and conception of priesthood and sacrifice and the New Testament, early Christian notions of liturgy and priesthood.[13] However, the fundamental transformation that took place in the Christian order cannot be underlined enough. We may characterize this as a spiritualization—indeed, more suggestively, as a *pneumaticization*—of sacrifice and priesthood in the Christian dispensation. Worship in the Spirit transformed the whole of Christian life into a living sacrifice. The temple became the people; priesthood was appropriated by the Spirit-filled body of the baptized; worship was no longer a cult, but *koinonia* in the Spirit.[14]

It was precisely this transformed, inclusive sense of Christian life and liturgy that began to be reversed in the self-understanding of the church in the medieval period, when a principle of exclusion came into play, largely through the reassertion of pre-Christian ideas of sacrifice, liturgy and priesthood. Therefore, liturgical acts would be seen as a means of gaining temporary access to sacred realities to which the baptized had no constitutional access.

The Stipend and the Dynamics of Exclusion

It would not be correct to romanticize the patristic period or to set it in opposition to the medieval. Indeed, significant modifications in ecclesiastical structure and liturgical practice had already begun to take place by the end of the patristic period. These found expression in the increasing exclusion of the people from the transactions of the liturgy and their marginalization in the structure of the church. Clericalization was quickly established as the church began to be reconceived structurally according to the imperial model. Increasingly the ministry of the ordained ceased to be understood as a charism within a community of believers and appeared instead as a personal authority complete in itself, ecclesiastically absolute, with ordination seen as accession to hierarchical power and official status.

The liturgy itself had unwittingly provided some internal impetus in this direction when it began to appropriate the style and ethos of imperial ceremonial. This gave rise to a set of symbols that would result in the transference to Christ of regal categories and thus to a changed relationship between Christ and believers. The latter began to be seen more as servants and unworthy dependents, and as a result there arose a growing sense of unworthiness and awe in the face of the *mysterium tremendum,* as the eucharist was increasingly called.[15]

The most significant expression of this was the decline in congregational communion. The seriousness of this development was recognized at once by such eminent bishops as John Chrysostom and Ambrose of Milan, both of whom campaigned against this trend.[16] The decline was not reversed, however, but only deepened in succeeding centuries.

The withdrawal of the people from communion may be regarded as the first of a series of radical shifts in the church's eucharistic transactions. The gifts were still prepared and offered by the people, *but no longer shared in communion.* This established a serious break in the giving and sharing of the gifts of the eucharist. The result was a profound modification, not only of the dynamics of eucharistic participation but also of the manner in which access to the sacred would be perceived thereafter.

Increasingly, penitential supplicatory elements came to dominate over the older ones of thanksgiving and communion; the spiritual sacrifice of the common life gave way to ritualism. There emerged a growing sense of the eucharist as a privileged act by which God's aid might be sought for various personal favors as well as for the benefit of others, living and dead. This resulted in a conception of the priest as the exclusive subject of the eucharist and on his personal act of offering and consecration as the central dynamic of eucharistic transactions.

The significance of this shift in the Christian praxis of the eucharist can hardly be exaggerated. The eucharist no longer appeared to believers primarily as expressing Christian identity in Christ, but as a privileged mode of access to divine favors and sacred realities to which there was virtually no other means of access. The subsequent history of eucharistic transactions may be read as the elaboration of this principle. Gifts and offerings were no longer transacted out of the fullness of eucharistic *koinonia* in the body of Christ but in order to gain access to eucharistic realities extrinsic to the self-definition of Christian believers. The priest was increasingly seen as the unique mediator, as having personal power over the blessings of the eucharist. Thus, offerings and gifts were no longer given to the clergy because the latter were servants of the eucharistic community and worthy of a living thereby, but because they were custodians and dispensers of eucharistic grace. The praxis of a priestly people was replaced by the praxis of an overly hierarchical society; a dynamic of inclusion was replaced by a dynamic of exclusion.

From the seventh century onward, the offering of money came increasingly to the fore and the offering of bread and wine was discontinued. The decrease in congregational communion led to a curtailment of the bringing of the gifts for communion. The more significant reason for this development was the transition from the use of leavened to unleavened eucharistic bread. It was this development, more than anything else, that signified the reemergence of Old Testament ideas about priesthood and liturgy.[17] The motivation behind this change was to remove eucharistic bread and its production from the sphere of the earthly and the profane and to ensure its worthiness for the Christian cult. The result was the ritualization of the process of producing eucharistic bread and the restriction of its production to the clergy and to monasteries. With this development, the people's role was curtailed once more, this time at the level of the originating action which the preparation and provision of material gifts for the eucharist represented.

This change had greater significance that might appear at first sight, as Mary Collins has shown in her exploration of the profound interplay between restrictions in the matter of eucharistic bread and restrictions in ecclesial roles and theological conceptions. The emergence of a new set of restrictive choices about eucharistic bread and the qualifications of those who produce it could not but shape and effect restrictive conceptions about redemption, holiness and access to God.[18] With this further exclusion, then, came the second major shift in the practice of the eucharist and the emergence of a set of conceptions that further contributed to a restrictive and exclusive eucharistic praxis.

By the twelfth century, the presentation of bread and wine by the people took place only on a very small number of occasions and, when practiced, had little more than dramatic value. Where the collection of money continued, it no longer had intrinsic connection with the eucharist or with alms for the poor.[19]

It was against this background that the practice of the Mass stipend had begun to emerge from the eighth century onward. Significantly, as Joseph Jungmann has shown, the point at which the Mass stipend proper emerged was the point at which the connection between eucharistic preparation and the presentation of the gifts had finally broken down. The particular character of the Mass stipend was of an honorarium paid in advance to obligate a priest to celebrate exclusively for the intention of the donor.[20] It was, thus, an *extra-eucharistic* transaction directed toward *obtaining* a special benefit available only through the exclusive mediation of the priest.

The earliest regulated accounts of Mass stipends are found in the eighth century rule of Chrodegang of Metz, in which it was granted that a priest might accept a stipend in return for a Mass celebrated for a donor and his intentions.[21] By the ninth century it was understood that such stipends were accepted in an exclusive way, as we know from the revisions undertaken by that time on the rule of Chrodegang.

The practice was not adopted without some reserve and even opposition, however. The ecclesial sensibility of many ecclesiastics led them to recoil from the exclusive, extra-eucharistic nature of the transaction. The Synod of Rome held in 826 rejected the practice, declaring that priests should not be allowed to take offerings from some persons to the exclusion of others.[22] As late as the twelfth century, the privatizing tendency of the Mass stipend practice was rejected by the Synod of York, which allowed priests to receive stipends only during the Mass.[23] However, at that time, the Mass stipend system was firmly established throughout the Western Church. Stipends were given more and more outside the liturgy and were increasingly attached in a permanent way to benefices of various kinds.

With the growing organization of the stipend system came the multiplication of votive Masses for various needs and an enormous increase in the number of priests whose sole duty was the celebration of Masses to fulfill the numerous requests. In this way there was firmly established the practice of private Masses and the principle that the giving of a stipend was effective even without the physical presence of the donor. The eucharist was increasingly removed from its ecclesial context, and the manner of its performance and effectiveness was defined without reference, except in the most minimal way, to the eucharistic congregation. In effect, the eucharist could now be transacted from beginning to end without the participation of the people. The congregation, when present, involved itself in the eucharist in a drastically curtailed manner, if at all.[24] In this exclusive and restrictive eucharistic praxis, the Mass stipend became virtually the only ritual means for the people to gain access to the most cherished graces of the eucharistic sacrifice.

It is not difficult to see that monetary transactions of this sort were related to the eucharist in a manner quite different from those of the post-apostolic and patristic periods. Because of the curtailment of the people's role in providing the elements for the eucharist and their exclusion from communion, as well as the many other manifestations of ecclesiastical and clerical exclusivism, the Mass stipend system of the medieval period had only a surface similarity to the offering of gifts in the early Christian eucharist. There is a world of difference between gifts transacted within the fullness of an inclusive Christian eucharist and gifts transacted in an attempt to gain access to a eucharistic and ecclesial system from which ordinary Christians are, in fact and theory, excluded. The offering of gifts was no longer a *symbol of participation* as it was earlier, but rather a *symbol of access*. Because of this, the medieval Mass stipend stood only in apparent continuity with the original practice of offering gifts. The whole ritual complex of the eucharist within which monetary transactions originally operated had been radically changed and modified and thus such transactions operated differently as a result, departing radically from their original meaning and function.

The dynamics represented in the movement from the early form of the offering of gifts to the medieval Mass stipend system bear comparison with what the anthropologist Schlomo Deshen has referred to as *profanation* in the process of change in symbolic operationality. Profanation occurs, according to Deshen, when a symbol is separated from the range of experience within which it originally operated and when a new range of experience becomes operative to the effect of violating the original integrity of the symbol.[25] This is lamentably what happened in the shift of modes of offering in the eucharist from the patristic to the medieval periods. The whole ecclesial and liturgical ethos within which the eucharistic offerings operated was no longer that of an inclusive, participatory order but of a clerical and exclusive order to which the people had access only in the manner of outsiders.

As a consequence, the popular modes of offering lost their original character and integrity.

An Economic Theology of the Eucharist

If praxis refers to the process by which practice shapes and generates theoretical understanding, then it should not be surprising that the medieval theology of the eucharist arose to a considerable extent out of the Mass stipend system, given the prominence this system had achieved by then. Nor should it be surprising that the language of economics and commerce should have entered into the conceptualization of eucharistic operationality and efficacy.[26]

Edward Kilmartin describes the results in the assertion that "the history of theological opinion concerning the value and fruits of the Mass is intimately associated with the history of the system of Mass stipends."[27] The fundamental issue for eucharistic theology in this regard was established by a practical consideration: If something may be gained from the Mass by one who offers a stipend to a priest which is independent of the donor's own attendance or non-attendance, then that gain must be in the objective order. Theologians affirmed the existence of such an objective quantity and thus was established the theory of the fruits of the Mass.

Amalar of Metz in the ninth century had suggested a threefold distinction that was now taken up and elaborated upon as a way of explaining how these fruits might be applied. The Mass, according to Amalar, is offered for the holy universal church, for those who offer alms and gifts, and for the priest.[28] Duns Scotus in the thirteenth century developed this scheme, asserting the existence of three distinct fruits of the Mass, applicable as follows: to the priest *(specialissime);* to the universal church *(generalissime);* and to the one who is the subject of the special intention *(specialiter).*[29] With this scheme came a set of assertions that were widely accepted thereafter: that the fruits available from each Mass are limited; that they are produced in an objective fashion independent of the dispositions of the priest and the participation of the people; and that the priest has the power to apply these fruits.

Here we have the logical conclusions to a practice of the eucharist that was restrictive, nonparticipatory and pointedly clerical. These principles also logically coincided with a disintegration of the profound sense of the unity between Christ, the church and the eucharist that had characterized the post-apostolic and patristic periods. It is telling, for example, that in the medieval church, "body of Christ" no longer referred to the communion of the church in Christ but only to the eucharist itself in a restricted fashion, while the church was regarded as the body of Christ only in a vague sense.[30] But if the church is separated from Christ, then great difficulty arises in maintaining the sense of how Christ and the eucharist are united.

We see this problem of disintegration operative also in medieval discussions about how the fruits of the Mass could be limited. The limitations can be accounted for, according to Scotus, by the fact that it is the church and not Christ which is the immediate subject of the eucharist. This thinking gained wide currency in the thirteenth century and after. It is significant, as Edward Kilmartin points out, that such considerations in the fourteenth and fifteenth centuries arose less from theological speculation than from "the practice of the Church which allows Mass to be offered for an individual and often forbids acceptance of more than one stipend for a single Mass."[31] A restrictive practice of the eucharist gave rise to a restrictive theology; in turn, a eucharistic theology that distanced Christ from the church's eucharistic operationality shaped a eucharistic practice that was self-centered and introverted.

It was only in the sixteenth century with Cardinal Cajetan that a new conceptualization of the question of limited fruits in the Mass was brought forward.[32] According to Cajetan, the Mass is of infinite value in itself because in it the sacrificial offering of the cross is present. At this level the Mass is unlimited. Where the limitation enters in, according to Cajetan, is at the level of the devotion of Christians. This position did not alter the practice of the eucharist in any way but it did provide a more adequate account of the relationship between the infinite value of the Mass and the limitations that were at the same time thought to attend its efficacy. The position of Cajetan became the dominant one and was widely held in the seventeenth century and after.

The question of the relationship between the stipend and the fruits of the Mass was not so easily resolved, however. A feature of this question was the necessity of distinguishing the stipendiary transaction from simony. Scotus's approach was to insist that the priest does not accept payment for the Mass, but only a gratuitous donation.[33] Thomas Aquinas interpreted the stipend in broader terms as a contribution to the priest's support.[34] A number of theories were presented during the medieval and post-medieval periods, each seeking to avoid, on the one hand, the danger of simony and, on the other, the notion that the acceptance of a stipend involves no more than a nonbinding promise on the part of the priest. A primary consideration in these theories was to preclude any impingement of the stipendiary transaction upon the essence of the eucharistic sacrifice and its fruits.[35] But it is precisely in this necessity that the ultimate irony of the whole stipendiary system appears. For theology's final defense against simony was to exclude the stipend from any intrinsic role in the eucharistic act. Considering the original form and conception of monetary transactions as a mode of participation and communion in the eucharist, we are thus given a signal of the extent of the problem that the final evolution of the Mass stipend represented. Within the early practice of the eucharist, monetary transactions were intrinsic expressions of *koinonia* and of care for the needy in the community (including the church's ministers); within the medieval eucharistic context, these monetary transactions bordered dangerously on the buying and selling of spiritual goods from a priest regarded as the exclusive subject of the church's power.

We can see, then, that from the medieval praxis in which the stipend came to play such a prominent role there was derived a theology of the monetary gifts as a ritual means of obtaining rights over eucharistic fruits; an ecclesiology and theology of orders that placed the ordinary Christian outside the realm of proper eucharistic subjectivity; and a popular spirituality concerned to great extent with personal gain viewed in overly commercial terms.

Toward a Renewed Eucharistic Praxis

The modern liturgical movement has had as one of its primary concerns the revitalization of the subjectivity of the baptized in the liturgy. Apart from the restoration of frequent communion during the pontificate of Pope Pius X, one of the earliest practical expressions of greater participation was the restoration of the offertory procession. The success experienced with this practice no doubt generated further interest in the achievement of a more profound theology of the role of the baptized in eucharistic offering and consequently of the Mass stipend.

In the twentieth century, two theologians had much influence in developing such a theology: Maurice de la Taille and Karl Rahner. De la Taille approached the question of eucharistic sacrifice and stipends by situating it in a biblical context. In his view, the stipend should be viewed as providing the material elements for the sacrifice, thereby drawing the donor into the role of active offering in the eucharist. In de la Taille's conception, while the power of eucharistic consecration belongs to the priest, the act of offering belongs to the one who provides the elements for the eucharist.[36] To support this view, he returned to the early practice of the offertory and from this drew the conclusion that "the authors of the sacrifice, in a manner which is proper and personal to them, are the faithful whose gifts are by the priest's hands addressed to God under the form of the Body and Blood of Jesus Christ."[37] This principle, he asserted, provides the only proper interpretation of the Mass stipend.

While de la Taille's approach would be faulted today on a number of grounds, not least because of the questionable analogies he drew between Old Testament sacrifices and the Christian eucharist, as well as his interpretations of patristic thought, he did provide a strong impetus toward the restoration of popular eucharistic subjectivity.

In a controversial essay published in 1949, Karl Rahner developed the general approach of de la Taille and attempted an interpretation of the question of the fruits of the Mass and their relationship to active participation.[38] Rahner's fundamental concern was to remove the Mass from the domain of mechanical and impersonal operation and to establish as a primary principle the efficacy of the Mass within the categories of active participation and *devotio*.[39] At the outset, Rahner proposed as the norm for the frequency of Masses that they be celebrated as often and only as often as *devotio* would be increased, and he contested the notion that the Mass gives glory to God by the simple fact that it is celebrated.[40] While at pains to insist that *devotio* is not the cause and origin of eucharistic operationality, he nevertheless made clear his conviction that the *effects* of the Mass are contingent completely upon personal *devotio*.

Regarding the fruits of the Mass, Rahner proposed that "union by grace in faith and love with Christ's sacrifice is the *one* effect of the sacrifice itself, the essentially single fruit of the sacrifice issuing from the sacrifice itself."[41] In applying this principle, Rahner denied any radical division in the fruits of the Mass. There is no *fructus specialissimus* acquired by the celebrant that is independent of his devotion; nor is there a *fructus specialis* that accrues to the one for whom the Mass is offered that is not dependent upon the *devotio* of the donor.[42] The Mass stipend, in Rahner's view, has no meaning apart from the quality of active participation in the eucharist by the person who makes the offering. It is, in effect, nothing other than a mode of participation in the Mass.

Rahner could be criticized for having put too much emphasis on eucharistic *devotio* and not enough on the eucharist as sacrament. It could be argued that it is the latter and its ecclesial authenticity that properly determines the frequency and operationality of the eucharist. Nevertheless, Rahner did advance theological understanding on a number of important points: namely, that the eucharist operates primarily as an act of communion in Christ; that the priest who presides has no more access to eucharistic realities than does the devout believer; and that the stipend has its fundamental validity as a symbol of eucharistic participation.[43]

At this point, the fundamental question of this essay may be raised: Does the Mass stipend have a future? To follow through a fundamental principle of this essay—that the stipend system cannot be dealt with apart from considerations about its operationality within a larger complex of eucharistic transactions—means that the answer cannot be a simple one; neither can it be given apart from wider considerations about the church, ministry, and the nature of liturgy. However, the conclusion cannot be avoided that the Mass stipend in its medieval and post-medieval form is a highly problematic institution. Its emergence to prominence in the Middle Ages was contingent upon a number of distorted factors in the church's ecclesial and liturgical praxis, and its subsequent evolution gave rise to a fractured, exclusive, and alienating theology of worship, church, and ministry.

The Mass stipend system, then, can only have an acceptable future within a liturgical and ecclesial environment in which there is vigilance about the problematic features of the history identified in this essay. The system must find fresh theological reformulation by contact with the original and most authentic role that monetary transactions performed in the early Christian eucharist. This, in turn, will mean a careful and intelligent practice of the Mass stipend system which avoids the dangers of commercialism, the improper multiplication of Masses, and the encouragement of an individualistic piety impervious to the communal nature of the liturgy.[44]

In order to propose a way forward here, three elements of the postconciliar praxis of the eucharist may be invoked. The first of these elements finds expression in the principle of *ecclesial subjectivity of the eucharist*. According to this principle, the primary subject of the eucharist is the church, not the ordained minister. While no local eucharistic assembly is valid in isolation from the catholicity and apostolicity of the church, sacramentalized and verified in the episcopal and presbyteral orders, it is nevertheless clear from the ancient tradition and its modern appropriation that the concrete, visible eucharistic subject is the local assembly.[45]

Accordingly, liturgical or pastoral practices that appropriate the eucharist to individuals or special groups or remove it from its public, communal context are offensive to the ecclesial constitution and purpose of the sacrament. Similarly unacceptable is the suggestion that the one who presides has fuller access to the eucharistic reality than is available to the liturgical assembly at large.

Since the Mass stipend system has contributed to these and similar theological distortions of understanding in the past, the continuance of the system can only be justified within a theological and pastoral framework careful about the reemergence of these problems. This will mean, for example, vigilance about the priestly celebration of the eucharist in private with little consideration given to the role of the community and with a special intention attached to a stipend as the dominating concern.[46]

What is being suggested here is that the stipend system be so modified in its practical elements that it will never appear merely as a private transaction between an individual and a priest, but always have a communal orientation. For instance, the intention for which a stipend is given should be incorporated formally into the eucharistic liturgy (in the general intercessions, for example), so that it will be not only the priest but the whole assembly that prays for the intention. The appeal is not only to the private prayer of the priest but to the public prayer of the eucharistic assembly.

Similarly, the stipend should be seen not as a commercial, remunerative transaction between an individual and a priest but as an expression of care for the church and its ministry on the part of the person requesting prayers. This point could be given effective expression in the creation of a pastoral system wherein the priest receiving the stipend places it in the charity fund of the parish or ecclesiastical institution. In this way, there would be restored a more intimate connection between the monetary transaction and the eucharist.

The model here would be that of the Pauline tradition in which the eucharist and communal charity were inseparably connected.

The second element in the postconciliar liturgical praxis, which it is appropriate to call upon here, is represented in the ongoing reconstitution of the *participatory dynamics of the eucharist.* This finds expression in the recognition that the eucharistic liturgy is primarily an *action* that unfolds in the hearing of the Word and participation in the communion of the Lord. This participatory conception of the liturgy stands in contrast with those phases of history in which the liturgical assembly was perceived in a passive and receptive mode vis-à-vis the sanctifying action of the priest. Recent renewal emphasizes that the eucharist sanctifies not in an automatic or mechanical way but in and through the very dynamics of the act of participation. This sanctification comes not from any intention of the priest to direct eucharistic graces to individuals or groups but from the fact that the people themselves participate in an intrinsically sanctifying action.

What this implies is that the liturgical assembly is itself the primary recipient of the operations and effects of every eucharistic celebration. No psychological intention on the part of the priest is necessary or able to open to the people more intense levels of grace or benefit. The priest is limited in his ability to dispose of the fruits of the Mass.

It follows from the participatory dynamics of the liturgy that prayer for the absent and the dead is not efficacious in a mechanical or automatic way. The eucharist does not assist such persons in the manner of legal transactions. Thinking in this way fails to respect the proper dynamics of eucharistic sanctification and it depersonalizes the process by which the absent and the dead are recipients of the grace and blessedness of the eucharist.

Historically, the Mass stipend system has offended against the participatory operationality of the eucharist by generating the notion that active participation need not be the primary consideration in receiving eucharistic grace. It encouraged the view that an absent person may actually gain more from the eucharist than one who is present but not included in the intention of the Mass. This has found expression in the notion that while the eucharist is always *celebrated* for the congregation present, it may be *offered* for another intention, often one known only to the priest and involving an absent donor.[47] Some corrective to this has been enshrined in the traditional requirement that the Mass be offered *pro populo* at least once a week.[48] However, the theology and practice of the ancient liturgical tradition, as well as the principles of postconciliar praxis, imply that the Mass is always and unavoidably *pro populo* and that the benefit to the absent and the dead arises from this foundational reality.

If the restoration of the participatory dynamics of the eucharist remains one of the primary tasks of ongoing renewal, then the practice of prayer for the absent and the dead in the liturgy will be reconceived and enriched by this restoration. This means a recognition that such prayer has a deeply personal basis in the devotion and care is incumbent upon the eucharistic community. Prayer of this kind will be conceived properly as an outpouring of love on the part of the church for particular persons and groups, living and dead, and for particular conditions of the church and the world. It will be understood as a conscious expression of love and solidarity founded in the requirements of true Christian conversion. The dynamics of the efficacy of this prayer will not be understood in terms of a private, legal transference of grace but will be recognized to have the shape of a loving act arising out of the edifying role of the eucharist within the communion of saints. As already suggested, the stipend attached to the request for such prayer will be seen properly as a material expression of the charity that flows from authentic Christian prayer.

The final element of the church's eucharistic praxis here concerns the *intrinsic economy of the liturgical order.* By economy is meant the complementary manner in which all the elements of the church's liturgy (the eucharist, the other sacraments, the liturgy of the hours, and so forth) are interrelated and unfold according to a calendar of days, times, feasts, and seasons. In this economy, different features of the mystery of faith come to the fore at different times and the church participates in the mystery of faith according to a carefully moderated understanding of the gradual processes of sanctification and edification. There is an inner rhythm and timeliness in the unfolding of the liturgy that is measured and wisely calculated.

That the stipend system habitually cuts across this liturgical economy is evident within the broad lines of the present analysis. We have already observed that this system offended against the communal nature of worship by separating the special intention of the Mass from the public prayer of the people. It offended similarly by ignoring the manner in which prayer for the living and the dead arises out of the prayer of the eucharistic assembly. The further problem that needs identification here is the tendency of special intentions and the transaction of stipends to take on an autonomy of their own unrelated to the economy of the liturgy. This problem is acutely represented, for example, in the popular premium placed on the multiplication of Mass intentions and in the view that the graces and benefits from such multiplication are cumulative and quantitative.

It is evident, for instance, that the multiplication of Masses for the dead impedes the proper integration of prayer for the dead into the whole structure of the eucharist and the liturgical season. Accordingly, the practice of prayer for the dead would gain greatly from a scheme based on the intrinsic economy of the liturgical year. It might be suggested, for instance, that the number of Masses for the dead be limited. A historical scheme worth recovering would be that of early Christianity, when Masses were celebrated on the third, seventh, and thirtieth days after burial.[49] This scheme was not primarily concerned with the accumulation or multiplication of the benefits of the eucharist, but rather it served to symbolize, in a public and processual way, the desire of the church to accompany and be in solidarity with the dead in their continuing pilgrimage toward blessedness in God's kingdom. In a similar way, Masses for the living could be carefully regulated and moderated to avoid any implication of intrinsic value in multiplication.

In general, all special intentions supported by stipends might be considered more suitable for weekday Masses. This would allow the preeminence of Sundays, major solemnities, and feasts to be celebrated with a more universal and ecclesially inclusive outlook with concern for all God's people and every condition of humanity and human need.

The emerging liturgical praxis of the eucharist, then, as outlined in this essay, would seek to reshape the practice of Mass stipends and special intentions by contact with the Pauline eucharistic model. In this model, gifts and money are brought to the eucharist, collected for the poor, and distributed out of the bounty of the church. The modern basis for this conception and practice of the gifts is established in the General Instruction of the Roman Missal of 1969, which speaks of the preparation of the gifts at the eucharist as "the time to bring forward or collect money for the poor and the church."[50] This involves a theological and pastoral conception of the gathering and presentation of the gifts as a transaction of liturgical *diakonia* that flows from the very nature of the eucharist. It means a corresponding movement away from the superficial view that the eucharistic collection has no more significant value than the utilitarian necessity of raising funds for the maintenance of ecclesiastical institutions. A richer understanding of the intrinsic eucharistic nature of the collection of the gifts is already being set in place in many congregations and Christian communities by the advancement of a theology of stewardship. In this perspective, the offering of money within the eucharist is seen as an integral feature of liturgical spirituality. By the same process, the stipend system can be purified and enriched by contact with the same rich and traditional theology and practice of eucharistic *diakonia*.

In short, the Mass stipend system can have a suitable future only if it continues to be subjected to the same critical scrutiny and positive theological and pastoral enrichment to which the liturgy in general has been subjected in the renewal advanced by the Second Vatican Council.

---

1. Edward Kilmartin, "The Sacrifice of Thanksgiving and Social Justice," in *Liturgy and Social Justice*, ed. Mark Searle (Collegeville, MN: The Liturgical Press, 1980) 58. While the 1983 Code of Canon Law has replaced the term *stipends* with *offerings*, the more familiar term is retained in this essay for clarity of subject matter.

2. Gregory Dix, *The Shape of the Liturgy* (New York: The Seabury Press, 1982) 48–50.

3. Justin Martyr, *Apologia I*, 67, PG 6, 430; translation from Lucien Deiss, *Springtime of the Liturgy: Liturgical Texts of the First Four Centuries*, trans. Matthew J. O'Connell (Collegeville, MN: The Liturgical Press, 1979) 94.

4. *La Tradition Apostolique de saint Hippolyte: Essai de reconstitution*, ed. Bernard Botte. LQF 39. (Münster: Aschendorff, 1963) 62; translation from Deiss, *Springtime of the Liturgy*, 145.

5. *Didascalia et Constitutiones Apostolorum*, ed. F. X. Funk (Paderborn: Schoeningh, 1895) 2, 58.

6. Cyprian of Carthage, *De opere et eleemosynis*, PL 4, 612–13.

7. Edward Kilmartin, "The Sacrifice of Thanksgiving and Social Justice," 57.

8. Tertullian, *De corona* 3, PL 2, 79.

9. See the chapter entitled "The Feasts of the Dead," in Frederik van der Meer, *Augustine the Bishop: The Life and Work of a Father of the Church* (New York: Sheed and Ward, 1961) 498–516.

10. Joseph Jungmann, *The Mass of the Roman Rite: Its Origin and Development* (New York: Benziger Brothers, 1955) vol. 1, 212–33.

11. There is no significant distinction between food offerings and money offerings in this early period. Some anthropologists have concluded, in fact, that shared food represented the earliest form of money, and that money itself had a fundamental link with ancient food rituals. See William H. Desmonde, *Magic, Myth, and Money: The Origin of Money in Religious Ritual* (New York: Free Press of Glencoe, 1962).

12. Jerome, *In Malachiam* 3:7, PL 25, 1571.

13. This vastly complex area is introduced in Robert J. Daly, *The Origins of the Christian Doctrine of Sacrifice* (Philadelphia: Fortress Press, 1978); see also David N. Power, "Words that Crack: The Uses of 'Sacrifice' in Eucharistic Doctrine," *Worship* 53 (1979) 386–404.

14. See John Hall Elliott, *The Elect and the Holy* (Leiden: E. J. Brill, 1966); Raymond Corriveau, *The Liturgy of Life: A Study of the Ethical Thought of St. Paul in his Letters to Early Christian Communities* (Brussels/Montreal: Desclée, 1970).

15. See Joseph Jungmann, *The Place of Christ in Liturgical Prayer* (New York: Alba House, 1965) 245–55.

16. ___, *The Mass of the Roman Rite*, vol. 2, 339–67.

17. ___, 33–41.

18. Mary Collins, "Critical Questions for Liturgical Theology," *Worship* 53 (1979) 302–17.

19. Joseph Jungman, *The Mass of the Roman Rite* vol. 2, 12–13; 25–26.

20. ___, 23–24.

21. Chrodegang, *Regula Canonicorum* 43, PL 89, 1076; see 32 PL 89, 1117. Historical and canonical studies of the Mass stipend system are available in the following: Adalbert Mayer, *Triebkräfte und Grundlinien der Entstehung des Messstipendiums*. Münchener theologische Studien III: Kanonistische Abteilung 34, (St. Ottilien: Eos, 1976); Charles Frederick Keller, *Mass Stipends* (St. Louis, Herder, 1926); Klaus Mörsdorf, "Erwägungen zum Begriff und zur Rechtfertigung des Messstipendiums," in *Theologie in Geschichte und Gegenwart*, ed. J. Auer and H. Volk (Munich: Karl Zink, 1957) 103–22; idem, "Mass Stipends," in *Sacramentum Mundi: An Encyclopedia of Theology,* ed. Karl Rahner et al. (New York: Herder and Herder, 1968), vol. 3, 429–31; A. Meunier, "Les offrandes des messes, *Revue ecclésiastique de Liège* 43 (1956), 107–16; T. Ortolan, "Honoraires de messes," DTC 7-1, 69–94; Colum Kenny, "Mass Stipends: Origin and Relevance, " *The Homiletic and Pastoral Review* 64 (1964) 842–50; C. Edward Gilpatric, "Mass Stipends and Mass Intentions," *Worship* 38 (1964) 190–201; Joseph A. Jungmann, "Mass Intentions and Mass Stipends," in

Unto the Altar: The Practice of Catholic Worship, ed. Alfons Kirchgaessner (New York: Herder and Herder, 1963) 23–31; Edward Kilmartin, "Money and the Ministry of the Sacraments," in *The Finances of the Church*, ed. William Bassett and Peter Huizing (*Concilium* 117), (New York: The Seabury Press, 1979) 104–11.

22. Canon 17, Mansi 14, 1005.

23. Decretum 3, Mansi 22, 653.

24. Two further expressions of the growing alienation of the people from active participation in eucharistic transactions were represented in the practice from the ninth century onward of giving communion to the people on the tongue rather than the hand and from the twelfth century onward of withholding the chalice from the people. See Jungmann, *The Mass of the Roman Rite*, vol. 2, 381–86.

25. Schlomo Deshen and Moshe Shokeid, *The Predicament of Homecoming: Cultural and Social Life of North African Immigrants in Israel* (Ithaca, NY: Cornell University Press, 1974) 162.

26. This development was represented in the use of ambiguous expressions such as *comparatio missae* and *missam comparare*. See Jungman, *The Mass of the Roman Rite* vol. 2, 24 n. 133. For a study of monetary factors in the formation of philosophical ideas in general, see Marc Shell, *Money, Language, and Thought: Literary and Philosophic Economies from the Medieval to the Modern Era* (Berkeley: University of California Press, 1982).

27. Edward Kilmartin, "The One Fruit or the Many Fruits of the Mass," *Proceedings of the Catholic Theological Society of America* 21 (1966) 37–38. On the development of theological ideas in this area, see Erwin Iserloh, "Der Wert der Messe in der Diskussion der Theologen vom Mittelalter bis zum 16. Jahrhundert," *Zeitschrift für Katholische Theologie* 83 (1961) 44–79.

28. Amalar of Metz, *De ecclesiasticis officiis* 3:23, PL 105, 1138.

29. Duns Scotus set out his thought on this matter in *Quaestio* 20 of the *Quaestiones Quodlibetales*. See *Opera Omnia* 26 (Paris: Vivés, 1895) 298–331.

30. See Henri de Lubac, *Corpus mysticum: L'eucharistie et l'église au moyen âge* (Paris: Aubier, 1944).

31. Edward Kilmartin, "The One Fruit," 53–54.

32. Thomas Cajetan, *Opuscula Omnia* 2 (Lyons: Tinghi, 1585) 147–49.

33. Duns Scotus, *Opera Omnia* 26, 324.

34. On this, see Kilmartin, "The One Fruit," 43–44.

35. See Thomas McDonnell, "Stipends and Simony," *The Irish Ecclesiastical Record* 54 (1938) 593–612; 55 (1939), 35–57, 159–75. On the notion of the

stipend as an ecclesiastical tax, see R. G. Renard, "Les honoraires de messe," *Revue de sciences philosophiques et théologiques* 28 (1939) 222–27.

36. Maurice de la Taille, *The Mystery of Faith and Human Opinion Contrasted and Defined* (New York: Longmans, Green and Co., 1930) 108ff; idem, The Mystery of Faith (New York: Sheed and Ward, 1950), vol. 2, 223–83.

37. De la Taille, *Mystery of Faith and Human Opinion*, 134.

38. Karl Rahner, "Die vielen Messen und das eine Opfer," *Zeitschrift für Katholische Theologie* 71 (1949) 257–317. This essay has been incorporated in a modified form into Karl Rahner and Angelus Häussling, *The Celebration of the Eucharist* (New York: Herder and Herder, 1968). Quotations are from this latter work.

39. See David B. Burrell, "Many Masses and One Sacrifice: A Study of the Thought of Karl Rahner," *Yearbook of Liturgical Studies* 2 (Notre Dame: Fides Publishers Association, 1961) 104.

40. Rahner and Häussling, *The Celebration of the Eucharist*, 1–12; 34–38; 91–96.

41. ___, 78.

42. ___, 79–84.

43. Rahner's views did not go unchallenged by the Roman magisterium at the time. See Pope Pius XII's address of 2 November 1954, AAS 46 (1954) 313–17; and his address of 22 September 1956, AAS 48 (1956) 711–25. That Rahner's positions are compatible with the magisterial positions set forth in *Cum Semper Oblatas* of Benedict XIV (1744) and *Auctorem Fidei* of Pius VI (1794) has been argued by Colum Kenny in "Mass Stipends: Doctrinal Problems, "*The Homiletic and Pastoral Review* 66 (1966) 306–11.

44. The 1983 Code of Canon Law incorporates a vigilant attitude regarding the proper theological understanding and pastoral practice of Mass stipends. See Code of Canon Law, canons 945 -58. See also John M. Huels, "Stipends in the New Code of Canon Law in *Living Bread, Saving Cup*, ed. R. Kevin Seasoltz (Collegeville, MN: The Liturgical Press, 1987) 347–56.

45. On the ecclesial subjectivity of the eucharist, see Yves M-J Conger, "L'ecclesia' ou communauté chrétienne, sujet intégral de l'action liturgique," in *La Liturgie après Vatican II*, ed. J-P. Joshua and Y. Congar (Paris: Cerf, 1967) 241–82. See also Herve-Marie Legrand, "The Presidency of the Eucharist According to the Ancient Tradition," *Worship* 53 (1979) 413–38. A valuable historical study on the question is also provided in Benedicta Droste, *"Celebrare" in de Römischen Liturgiesprache. Eine Liturgie-Theologische Untersuchung* (Munich: Max Hueber Verlag, 1963).

46. The more questionable practices generated in this regard are among religious congregations that operate mail-order Mass association and purgatorial societies, which even advertise for Mass stipends through Catholic periodicals. Such

practices fall short of exemplifying the qualities of ecclesial and liturgical integrity promoted in postconciliar renewal. There is also the troublesome practice of priestly concelebrations at which all or some of the priests present accept stipends for individual intentions. On this, see Kevin Seasoltz, *New Liturgy, New Laws* (Collegeville, MN: The Liturgical Press, 1979) 88–91.

47. On this see George St. Hilaire, "Eliminating Mass Stipends," *The Homiletic and Pastoral Review* 66 (1966) 845–52.

48. The requirement finds expression in the 1983 Code of Canon Law in canon 534.

49. See Geoffrey, Rowell, *The Liturgy of Christian Burial: An Introductory Survey of the Historical Development of Christian Burial Rites* (London: Alcuin Club/S.P.C.K., 1977) esp. 12–13. Rowell shows how the schematization of postburial observances varied from place to place. See also Robert J. Hoeffner, "A Pastoral Evaluation of the Rite of Funerals," *Worship* 55 (1981) 482–99.

50. The General Instruction on the Roman Missal, 49. Text in *Vatican Council II: The Conciliar and Post Conciliar Documents*, ed. Austin Flannery (Collegeville, MN: The Liturgical Press, 1975) 175.

Chapter 3

Catholic Worship and the Dynamics of Congregationalism

Who celebrates the eucharist: the priest or the Christian assembly? What does it mean to say that the role of the priest is to preside at Mass? In what sense is the liturgy a celebration of communal faith? Such questions are discussed today in endless variety both in scholarly and pastoral circles. A great deal that is controversial in Catholic life is condensed in disagreement over these matters. Fundamentally, these questions are about the proper relationship between the congregation or people, the ordained priest, and the ritual or liturgical form. Which comes first? Is one more foundational than the others? What is the proper theoretical and practical balance between them?

These questions are capable of quite diverse answers and it would be unwise to lock them into an overly rigid or narrow framework. In this essay, I want to suggest, however, that in order to be adequate to Catholic ecclesiology, answers to these questions must enshrine the recognition that in Catholic eucharistic structure the elements of people, priest, and rite are irreducibly distinct. Because of this, none of these can be regarded as a function of the other or be collapsed into the others. These elements are not, of course, isolated or detached from each other. The eucharistic action is the synergistic, dynamic, and complex cooperation and interaction of the three.

This principle of tripartite irreducibility receives some historical verification in the fact that when breakdown occurs in the church's eucharistic life, it can often be located in the breakdown of one of these elements or in some imbalance in the interrelationship of the three. When any one element begins to operate to the detriment of the others or to assume the operations of the others or when any one compromises the irreducible character of the others, then there is enacted one of three distortions that are recurring features of Christian liturgical history: clericalism, ritualism, and congregationalism.

CLERICALISM, RITUALISM, CONGREGATIONALISM

Let me take each of these in turn. Clericalism occurs when the tripartite irreducibility of the church's eucharistic structure theoretically or practically collapses so that the role of the ordained minister radicalizes, that is, becomes the principle, source, and origin of the ritual form and/or the congregation. Clericalism, in short, is the subordination of both rite and people to the priestly role.

History provides more than adequate evidence of the process of clerical radicalization, especially in the privatization of the Mass and the isolation of the eucharist from actual worshiping communities. Many are old enough to remember when Masses were celebrated in parish churches and religious houses by priests with no more than an altar boy in attendance. There are, of course, complex reasons for this historical phenomenon and facile condemnation is unwise. Yet, as the modern liturgical movement and the Second Vatican Council pointed out, the fullness of liturgical reality is verified when the eucharist is celebrated in a communal setting with the active participation of the people. This principle is expressed in an important affirmation of the Constitution on the Sacred Liturgy of Vatican II: "Mother Church earnestly desires that all the faithful should be led to that full, conscious, and active participation in liturgical celebration *which is demanded by the very nature of the liturgy.*"[1]

The clericalism of the past is, for the most part, unknown today. Yet, it can take new and unwitting forms. The presidential "style" of priests can sometimes be such that their behavior overpowers both rite and congregation. The "game show host" approach to eucharistic presidency serves to focus unduly on the priestly role. The people (even when entertained) are passive spectators at a priestly event. By the same token, when priests take liberties in changing official texts or improvising on ritual elements, the liturgical rite is destabilized and the people are disenfranchised and marginalized.

By the same process as I am describing, the phenomenon of ritualism emerges when the roles of the ordained and/or the congregation are in theory or in practice relativized by, and made subservient to, the ritual form. Liturgical rite then takes on a quasi-automatic, overly objectified, excessively autonomous character.

Historic Catholicism has not been free of moments of ritualism of one shade or another. That the liturgy was celebrated in Latin into modern times and was therefore somewhat inaccessible to Catholic worshipers indicates notable elements of ritualism. The operationality of the liturgy was so understood that its connections to the faithful participation of worshipers, as well as to the ministerial order of the church, was inadequately apprehended. At a theological level, the *opus operatum* principle of sacramental theology became disconnected from its necessary correlative in the *opus operantis* principle. An absorption with the rubrical deflected attention from the fundamental sacramental reality.

Ritualism is less a problem in Catholicism today, although it finds veiled expression in an overly aesthetic appreciation of the liturgy, as well as in some types of commitment to the so-called Tridentine Mass and the Latin language liturgy. Because of its anti-ritual bias, modern culture does not easily support a ritualistic outlook. Yet, ritualism continues to have some interesting expressions in other sectors of Christianity. I recall, for instance, Evensong at King's College, Cambridge, where on a particular Sunday I witnessed one of the liturgical and musical glories of Christendom performed to perfection for an audience of tourists and aesthetes and presided over by a Church of England priest, a self-proclaimed atheist who was barely active ministerially in the liturgy.

The third problem, that of congregationalism, results from the process by which rite and/or ordained ministry are relativized to the operationality of the worshiping community. In the congregationalist outlook, ritual forms are regarded as the product, creation, and property of the congregation. Rite lacks symbolic density, authority, and objectivity and becomes experimental, temporary, and functional. The history of Protestant worship amply demonstrates the pattern here. In the Protestant congregationalist outlook, there is an inherent adversity to ascribing sacramental character to the material and the ritual. Rite derives its significance and power from congregational spirituality.

Similarly, ordained ministry loses its irreducible character and is regarded as a function or extension of the general ministry of the congregation. Consistent with this, Protestant congregationalism denies the sacramental and hierarchical nature of the ordained. Those knowledgeable about the history of orders since the Reformation and attentive to modern ecumenical discussions on the theology of ordained ministry will be familiar with these dynamics.

Given its intrinsic character, Catholicism has offered historically little in the way of congregationalist patterns. Thus it is all the more remarkable that this trend seems to be on the ascendancy in the church's liturgical life in the decades since the Second Vatican Council. The congregationalist trend occasionally finds quite radical expression. Eucharistic events devised by household communities and presided over by non-ordained persons are not unknown. Less radical congregational impulses are found in the way the priestly role is regarded in some more mainstream communities. In one university chaplaincy with which I am familiar, the priest is "empowered" at the beginning of Mass by a congregational laying on of hands to preside with the authority of the community. In other situations, groups or communities search out and invite as eucharistic presiders priests agreeable to the spiritualities and sensitivities of the groups.

Congregationalist attitudes are exhibited in parishes and communities in processes of liturgical planning and celebration wherein the given rites are modified or even rejected in favor of local creativity. The operative conviction is that, to be authentic and effective, liturgical events must emerge from the spirituality and creativity of the group rather than be received from tradition or hierarchy.

The problems of clericalism and ritualism are lesser temptations in the church's liturgical life today, although they merit ongoing vigilance. The problem of congregationalism is, however, much more pronounced. In my opinion, the congregationalist trend represents possibly the most serious danger today to the integrity of Catholic liturgical life and to the ongoing renewal of the church. Accordingly, I want to explore this phenomenon further by examining three familiar and foundational convictions of popular liturgical theology. The first concerns the assembly as celebrant of the eucharist. The second focuses on the priest as eucharistic presider. The third relates to sacraments as celebrations of communal faith.

The Assembly Celebrates

Present-day liturgical theology espouses the axiom that the whole assembly, not just the presiding priest, is the proper celebrant of the liturgy. This conviction stands in some contrast with post-Tridentine theology, which spoke of the priest as the celebrant and subject of the eucharistic sacrifice. This conviction was related to Counter-Reformation concerns about the priest's indispensable role in eucharistic action. What was lacking in that theological tradition, however, was an adequate statement of the role of the people in the Mass. The important modern research of Henri Chirat, Aimé-George Martimort, and Thierry Maertens on the early Christian theology of the assembly and of Rupert Berger and Benedicta Droste on the corporate character of eucharistic offering and celebration in the early tradition indicated that the perspective operative in recent centuries needed considerable enrichment. In *Mystici Corporis* and *Mediator Dei,* Pope Pius XII assumed this renewed theology of the assembly as active liturgical agent, and he reestablished the normative role of the people in the structure of the liturgy, correcting a somewhat one-sided emphasis on the role of the priest. The new appreciation of the assembly as a vital corporate reality was represented amply in the Constitution on the Sacred Liturgy of Vatican II and in postconciliar liturgical documents.

However, the important theological achievement of a more adequate theology of the assembly is in serious danger today of being corrupted and reduced to simple congregationalism. By the term "assembly," the scholars of the earlier liturgical movement understood not a simple undifferentiated body, but the complex interaction of worshiping congregation and ordained priest. Never did they understand "assembly" as the congregation primarily or congregation without priest. Priest and congregation were regarded as *irreducibly* distinct yet cooperative actors in eucharistic agency, each acting according to hierarchically ordered roles.

In the past two decades or so, however, the agency of the eucharistic assembly has begun to be understood without its earlier complexity and subtlety and it now habitually appears in popular pastoral theology in a thoroughly congregationalist form. The role of the ordained priest is collapsed into that of the congregation, so that the term "assembly" now often means congregation without remainder, instead of congregation and priest irreducibly cooperating in the complex act of the liturgy.

Clearly, a proper conceptual and practical balance needs to be recovered in theologies of the eucharistic assembly if the process of congregationalism is to be checked. Not for a moment am I suggesting the restoration of an exaggerated understanding of the priestly role or the devaluation of the congregation. The dignity of the worshiping people can never be highlighted enough. An exaltation of ordained ministry at the expense of the people who gather for worship is not in keeping with the rich ecclesiology espoused by the Second Vatican Council. Ordained ministry and the worshiping congregation are powerfully intended toward each other. Neither, however, is served by the extremes of clericalism and congregationalism.

The Priest as Presider

This brings me to the second affirmation of popular theology, which is today subject to the congregationalist tendency. This relates directly to the foregoing and it has to do with the presidential role of the priest at Mass. To speak of the priest as liturgical "presider" of "president" is a standard part of modern Catholic parlance, as is evident from the 1969 Sacramentary. "Conservative" objections to this language are not well founded in liturgical history or theology. Yet, the terms "presider" and "president" are often popularly understood today in a theologically weak and sacramentally denuded sense. That the priest contributes to the eucharist anything radically constitutive beyond that of functional leader or animator is set in question by a congregationalist understanding of priestly presidency. The congregationalist understanding, typified at a popular level in the writings of Bernard Cooke, James Empereur, and others, disconnects priestly presidency from much of the dense theological parlance about priesthood in Catholic tradition. The elements of the tradition that in any way set the priest "over against" the congregation are today quite unpopular. Included are notions of the priest as acting in *persona Christi*, as sacramental icon of Christ, as Bridegroom and New Adam. Indeed, the sacerdotal language of "priesthood" and "offering" is today offensive to many. The affirmation of the Dogmatic Constitution on the Church of the Second Vatican Council that the ministerial priesthood and the priesthood of the laity differ essentially and not only in degree has trouble surviving in this climate, as do hierarchical and sacramental understandings of priestly identity and role. Edward Schillebeeckx's rejection of ontological conceptions of priesthood as a fabrication of the medieval church has effectively trickled down to popular level. Some theologians propose the theory that, at least in emergencies, a priest is not necessary for a valid eucharist. For instance, to the question, what is a eucharist without a priest? Tad Guzie responds, "The only answer I can give is that it is a eucharist without a priest."[2] On the growing phenomenon of Sunday eucharistic services in the absence of a priest, Richard T. Szafranski comments: "Perhaps a part of the bread should be taken to the priest since he is the one who could not be part of the eucharistic meal."[3] This suggestion captures the essential conceptual dynamics of the congregationalist reduction of priestly presidency.

What is compromised here is the conviction of Catholic tradition that the priest not only orchestrates or gives voice to the prayer of the congregation at the eucharist, but brings to it an irreducibly constitutive element. The priestly office "adds" to the eucharist, according to Cardinal Ratzinger, a link with the whole church that is not merely catechetically edifying or an expressive nicety but "a central inner dimension of the very mystery of the Eucharist."[4] In the cardinal's words, "No group can constitute itself a church but becomes a church only by being received as such by the universal Church."[5] For this reason, the link between eucharistic celebration and priestly order is absolutely crucial. No doubt, the modern desire to humanize the priest, to connect him to the congregation, and to encourage humble and sensitive service within the liturgy is entirely worthy and it should not be undervalued. This desire can (and must) be incorporated into the liturgical order of the church, but not at the expense of a reductionism which will, in the long run, be to the detriment of the whole church. What is called for, once again, is a proper balance in the principal elements of the church's liturgical life.

Liturgy as Celebration

This brings me finally to the third way in which the congregationalist reduction of the liturgy can occur. This relates to understandings of the eucharist as a celebration of communal faith. Once again, the notion of the liturgy as "celebration" is perfectly valid when understood in a manner that respects the tripartite irreducibility of people, rite, and priest. A rejection of the language of "celebration" in speaking about the liturgy demonstrates an inadequate knowledge of liturgical history. The problem sets in only at the point where the language of sacramental "celebration" is placed in the framework of congregationalist reductionism and when celebrative theories of sacrament take on an anti-mediatorial character. Mediatorial theories of sacraments accord the church's sacramental actions a "high" and revered status. Sacraments are understood as indispensable media of divine presence and activity. They "confer" grace and bring about a sanctifying result in the life of the church. Most traditional Catholic sacramental theologies belong in this category.

Modern liturgical renewal rightly observed a certain extrinsicism in mediatorial theories of sacrament. Sacramental spirituality therein was often disconnected from human experience; it failed to account adequately for the graced character of ordinary life; and it lacked a festive, celebratory dimension. In order to overcome this imbalance, the liturgical movement sought to restore the celebrative aspect of liturgy.

Modern celebrative theories of sacrament found their more systematic expressions in the writings of Karl Rahner and Piet Fransen. Rahner even spoke of a "Copernican revolution" in sacramental theology, by which he meant that the grace of sacramental events was deeply connected to existent human reality. Yet, as he advanced a celebrative dimension, Rahner never abandoned the traditional mediatorial schematization of Catholic sacramental theology. However, in its more recent expressions in the writings of George S. Worgul, Tad Guzie, and James Empereur, the celebrative model of sacrament assumes the necessity of questioning whether anything mediatorial at a theological level occurs in worship at all. In this perspective, liturgy expresses much more than it constitutes or mediates. A celebrative theory of sacrament holds that sacraments concentrate, manifest, and give expression to divine grace present in the world—specifically the world of the local community—but do not establish or constitute the reality of grace in any traditional sense. This translates into the conviction that the primary symbol and the fundamental reality of the liturgy is the gathered assembly and not the ritual actions or media. Accordingly, Christ is thought to be present in the eucharistic elements as an expression of his presence in the eucharistic assembly. Ritual objects and symbols are regarded as holy in a manner secondary to the holiness of the worshiping people.

From this conviction, it is only a short step to the notion that sacramental celebration does not depend fundamentally upon or require much more than the expressive symbolic resources of the local community. The difference between a Mass presided over by a priest and a lay-led communion rite is not greatly significant. Nor are the sacramental shape, formulaic validity, or hierarchical origin of the liturgy of notable import. Sacramental validity and effectiveness become matters of immediate symbolic expressiveness.

Once again, the renewal of a proper conceptual and practical balance in the relationship between rite and congregation requires the reappropriation of a profoundly sacramental view of liturgical rites, a recognition that sacraments are instruments of divine activity rather than simply the self-referential resources of a local community. Only in such a framework can a celebrative understanding of sacraments maintain theological authenticity and avoid a congregationalist reduction.

Is Catholic liturgical theology and practice today being caught up in the dynamism of congregationalism? In my opinion, it is. To say so is not to ascribe ill will to individuals or groups in the church. On the contrary, many of the fundamental impulses operative are quite meritorious and appropriate: advancing the dignity of the assembly; integrating the priestly role more adequately into liturgical events; and promoting a celebrative and festive dimension in Christian worship. These tasks should and must continue. The sacramental and spiritual richness of Catholicism and its liturgical life will, however, be seriously compromised if they are advanced within a congregationalist framework.

---

1. No. 14 (emphasis added); text from *Vatican Council II. The Conciliar and Post-Conciliar Documents,* Austin Flannery, gen. ed. (Collegeville, MN: Liturgical Press, 1975/1984) 7.

2. Tad Guzie, "Reclaiming the Eucharist," *Liturgy* 7:1 (1987) 32.

3. Richard T. Szafranski, "The One Who Presides at Eucharist," *Worship* 63:4 (1989) 315.

4. Joseph Cardinal Ratzinger, *Principles of Catholic Theology: Building Stones for a Fundamental Theology* (San Francisco: Ignatius Press, 1987) 294.

5. ___, 293.

Part II

Liturgy and Culture

Chapter 4

Liturgy and the Present Crisis of Culture

The relationship between liturgy and culture continues to be one of the most complex and challenging issues for the church as it seeks to advance the trajectory of reform established by the Second Vatican Council. This essay will be concerned with two related aspects of this issue: first, the degree of success of the modern liturgy in generating social and cultural transformation; and second, the impact of modern culture on the perception and practice of the liturgy.

The success of the modern liturgy in bringing about the transformation of culture is usefully measured within the history of the liturgical generativity of culture. The work of cultural historian Christopher Dawson, whose writings are the subject of renewed interest today, provides a revealing starting point. In his book *Religion and the Rise of Western Culture,* Dawson analyzes the manner in which the origin of Western culture is to be found in the spiritual community which emerged from the ruins of the Roman Empire. According to Dawson, this spiritual community, of which the Latin fathers Ambrose, Augustine, Leo, and Gregory were the progenitors, filled the void created by the fall of the empire and prepared the way for the unified spiritual culture of Western Christendom.[1]

What is interesting in Dawson's analysis is the role that liturgy played in the generation of the new culture. In his view, it was in the liturgy more than anything else that "the whole Christian world, Roman, Byzantine and barbarian, found an inner principle of unity."[2] In fact, the liturgy was "the means by which the mind of the gentiles and the barbarians was attuned to a new view of life and a new concept of history."[3] Thus, Dawson says, "in the West, after the fall of the Empire, the Church possessed in the liturgy a rich tradition of Christian culture as an order of worship, a structure of thought and a principle of life."[4] Accordingly, "the preservation and development of this liturgical tradition was one of the main preoccupations of the Church in the dark ages that followed the barbarian conquest, since it was in this way that the vitality and continuity of the inner life of Christendom which was the seed of the new order were preserved."[5]

In Dawson's view, this was an age of great liturgical creativity. The Christian cult operated to transfuse the extant barbarian traditions with a new ethical and spiritual quality. So impressive was this transfusion that, in Dawson's words, "it is almost impossible to convey to the modern mind the realism and objectivity with which the Christians of those ages viewed this liturgical participation in the mysteries of salvation."[6]

The dynamic relationship between liturgy and culture that Dawson saw operative in the formation of the middle ages was strongly invoked at the beginning of the modern liturgical movement. The figure that stood at the head of this movement was Dom Prosper Guéranger, abbot of Solesmes from 1837 to 1875. Guéranger's reputation was for a long time that of an ultramontane reactionary intent on destroying the liturgical diversity of France in favor of the pure Roman rite. However, more recent scholarship has underlined the importance of Guéranger in establishing a strong connection between liturgical renewal and the transformation of culture and society.

According to R. W. Franklin, one of the strengths of Guéranger's early work was the "vision of worship as a means to solve one of the greatest problems of the nineteenth century—the reintegration of matter and spirit."[7] Accordingly, Guéranger regarded the liturgy as "the instrument for an attack on the dissociation of the material and the spiritual in a predominately materialistic civilization which divided society into a secular sphere and an increasingly unimportant otherworldly sphere."[8] In a society torn apart by individualism, capitalism, and revolution, the liturgy would become, in Guéranger's vision, a force integrating individual and community, labor and spirituality, religion and life. The transcendent and inspiring character of worship and the intrinsic unifying power of Christian liturgy would reverse social disarray and restore the communitarian ethos of authentic Christian civilization.

Guéranger's dream was not, of course, realized. The social effects of the early liturgical movement in France bear little positive comparison with the powerful influence of the liturgy in the formation of the early middle ages as noted by Dawson.

The same vision found notable expression in some of the pioneers of the early liturgical movement in the United States. The recognized leader of this movement was Father Virgil Michel, a monk at St. John's Abbey, Collegeville, Minnesota, until his death in 1938. Michel was an eloquent and prodigious exponent of the social power of the liturgy. Writing in *Orate Fratres* in 1935, he expressed his overwhelming conviction that the liturgy "is the one true basis of Christian culture and civilization."[9] The liturgy, he declared, "understood and lived after the mind of Christ and His Church—therefore lived both individually and socially—cannot but flower out into a genuine Christian culture that embraces every aspect of life and human experience."[10]

Michel's conception of culture was notably inclusive. Culture, he held, "embraces all the activities and abilities of man, all the aspirations and inspirations of his nature, the entire field of human existence."[11] It includes individual and society, the intellectual and the material, belief and morality, art, custom, and law. For Michel, consequently, if the whole culture is to be changed and transformed, this can only be achieved by a vigorous living out of a true Christian spirit. For this reason, the living of the liturgical life must have as its aim "the penetration of all human contacts and activities with the spirit of Christ."[12] This recognition of the social power of the liturgy was, for Michel, "a most important truth for our day, when the Holy Father calls for a Christian reconstruction of the social order, when we are living in a world torn by a struggle of cultures, and when we are a minority group in a pagan, materialistic, naturalistic culture and civilization, much as were the early Christians."[13] Accordingly, for Michel, there was an inner connection between the liturgical apostolate and Catholic social teaching.[14]

The question that may be asked in the light of this brief historical sketch is whether or not the liturgy of the postconciliar church has yielded the social and cultural transformation proclaimed in the modern liturgical movement and invoked by Dawson. The answer must, unfortunately, be a negative one. It is noteworthy that J. Bryan Hehir, the scholar most identified with the 1986 Pastoral Letter on Catholic Social Teaching and the U.S. Economy issued by the United

States National Conference of Catholic Bishops, is no less negative about the promised liturgical transformation of culture. Writing in 1980, Hehir concluded that "fifteen years after the Council this potential remains largely unfulfilled in the Church in the United States."[15] Two decades later, that judgment warrants little modification.

While there continues to be much energetic discussion today about the commitment to justice in the church, this discussion does not appear to be matched with effective results. What is no less problematic is that the vision of the social and cultural power of the liturgy analyzed by Dawson and embodied in the key figures of the modern liturgical movement is often not operative in discussions about justice and social transformation.

I want to suggest some reasons for this absence of vision by taking up the matter of the impact of modern culture on the perception and practice of the liturgy. I will suggest, accordingly, that the fundamental reason why liturgy has lost much of its cultural and social power is related to the absorption into postconciliar American Catholicism of profoundly negative dynamics operative in modern secular culture. I will argue that the appropriation of these dynamics has generated conceptions of liturgy that are exceedingly destructive and disorienting of the social and cultural generativity of liturgy.

The cultural dynamics that I shall identify are the following: the subjectification of reality; the intimization of society; and the politicization of culture. I will deal with these in turn, recognizing that each contributes to the cumulative effect of liturgical dysfunction. I will conclude the essay by offering some suggestions for renewing the power of the liturgy to generate social and cultural transformation.

THE SUBJECTIFICATION OF REALITY

The subjectification of reality as a pervasive social phenomenon is a matter about which much has been written recently. *Habits of the Heart*, written by Robert Bellah and a team of social scientists, documents the widespread assumption in modern American culture that the individual person rather than institutions or traditions is the locus and origin of meaning and values. This view, which *Habits of the Heart* describes as "ontological individualism," embodies the conviction that "the individual has a primary reality whereas society is a second-order, derived or artificial construct."[16]

Christopher Lasch, following a similar thesis, has shown that the ontologization of individual experience is accompanied by a loss of confidence in history, future vision, politics, and social and cultural institutions.[17] Accordingly, the structures and institutions that have traditionally embodied meaning and values lose their mediating power. The narcissistic individual created in the process becomes "the minimal self" existing in survival state, shunning commitment to relationships and public life. As a result, personal energy is focused on the relentless pursuit of selfish needs and the public world is scorned as meaningless and humanly irrelevant.

Congruent with this pattern, there emerges what Lasch calls the "therapeutic sensibility," in which psychology and psychiatry replace the social institutions and modes that traditionally mediated personal growth and maturation.[18] In this climate, moral traditions and ethical systems survive only by being appropriated into psychological and therapeutic modes for the articulation and expression of personal meaning and value. Correlatively, the idioms of therapy invade education, culture, and spirituality and undermine the objective status traditionally accorded to moral codes and systems.[19]

One of the consequences of the process of subjectification and its attendant psychologization is the abandonment of the social and cultural arenas to consumerism and the propaganda of mass advertising. T. J. Jackson Lears has pointed out that "the decline of symbolic structures outside the self has been a central process in the development of a consumer culture joining advertising strategies and the therapeutic ethos.[20] In modern times, he holds, "advertisers began speaking to many of the same preoccupations addressed by liberal ministers, psychologists, and other therapeutic ideologues."[21] Lears characterizes the world in which we live, accordingly, as one in which the phenomenon of consumerism operates as a comprehensive cultural ideal, as a "way of seeing" wherein all significance evaporates from social institutions and a sense of trivialization and "weightlessness" prevails.

This process of trivialization is further compounded by the manner in which the electronic media reduce public life, education, art, and history to show business and entertainment. Every institution and idea that has some potential for therapeutic or consumer value is subject to appropriation by the entertainment media and loses, thereby, its moral seriousness and its integral value as autonomous agents of social edification.[22] It is no secret that the subjectification of reality has had profound effects upon the conception and practice of religion in America. The authors of *Habits of the Heart* point out that the disposition to regard religion in a privatized manner has deep roots in the history of American individualism. The earlier tradition, however, did assume "a certain priority of the religious community over the individual."[23] More recently, that pattern has experienced a reversal, so that the majority of Americans now assume a personal rather than a social or ecclesiastical source for their religious beliefs. God is conceived more likely as an "inner voice" than as the voice of community or tradition.

The modern subjectification of reality has its philosophical roots in the eighteenth-century "turn to the subject" and it finds contemporary articulation in what George Lindbeck describes as "experiential-expressive" modes of religion and religious reflection. According to Lindbeck, "the structures of modernity press individuals to meet God first in the depths of their souls and then, perhaps, if they find something personally congenial, to become part of a tradition or enter a church."[24] Religion, in this view, is a radically private and individual matter. Consequently, "increasing numbers of people regard all religions as possible sources of symbols to be used eclectically in articulating, clarifying, and organizing the experiences of the inner self."[25] In line with this approach, doctrines are understood as "noninformative and nondiscursive symbols of inner feelings, attitudes, or existential orientations."[26]

In similar manner, authentic morality is thought to be generated in personal conscience, with little reference to traditions of law or virtue. Alasdair MacIntyre has identified the problem of liberal ethics in an atomic view of individual existence in which personal will and feeling become the ultimate sources of morality. Consequently, "everything may be criticized from whatever standpoint the self has adopted, including the self's choice of a standpoint to adopt."[27] MacIntyre characterizes this ethical position as emotivism, according to which the meaning of a moral judgment resides in the emotional quality of the individual response to an action or personal encounter. This generates the attitude, he writes, that "evaluative utterance can in the end have no point or use but the expression of my own feelings or attitudes and the transformation of the feelings and attitudes of others."[28]

The effects of the process of subjectification upon the whole range of Christian institutions are devastating. The Bible, worship, preaching, ministry, doctrine, ecclesiastical structures, and communal life are thought useful to the extent that they serve the experience of inner truth and personal encounter with the divine. They become little more than functional guides for the discovery of inner realities and personal dispositions.

There is ample evidence that the subjectification of reality has become systemically operative in American Catholicism since at least the late 1960s. This finds liturgical expression in what Nathan Mitchell has identified as a shift in the apprehension of the sacred. The "sense of the sacred has moved, shifted its location,"[29] and has become progressively disengaged from its traditional location in the church gathered at public worship. Now the sense of the sacred "is located 'inside,' in the personal history and geography of the self."[30] Consequently, "the sacred is closely attached to the *self*, not to rituals celebrated and shared in public."[31] The result is that modern Americans "look for the holy to reveal itself, not in the awe-inspiring rites of baptism and Eucharist, but in the awesome precincts of the self."[32]

In this movement, liturgy begins to be reconceived as a resource for getting in touch with the inward God or for celebrating inwardly constituted faith. The focus of engagement shifts from the transcendent God to the God apprehended in the mystery of the self. In this perspective, liturgy provides a non-intrusive space within which the Spirit may become operative in the heart and mind of the individual. Indeed, liturgy is regarded not as mediating divine presence, but as merely giving it shape and expression. Consequently, the real operations of worship are easily viewed as taking place outside formal liturgical contexts.

In this climate, the performance of liturgical rites takes on an experimental and improvisatory character. The search for liturgical expressions adequate to interior personal disposition, crisis, or need appears as a constant and intense preoccupation. Accordingly, the official and inherited liturgical forms tend to be regarded as of lesser value in themselves and are routinely replaced or supplemented by novel forms thought more authentic because they arise from the experience of individuals or groups in particular moments or situations.

The experiential-expressive framework imposed on liturgy as subjectification develops tends to recast evaluative criteria almost exclusively in terms of the inward needs of participants. Indeed, ritual forms will be so evaluated that what appears as therapeutically valuable will move into high relief while the more formal, complex, and ceremonial elements which mediate ecclesial significance will be reduced in importance.

If Lears and others are correct in seeing a connection between the therapeutic ethos and cultural consumerism, it should not be surprising that the subjectification of liturgical consciousness opens the way for the entrance of inferior and inappropriate artistic and communicative modes into the liturgy. Many commentators note a further consequence in the progressive appearance of a lack of dignity, seriousness, and reverence in liturgical celebration.

Those concerned about the subjectification of worship and liturgy believe that the process will, in the long run, reap a bitter harvest. As Mary Douglas pointed out over three decades ago, the loss or rejection of the integrity of ritual traditions ultimately involves the loss of the means by which religious conceptions and motivations are mediated and maintained. The collapse of ritual, according to Douglas, leads to the privatization of religious experience and finally to a reduction of the religious sense to humanistic philanthropy.[33] Without traditional rites, Christians are bereft of the necessary language by which faith is formed and motivated. Without engagement with an objective liturgical system, the individual is literally cut off from the necessary sources of Christian existence. There occurs a loss of confidence not only in the church and its rites and institutions but ultimately in meaningful inner experience, as the believer, left to his or her own devices, finds nothing "inside" and, in disillusionment, loses faith.

The process of subjectification is, I believe, partly to blame for the profound disengagement of the liturgy from its traditional role in social and cultural transformation. With the pervasive tendency toward subjectification in the postconciliar church, there has emerged a massive loss of confidence in the social and cultural orders and, consequently, a dissolution of interest and commitment in efforts to transform them. If society and its institutions are regarded as irrelevant to authentic human existence, then the traditional role of the church in transforming society is dismissed as romanticism or imperialism or (as we shall see later) collapsed into political action. In turn, because of the tendency to withdraw into individual subjectivity as the foundational source of meaning and value, the liturgy is shorn of its traditional, sacramental formality and reconceived and practiced as therapy. In the process, the liturgy loses its power to embody a vision of social transformation and its ability to elicit commitment to the social project is vitiated.

THE INTIMIZATION OF SOCIETY

The second pervasive dynamic with negative effects on the liturgy and its transforming agency derives from what I call (for want of a better expression) the intimization of society. This process is a logical outgrowth of the subjectification of reality and the attendant loss of confidence in social and cultural institutions. By the intimization of society I mean the process by which social complexity is eschewed in favor of a model of human coexistence that puts ultimate value on bonds of intimacy, personal closeness and radical familiarity.

In *The Fall of Public Man,* Richard Sennett has analyzed the modern collapse of the social in favor of the personal and the intimate. According to Sennett, "the reigning belief today is that closeness between persons is a moral good. The reigning aspiration today is to develop individual personality through experiences of closeness and warmth with others. The reigning myth today is that the evils of society can all be understood as evils of impersonality, alienation, and coldness."[34]

These convictions constitute what Sennett calls the "ideology of intimacy."[35] This ideology carries the pervasive conviction that "social relationships of all kinds are real, believable, and authentic the closer they approach the inner psychological concerns of each person."[36] These convictions have their origin, according to Sennett, in narcissism (the cult of the self-obsessed personality) and *destructive* gemeinschaft, which had its origin in the dramatic emergence of personality into the public realm in the nineteenth century. In the view of intimate community which emerged at that time, social interchange was thought to involve of necessity the revelation of personality, and society itself began to be conceived as a collective personality.[37] In this perspective, "all social phenomena, no matter how impersonal in structure, are converted into matters of personality in order to have meaning."[38] Indeed, society itself becomes meaningful only to the extent that it is converted into "a grand psychic system."[39]

The most notable effect of the process of intimization is that people have come to expect psychological benefits through the whole range of human experience. As a result, they are unable to appreciate as meaningful those social elements and institutions that embody impersonality, public distance, and relational complexity. Thus, the public world seems to them empty and stale. Political life becomes a matter of formal obligation. Interchanges with strangers are looked upon as dry, formal, and inauthentic. Indeed, the stranger is regarded as a threatening figure.[40]

This whole process is accompanied by a commitment to social unmasking. In Sennett's words, as intimization advances, people "put pressure on each other to strip away the barriers of custom, manners, and gesture which stand in the way of frankness and mutual openness."[41] Diplomacy is thought to be incompatible with honesty and reticence in self-revelation is regarded as a barrier to openness and real communication with others.

This process signifies for Sennett the end of public culture and of the codes of civility which allow for a wide variety of social relationships and the forging of bonds based on social distance.[42] Sennett complains that, unlike in traditional societies, there no longer remain today codes by which strangers recognize and greet each other in public. For that reason, public space is abandoned as "empty" and "dead."[43] Conventions which function as "rules for behavior at a distance from the immediate desires of the self" are abandoned.[44] Society and its institutions begin to be viewed as instrumental matters, as practical necessities, rather than as expressive of an order of reality within which commitment is appropriate and meaningful.[45]

In light of Sennett's analysis, it becomes clear why the rejection of systems of etiquette, protocol and manners in our society represents more than a dismissal of the old-fashioned. Such rejection represents, rather, disillusionment with the complex nature of social existence. As a result, there occurs an unwitting loss of the ritual codes and systems that allow the negotiation of relations and commitments in the public world. All that remain are what Erving Goffman calls the "brief rituals" of interpersonal behavior and the "little pieties" exchanged between individuals.[46]

Like the subjectification of reality, the intimization of society has become operative at a profound level in American religion. The pervasiveness of convictions about the values of intimization in the religious sphere is documented in *Habits of the Heart*. The authors point out how the church has come to be understood today primarily as a friendly gathering place for individuals who have experienced the divine or holy in their personal lives. Typically, the church is regarded as "an association of loving individuals" or "a community of empathetic sharing."[47] It becomes commonplace to think of the ultimate meaning and purpose of the church in expressive-individualistic terms. Thus it is commonly held that "its value is as a loving community in which individuals can express the joy of belonging."[48]

The authors of *Habits of the Heart* indicate that this perspective is not uncommon among American Catholics. They refer to a national study by Dean Hoge of The Catholic University of America, which shows that the two values that American Catholics seek most are "personal and accessible priests" and "warmer, more personal parishes."[49]

Margaret O'Brien Steinfels has identified a significant strand in popular writing on church and ministry which is convinced that "the ideal structure is community; the ideal relationship, intimate; and the ideal size, small."[50] To those who hold these convictions, the larger church appears cumbersome, inauthentic, and resistant to faith development. Ecclesial structures and operations are regarded as at best little more than functional resources.

Dick Westley of Loyola University of Chicago has proposed that the parish is a secondary community "whose major purpose is to offer programs and services."[51] For that reason, he says, the parish must be "built on primary communities where intimacy, interpersonal relations, and faith sharing can occur with regularity."[52] Westley proposes the highly problematic thesis that redemption is essentially a matter of intimacy. Indeed, he says, "redemption is just another name for learning the lessons of intimacy."[53] The difficulty with this radical association of redemption and intimacy is the implication of the absence of redemptive mediation in the public, formal structures, and operations of ecclesial life.

Parker Palmer has pointed out that the kind of ecclesial coexistence which emerges from intimization both constricts ecclesial life and profoundly vitiates the church's public role. "When an idealized image of family is imposed upon the church, our experience in the congregation becomes restricted."[54] Thus, "the church where we might experience creative conflict, heterogeneity, and freedom for innovation—becomes dominated by the expectation of closeness and warmth."[55] In such a community, "people with whom we cannot achieve intimacy, or with whom we do not want to be intimate, are squeezed out."[56] The church easily becomes a preserve for persons of similar class and status. The strange is eliminated and the familiar is cultivated. However, "such a church can neither welcome the stranger nor allow the stranger in each of us to emerge."[57]

This constriction operates, understandably, as a barrier to public life. The loss of confidence in the public, social arena and in the mediating power of ecclesiastical institutions leads to a loss of what *Habits of the Heart* describes as "a language genuinely able to mediate among self, society, the natural world, and ultimate reality."[58] Christians formed in this climate become singularly bereft of social literacy and of the means to understand and negotiate the relevance of Gospel values within the complexity of society. This evasion of the public world gives rise, in turn, to what Richard Neuhaus calls "the naked public square," that is, the public world sanitized of religious and moral values.[59] The church becomes a sect closed in upon itself, while the public world conducts its affairs impervious to religious and moral values.

The dynamics of the process of intimization are increasingly evident in the popular conception and practice of the liturgy. Indeed, in the light of social-scientific criticism, it is surprising that intimization is so widely and enthusiastically promoted at virtually every level of pastoral and liturgical renewal. Parker Palmer, in adverting to the original definition of liturgy as a "public work," laments the fact that "the church in our time has lost the sense of public worship."[60] According to Nathan Mitchell, today Christians identify their deepest religious experiences "not with public ritual and worship, but with private, personal experiences of intimacy and relationship."[61] Indeed, he says, our primary model for the sacred today "is *intimacy, not liturgy.*"[62]

The pervasiveness of this shift accounts, in part, for the considerable emphasis today on the small group as the ideal configuration of the liturgical assembly. Accordingly, a high priority is placed on the promotion of intimacy, closeness, and familiarity in liturgical gatherings. The large, traditional congregation is rejected as anonymous, alienating, and as a barrier to authentic communal faith and worship.

In the shift toward intimacy, personality rather than rite tends to become the medium of liturgical communication and performance. Indeed, the personalities and charismatic qualities of clergy and liturgical ministers easily become the crucial success factors in liturgical celebration. With this comes a rejection of the formal and the impersonal in the liturgy and an amplification of the "little pieties" and "brief rituals" focused on moments of interpersonal sharing. Conventions of social distance are left behind in favor of the criteria of mutual intimacy. The ministry of hospitality is often understood as creating friends and intimates, rather than graceful and respectful interaction between the friends, fellow citizens and strangers that make up the Christian body.[63]

In the process of intimization, liturgical rites and symbols lose the scale and complexity capable of engaging the Christian assembly with society, tradition, and history. As liturgy is conceptually repositioned within the configuration of intimate groups, it is shorn of broader cosmic symbolism and consequently loses the traditional ethos of grandeur, glory, and majesty. In effect, the journey into the intimate community is a journey out of the public world.

As with the subjectification of reality, the ecclesial appropriation of the dynamics of intimization distorts the power of the liturgy to transform society. In a church where the process of intimization is advanced, social and ecclesial complexity is conceptually and practically rejected and the institutional experiences a loss of confidence. Consistent with this, the liturgy is tailored to meet the characteristic needs of intimate groups. It is deprived of public, social symbolism. Consequently, the liturgy no longer stands as a model of redeemed society, and for that reason retains little ability to generate enthusiasm for social and cultural transformation.

The Politicization of Culture

Let me turn finally to the politicization of culture. Raymond Williams provides a definition of culture that usefully introduces the issue here. Culture, he says, "is the *signifying system* through which a social order is communicated, reproduced, experienced and explored."[64] This definition captures well the nature of culture as the total complex of symbols and codes which penetrates every facet of human existence, generating common orientation, meaning, and commitment. Culture incorporates individual and society, nature and art, religion, morality, and history within an ordered, complex configuration of reality.

The politicization of culture, then, refers to the collapse of the multimodal processes and codes of culture into the single process of political activity. Though the politicization of life as a modern phenomenon is a complex matter and can be accounted for in a wide variety of ways, it is clear that it finds its systemic origins partly in the processes of subjectification and intimization.

The politicization of culture and its relationship to the processes of subjectification and intimization can be set forth in the following way. In a world where these latter processes are advanced, the public, institutional arena does not cease to exist when ignored or neglected. The complexity of life beyond the individual and intimate group does not disappear. Social complexity and public affairs continue to impinge upon the individual and to assert claims. Individuals are still forced to grapple with the larger, more complex world. This engagement, however, shorn of traditional modes, is reduced to the processes of working out legal and political conventions by which mutual respect for individual freedom, self-determination and personal autonomy can be created and maintained. Consequently, the securing of freedom to pursue personal goals, to express oneself fully and to secure a level of material well-being becomes the principal and virtually only public and social issue. In this way, society is reduced to a set of political and legal contracts into which individuals enter for the purpose of the autonomous advancement of individual interests.

Richard Neuhaus has described the process by which the politicization of public life is advanced. As religion and cultural values are relegated to the private realm, there is created "the naked public square" devoid of moral and religious values. However, "when the value-bearing institutions of religion and culture are excluded, the value-laden concerns of human life flow back into the square under the banner of politics."[65] Though the relegation of religious and human values to the private sphere sterilizes public institutions of significance, the naked square "refuses to stay naked" and thus social meaning and values are politicized and culture is subsumed into the state. In this way, what Neuhaus calls "the pan-politicizing of life" is completed.[66]

A significant example of politicization is identified in what Neuhaus describes as "the growing litigiousness of the American people."[67] By this he means the increasing incidence of conflict issues in interpersonal relations finding their way into the law courts. It is clear that this process intensifies in proportion to the degree of breakdown of the conventions, formalities and codes of civility that have traditionally operated to resolve social conflict. Thus the means for the working out of conflict and cooperation are restricted to legal or political action.

Legal scholar Jethro Liebermann has analyzed similarly the manner in which appeal to the law courts has become a social epidemic.[68] Like Neuhaus, he is concerned that the traditional means of settling disputes have fallen away in favor of litigation. He argues that the litigiousness is essentially a social rather than a legal problem. "It is born of a breakdown in community, a breakdown that exacerbates and is exacerbated by the growth of law."[69] Thus the courts have become the last repositories of social trust and will remain so, in Liebermann's view, until there is a restoration of trust in public institutions and a resurgence of commitment to social ethics.

This general process of politicization arises out of and intensifies the corruption and abandonment of the symbolic structures of culture, the "signifying systems" described by Williams. Michael Warren speaks of "cultural pollution," by which he means "the despoiling of the chain, not of biogenerative processes, but of the processes of human signification, of human meaning."[70] Cultural pollution, he says, "proceeds to cause a breakdown of the processes of human valuing and understanding."[71] When cultural symbol systems collapse or become distorted, so too does the possibility of meaningful and civilized coexistence.

Other educators have spoken of a severe process of "deculturation" at work in the modern era.[72] They rightly observe that healthy societies have traditionally mustered and maintained social cohesiveness around a vital "cult," a vital set of symbols generating a deep veneration of life in all its expressions.[73] For that reason, the process of deculturation represents not only a loss of vital symbols, but a critical loss of transcendence and a collapse of the proper relationships between individual, nature, and society. "The result is that in our time the best and brightest have little support to dedicate themselves to art, genuine religion, scientific research, teaching, healing, parenting, or any of the other primary services of truth and human betterment."[74] In other words, "the movement toward transcendence having vacated the public scene, bad music, athletic displays, and a politics of power-plays command the center stage."[75] Essentially, this deculturation results in "a populace grown content with vulgarity."[76]

Whether we speak of cultural pollution despoiling the chain of signification or of deculturation leading to social vulgarity, the effect is the same: the arts, education, intellectual life, social and religious traditions, the discipline of family life, codes of civility and decorum, and the wise stewardship of creation survive as public and social matters only by reconstitution under the modes of politics and law.

The process of politicization has had a significant influence on the life of the church in recent decades and, consequently, has had notable results in the contemporary conception and practice of the liturgy. Without doubt, the heightened concern for social justice and for Christian commitment to systemic social reform is one of the most remarkable elements to emerge from the renewal set in motion by the Second Vatican Council. The problem, however, appears in the post-conciliar trend (very advanced in some regions of the church) to interpret all social and cultural issues as primarily political. This goes hand in hand with the abandonment of concerns for the organic transformation of society in a comprehensive and multimodal manner. The traditional methods of social transformation are left aside in favor of narrower legal or political action. In the process, the theoretical complexity of social transformation is relativized to political concepts of social justice.

Avery Dulles has argued for "the legitimacy of the church's concern for social order while at the same time cautioning against the politicization of religion."[77] He believes that while the church has an inescapable mission to proclaim the reign of God, it must avoid doing so in a manner that ties the Gospel too closely to partisan or political agendas. Indeed, he says, "as a general rule, faithfulness to Jesus will incline the ecclesiastical authority to avoid entanglement in economic and political struggles."[78]

In a similar vein, J. Brian Benestad has argued against the trend of collapsing the comprehensive, organic understanding of social justice into a narrow political scheme. He decries the fact that "the contemporary concern for social justice leads primarily to stress on public-policy initiatives, to a reorganization of the system, to social reform."[79] Accordingly, Benestad appeals to those elements of traditional Catholic social thought that focus on the comprehensive transformation of society at all levels and through many non-political modes. Social justice, he says, focuses not only on the political and economic sectors of society, but on the comprehensive common good of the whole society. For Benestad, then, the point of departure for social justice is primarily the action and commitment of virtuous and converted persons, not political action. For this reason, he is unhappy that today "the intellectual, moral and theological virtues are hardly mentioned in social-justice circles."[80] Regrettably, in his view, social justice as presently understood and promoted has little to do with virtuous action or with concepts of virtue that incline persons to fulfill duties toward society.

It becomes increasingly apparent that the dissociation of social transformation from traditional and cultural systems leads to frustration. As concepts of justice lose their concreteness and specificity and are disconnected from the integral elements of transformation embodied in the arts, education, family life, and in the codes of personal and civic virtue, they become abstract and ideological. Wolfhart Pennenberg and Stanley Hauerwas have identified from different perspectives the lack of reality and focus that attends the disconnection of the theory and practice of social justice from spirituality and the practice of virtue.[81] They show that purely political conceptions of the social order and of human commitment easily end in failure and frustration and cannot, given their abstract and unfocused character, yield a more just social order.

The politicization of ecclesial life that we are describing is reflected in modern theories and practices of liturgy formed in political visions of human action and of the world in general. The effect of politicization is essentially one of narrowing and even overriding the intrinsic social vision of the liturgy itself and of redirecting its transforming operationality into political and legal channels. Accordingly, the process of politicization effects a kind of deculturation of the liturgy, so that rites and symbols lose their power to generate social transformation according to their complex integral processes. Concern for the formation of personal virtue, civility, and intellect fades as the impetus for systemic political action assumes dominance in liturgical processes. Liturgical formation, conversion, and commitment are seen in activist terms rather than in terms of personal and communal holiness and sanctification. Concern for the poor and the oppressed is easily cast in the mold of political and legal reform.

When a left-wing ethos generated in radical or liberation movements becomes operative, the political edge becomes even more pronounced and a notably more intense character is generated. In this framework, liturgy quickly assumes an attitude of protest and rage. The agendas advanced in this context have a habitual orientation toward interest in the overthrow of unjust regimes, the restoration of human rights, the advancement of agrarian reform, or the rights of minorities. The imposition on the liturgy of multicultural politics has the effect of generating severe divisions within the liturgical assembly, so that the liturgy divides rather than unites.

Ironically, even the liturgy itself becomes the subject of ideological and political critiques. Where, for instance, the eucharist does not directly promote the cause of political liberation, it is prone to being regarded as in captivity to false powers.[82] The imposition of an ideological feminist critique will yield the view that "the Eucharist has become the ritual symbolization of the structural evil of sexism."[83]

The process of politicization, usually at work in much more subtle and diverse ways than I have outlined here, represents an inevitable manipulation of the liturgy. It is clear that such manipulation occurs when Christians "try to impose on the liturgy a social message it does not proclaim—even though, at the same time, they allow no sound of the liberating call proper to the liturgy."[84] This imposition overrides what Joseph Gelineau has called "the paschal dynamics of the Christian mystery."[85] By this he means those dynamics flowing from Christ's death and resurrection that intend "the total transformation of relations between God, man and the cosmos."[86]

The appropriation of the dynamics of politicization into the liturgy represents, then, another explanation of the inability of post-conciliar liturgical practice to advance the ideal of social transformation promoted by the modern liturgical movement. It is clear that the phenomenon of politicization impoverishes the vast complex of human culture, distorts the Christian message and severely restricts the ability of the liturgy to be an effective agent of social and cultural transformation.

This brings us back to our starting point in the social and cultural vision of the liturgy presented by Dawson, Guéranger, and Michel. It is clear that their vision was cultural rather than political. It embodied the recognition that the liturgy is effective as an agent of social transformation only when it generates intense commitment to spirituality, art, education, intellectual life, the discipline of the Christian household, public virtue, and codes of civility. In short, the perspective of these figures makes it clear that the commitment to justice becomes effective only when generated and supported by a wide cultural view rather than a narrow political vision.

The Way Forward

If the liturgy is to recover once again its power to transform the social and cultural environments, it will be necessary for the church and those in positions of leadership and influence to confront the deleterious dynamics presently operative in liturgical theology and practice. This cannot, of course, be a purely negative project. While I have been severely critical of the ecclesial and liturgical appropriations of the cultural dynamics identified in this essay, these dynamics should not be confused with some important features of the modern sensibility and of postconciliar reform. Accordingly, the positive features must be identified and appropriately incorporated into liturgical theory and practice.

While strong criticism must be maintained against the systemic subjectification of reality, it cannot be denied that the modern emphasis on subjectivity has had important positive benefits for the understanding and living of Christian faith. Many have rightly pointed to a certain extrinsicism in preconciliar Roman Catholicism as a result of which faith and doctrine were inadequately related to human experience. The Second Vatican Council is correctly understood to have introduced a reversal of extrinsicism through its incorporation of an emphasis on subjectivity in the renewal of doctrine, liturgy, and Christian life.

The fundamental problem, then, is not with a strong emphasis on subjectivity, but on subjectivity as the first principle of theological systems. Accordingly, we are not rejecting here the proper theological corrections that have been derived from modern phenomenologies of subjectivity, but only the radical subjectification of reality that is widely pervasive in ecclesial and liturgical theory and practice today. I agree with Parker Palmer and the authors of *Habits of the Heart* that religious inwardness and subjectivity are not to be rejected, but rather disciplined and reconnected to the public, institutional realm.[87] In the area of liturgy, this means not a rejection of concerns for subjective experience and interiority, but a conceptual and practical restoration of the liturgy as the origin and context of authentic subjectivity and spirituality.[88]

In a similar vein, the emphasis on community and concern for active participation are indisputably valid features of councilor and postconciliar liturgical reform. Likewise, the development and promotion of prayer meetings, spiritual support groups, and the advancement of faith through small gatherings have well-documented value in pastoral renewal.

The problem is not essentially in the search for an experience of the church that is hospitable, involving, and supportive, but in the tendency to absolutize intimacy as the principal element of authentic Christian community to the effect that the public, formal, and institutional elements of the church are rejected as meaningless and inauthentic. The challenge, then is to incorporate pastoral possibilities for hospitality and for mutual engagement and support into parish and ecclesiastical communities without generating the ideology of intimacy and its anti-institutional consequences. The choice, accordingly, is not between models of radical intimacy and of inhospitality and alienation. Parker Palmer describes the proper attitude when he suggests the paradox that the church must be "a company of strangers." The church must create communities, he says, "which are not mere extensions of private security, but which bridge the private and the public, leading us from the familiarities of private life into the strangeness of the public realm."[89] Thus, while the church does not disavow the values of intimacy, it does recognize that the only authentic intimacy is with and through God, for "in the spacious hospitality of God's love, the Christian can become 'intimate' even with people seen once, or not at all."[90]

Given the importance of images and metaphors in shaping and orienting faith, the image of the church as city seems, in the present context, more adequate than images of church as family or community of friends. Indeed, only when conceived as a city rather than an intimate community can the vocation of the church to possess and redeem all the dimensions of social reality emerge into proper relief. Consequently, only in a church truly public and publicly concerned will the liturgy be able to speak to and generate commitment to the transformation of the social and cultural environments.[91]

The politicization of the Gospel is not the same thing as genuine Christian commitment to service of the poor and the oppressed. The 1971 Synod of Bishops made the depth of the latter commitment clear when it declared that "action on behalf of justice and participation in the transformation of the world fully appear to us as a constitutive dimension of the preaching of the Gospel, or, in other words, of the Church's mission for the redemption of the human race and its liberation from every oppressive situation."[92] Undoubtedly, Christians have in the past often failed to enact this commitment in the realm of systemic and structural reform. For that reason, the need for this kind of reform is properly recognized today. Nevertheless, the systemic and political cannot become the principal or exclusive focus of social transformation.

The essential objection, then, to the politicization of the church's social mission is that it narrows the scope of this mission, robs it of the richness of vision that emerges from an organic conception of society, and effectively restricts the work of transformation to a very few. By contrast, the vision of the church's social mission embodied in the liturgy itself generates concern for the transformation of the total human city. It inspires political action according to the most profound sense of serving and preparing the way for the heavenly city, the New Jerusalem.[93] The kind of commitment that emerges is shot through with an ethos of praise, thanksgiving, and sacrifice and remains fundamentally subject to the power of Christ risen and exalted.[94] The rich and diverse symbolic operations of the liturgy point Christians to the great variety of ways by which the transformation of society and human culture can be achieved. They provide the energy for transformation within the diverse orders of personal existence, household and community, city and nation. Most of all, the liturgy directs Christians not to grand political schemes but to virtuous action, to the recognition proposed by Stanley Hauerwas that "justice often demands no more than the most common acts of care."[95]

---

1. Christopher Dawson, *Religion and the Rise of Western Culture* (Garden City, NJ: Image Books, 1958), 26ff.

2. ___, 41.

3. ___.

4. ___, 43.

5. ___.

6. ___, 42. See also the chapter entitled "The Influence of Liturgy and Theology on the Development of Byzantine Culture," in Christopher Dawson, *The Formation of Christendom* (New York: Sheed and Ward, 1967) 136–53.

7. R. W. Franklin, "The Nineteenth Century Liturgical Movement," *Worship* 53 (1979) 25.

8. ___. See also by R. W. Franklin: "Guéranger: A View on the Centenary of His Death," *Worship* 49 (1975) 318–28; "Guéranger and Pastoral Liturgy: A Nineteenth-Century Context," *Worship* 50 (1976) 146–62; "Guéranger and Variety in Unity," *Worship* 51 (1977) 378–99; "Response: Humanism and Transcendence in the Nineteenth Century Liturgical Movement," *Worship* 59 (1985) 342–53.

9. Virgil Michel, "Nine Years After," *Orate Fratres* 10 (1935–36) 5.

10. ___.

11. Virgil Michel, "Liturgy and Catholic Life," 193 (unpublished manuscript), quoted in Paul B. Marx, *Virgil Michel and the Liturgical Movement* (Collegeville, MN: The Liturgical Press, 1957) 257.

12. Michel, "Nine Years After," 6.

13. ___, 5.

14. H. A. Reinhold commented that "for Virgil Michel the labor encyclicals of Leo XIII and the liturgical reforms of Pius X did not just by accident happen within one generation, but were responses to cries of the masses for Christ, who had power and gave the good tidings. They belonged together." H. A. Reinhold, "The Liturgical Movement to Date," *National Liturgical Week–1947*, 11. Michel was careful to point out, however, that "the liturgy does not offer a detailed scheme of economic reconstruction, or anything of the kind. But it does give us a proper concept and understanding of what society is like, through its model, the Mystical Body." Letter to Martin Schirber, OSB, November 27, 1935, quoted in Marx, *Virgil Michel and the Liturgical Movement*, 205. See also *The Social Question: Essays on Capitalism and Christianity by Father Virgil Michel, OSB*, selected and edited by Robert L. Spaeth (Collegeville, MN: Office of Academic Affairs, St. John's University, 1987).

15. J. Bryan Hehir, foreword to *Liturgy and Social Justice*, ed. Mark Searle (Collegeville, MN: The Liturgical Press, 1980) 10.

16. Robert N. Bellah, et al., *Habits of the Heart: Individualism and Commitment in American Life* (New York: Harper and Row, 1985) 334.

17. Christopher Lasch, *The Culture of Narcissism: American Life in an Age of Diminishing Expectations* (New York: Warner Books, 1979); also *The Minimal Self: Psychic Survival in Troubled Times* (New York: W. W. Norton, 1984).

18. Lasch, *The Culture of Narcissism*, 33.

19. See Philip Rieff, *The Triumph of the Therapeutic: Uses of Faith After Freud* (New York: Harper and Row, 1966).

20. T. J. Jackson Lears, "From Salvation to Self-Realization: Advertizing and the Therapeutic Roots of the Consumer Culture, 1880–1930," in *The Culture of Consumption: Critical Essays in American History, 1880–1980*, ed. Richard Wightman Fox and T. J. Jackson Lears (New York: Pantheon Books, 1983) 21.

21. ___, 4.

22. See Neil Postman, *Amusing Ourselves to Death: Public Discourse in the Age of Show Business* (New York: Viking Penguin, 1985).

23. Bellah, et al., *Habits of the Heart*, 227.

24. George Lindbeck, *The Nature of Doctrine: Religion and Theology in a Postliberal Age* (Philadelphia: The Westminster Press, 1984) 22.

25. ___.

26. ___, 16.

27. Alasdair MacIntyre, *After Virtue: A Study in Moral Theory* (Notre Dame, IN: University of Notre Dame Press, 1984, second edition) 31.

28. ___, 24.

29. Nathan Mitchell, "The Sense of the Sacred," in *Parish: A Place for Worship,* ed. Mark Searle (Collegeville, MN: The Liturgical Press, 1981) 74.

30. ___, 72.

31. ___, 69.

32. ___.

33. Mary Douglas, *Natural Symbols: Explorations in Cosmology* (London: Pelican Books, 1973) 19ff.

34. Richard Sennett, *The Fall of Public Man* (New York: Alfred A. Knopf, 1977) 259.

35. ___.

36. ___.

37. ___, 219ff.

38. ___, 219.

39. ___, 4.

40. ___, 3ff.

41. ___, 338.

42. ___, 259ff.

43. ___, 12.

44. ___, 266.

45. ___, 263. The effects of this process upon family life are analyzed in Christopher Lasch, *Haven in a Heartless World: The Family Besieged* (New York: Basic Books, 1977).

46. Erving Goffman, *Relations in Public* (New York: Harper and Row, 1971) 63.

47. Bellah, et al., *Habits of the Heart,* 228.

48. ___, 230.

49. ___, 232. See Dean R. Hoge, *Converts, Dropouts, Returnees: A Study of Religious Change Among Catholics* (Washington, DC: United States Catholic Conference; New York: Pilgrim Press, 1981) 167.

50. Margaret O'Brien Steinfels, "The Laity: Not of One Mind," *Church* 3 (Fall 1987) 52.

51. Dick Westley, *Redemptive Intimacy: A New Perspective for the Journey to Adult Faith* (Mystic, CT: Twenty-third Publications, 1981) 140.

52. ___. Emphasis in original.

53. ___, 103.

54. Parker Palmer, *The Company of Strangers: Christians and the Renewal of America's Public Life* (New York: Crossroad, 1983) 120.

55. ___.

56. ___.

57. ___. The comment of the authors of *Habits of the Heart* on the superficial quality of intimization is instructive. The need for personal intimacy, they say, "suggests why the local church, like so many other voluntary communities, indeed like the contemporary family, is so fragile, requires so much energy to keep it going, and has so faint a hold on commitment when such needs are not met" (232).

58. Bellah, et al., *Habits of the Heart*, 237.

59. Richard Neuhaus, *The Naked Public Square: Religion and Democracy in America* (Grand Rapids, MI: William B. Eerdmans Publishing Company, 1984).

60. Palmer, *The Company of Strangers*, 136.

61. Mitchell, "The Sense of the Sacred," 71.

62. ___. Emphasis in the original.

63. On this, see Robert E. Meagher, "Strangers at the Gates: Ancient Rites of Hospitality," in *Parabola* 2:4 (1977) 10–15.

64. Raymond Williams, *The Sociology of Culture* (New York: Schocken Books, 1982) 13. Emphasis in original.

65. Neuhaus, *The Naked Public Square*, 159.

66. ___, 158.

67. ___, 157.

68. Jethro Liebermann, *The Litigious Society* (New York: Basic Books, 1983).

69. ___, 186.

70. Michael Warren, "Catechesis and the Problem of 'Popular' Culture," *The Living Light* 23 (1987) 133.

71. ___.

72. Denise Lardner Carmody and John Tully Carmody, "Voegelin and the Restoration of Order: A Meditation," *Horizons* 14:1 (1987) 82–96.

73. ___, 82–83.

74. ___, 84.

75. ___.

76. ___.

77. Avery Dulles, "The Gospel, the Church and Politics," *Origins* 16 (1987) 637.

78. ___, 646.

79. J. Brian Benestad, "The Catholic Concept of Social Justice: A Historical Perspective," *Communio* 11 (1984) 364.

80. ___.

81. See the chapter entitled "Sanctification and Politics" in Wolfhart Pannenberg, *Christian Spirituality* (Philadelphia: The Westminster Press, 1983) 50–70. For a summary of the views of Hauerwas on this matter, see his essay, "Should Christians Talk So Much About Justice?" in *Books and Religion* 14:5/6 (1986) 5, 14–15.

82. This is the thesis of Tissa Balasuriya, *The Eucharist and Human Liberation* (Maryknoll: Orbis Books, 1979).

83. Elisabeth Schüssler Fiorenza, "Tablesharing and the Celebration of the Eucharist" in *Can We Always Celebrate the Eucharist?* (*Concilium* 152), ed. Mary Collins and David Power (New York: The Seabury Press/Edinburgh: T. and T. Clark, Ltd., 1982) 4. Though we cannot go into it here, it is noteworthy that liberation and feminist theologies have their roots in systems other than liberalism and, therefore, the kind of politicization they represent is related only indirectly to the processes of subjectification and intimization.

84. P. de Béthunes, quoted in Joseph Gelineau, "Celebrating the Paschal Liberation," in *Politics and Liturgy* (*Concilium* 92), ed. Herman Schmidt and David Power (New York: Herder and Herder, 1974) 111.

85. Gelineau, "Celebrating the Paschal Liberation," 111.

86. ___, 113.

87. Bellah, et al., *Habits of the Heart,* 163, 248; Palmer, *The Company of Strangers,* 155.

88. For a similar suggestion, see Carol Doran and Thomas H. Troeger, "Reclaiming the Corporate Self: The Meaning and Ministry of *Worship* in a Privatistic Culture," Worship 60 (1986) 200–10.

89. Palmer, *The Company of Strangers,* 121.

90. ___, 110.

91. See the chapter entitled "The City" in Urban T. Holmes III, *Ministry and Imagination* (New York: Seabury Press, 1976) 13–34; also Aidan Kavanagh, *On Liturgical Theology* (New York: Pueblo Publishing Company, 1984), especially the chapter entitled "The Church," 39–51.

92. Introduction, *Justice in the World.* Text in *Justice in the Marketplace: Collected Statements of the Vatican and the United States Catholic Bishops on Economic Policy, 1891–1984* (Washington, DC: United States Catholic Conference, 1985) 250.

93. See Herman Schmidt, "Lines of Political Action and Contemporary Liturgy," in *Politics and Liturgy* (*Concilium* 92) 13–33.

94. On this, see the chapter entitled "Ethics" in Geoffrey Wainwright, *Doxology: The Praise of God in Worship, Doctrine, and Life* (New York: Oxford University Press, 1980) 399–434; also Mark Searle, "Serving the Lord with Justice," in *Liturgy and Social Justice*, 13–35.

95. Hauerwas, "Should Christians Talk So Much About Justice?" 14.

Chapter 5

Sunday in Modern America: A Cultural Perspective

The tension that exists between Catholic liturgical tradition and modern North American culture is more severely in evidence in the area of Sunday observance than in the area of Christian practice that include baptisms, weddings, and funerals for the reason that the latter have a more socially functional and "necessary" character than does Sunday observance. Accordingly, what I shall say about the problems attending Sunday observance in North America today has an application, even if less noticeably, to the whole liturgical system. Correlatively, the problems that attend the church's liturgy in North American cultural context may be seen to be enlarged in the area of Sunday observance.

In this essay, I shall suggest the existence of a number of conditions that make Sunday observance problematic in present-day North American Catholicism. Five of these have their origin in the larger culture and seven within the church's own life. It will be evident that there is considerable overlap in these twelve elements, as well as significant complexity in the relationship between their ecclesial and cultural origins.

The five culturally generated conditions that create a barrier to the full flowering of Catholic Sunday observance today are: the individualism of mainline American religiosity; the experiential-expressive understanding of the holy; the pervasiveness of cultural consumerism; the fragmentation of culture; and the excessive optimism of the American religious ethos.

Individualistic Religiosity

While a number of religious traditions in America remain deeply communal and social, mainline American religiosity, which generally corresponds to liberal Protestantism, is profoundly individualistic. In the 1830s, the French social philosopher Alexis de Tocqueville observed the emergence of this feature of the American character and recorded it in his celebrated *Democracy In America*. De Tocqueville saw that the emergent individualism was in danger of uprooting the communitarian strands which had traditionally provided American life with a profoundly cohesive character. If the communitarian traditions (founded in biblical and republican conceptions) are what bind men and women to each other and establish common identities, destinies, and strivings, individualism is what separates, leading each to isolation and detachment. "Individualism," wrote De Tocqueville, is "a mature and calm feeling, which disposes each member of the community to sever himself from the mass of his fellows," so that he "willingly leaves society at large to itself." In such an atmosphere, people increasingly look firstly to their own needs. "They owe nothing to any man, they expect nothing from any man; they acquire the habit of always considering themselves as standing alone, and they are apt to imagine that their whole destiny is in their own hands."[1]

The authors of the 1980s bestseller *Habits of the Heart* have traced the effects of this individualism on American religion, showing how, for instance, the individualistic strand has long triumphed over the public communal religious traditions of New England colonial religion. An incident recorded in the research process is instructive here: "One person we interviewed has actually named her religion (she calls it her 'faith') after herself." Her religion is "Sheilaism." These are Sheila's words: " 'I believe in God. I'm not a religious fanatic. I can't remember the last time I went to church. My faith has carried me a long way. It's Sheilaism' "[2]

It takes no great insight to predict the negative impact of religious individualism on public worship. While the biblical and republican strands of American culture traditionally undergirded the meaningfulness of public worship and the institutions of Sunday observance, individualism, even of a religious kind, sees little need for public liturgy and for Sunday observance.

Catholicism in America traditionally sustained a vigorously communal and public character largely by isolation from the wider culture. However, with the post-1960s entry into the American cultural mainstream, the religiosity of American Catholics has taken on individualistic characteristics, giving rise to an understandably negative impact on participation in liturgical worship and in Sunday observance in particular.

EXPERIENTIAL-EXPRESSIVISM

In tandem with an individualistic conception of religion there has emerged a profoundly subjectivist appreciation of the holy in mainstream American religion. The Yale theologian George Lindbeck describes this conception of religion as "experiential-expressive." According to Lindbeck, "the structures of modernity press individuals to meet God first in the depths of their souls and then, perhaps, if they find something personally congenial, to become part of a tradition or join a church."[3] This corresponds well to the "Sheilaism" identified in *Habits of the Heart* which understands religion primarily as "just my own little voice."[4]

In a subjectivist understanding and practice of religion, God's presence and activity have their primary locus in the human heart and conscience, not in objective religious forms and sacraments. If God can be encountered more authentically in the silence of the individual heart, in music and art, in personal meditation, or on the ski slopes, it is not surprising that there should occur a certain alienation from formal worship and a growing conviction of the irrelevance of a defined holy day.

Experiential-expressivism has become notably operative in modern Catholic sensibilities in recent decades. Nathan Mitchell has identified a significant shift in Catholic attitudes when he asserts that the "sense of the sacred has moved, shifted its location." Experience of the divine has become detached from its traditional location in the worshiping church and now "is located 'inside,' in the personal history and geography of the self." As a result, "the sacred is closely attached to the self, not to rituals celebrated and shared in public." Modern American Catholics, according to Mitchell, "look for the holy to reveal itself, not in the awe-inspiring rites of baptism and eucharist, but in the awesome precincts of the self."[5] The impact of this shift in religious sensibility upon Sunday worship is fairly self-evident.

Cultural Consumerism

The individualism and experiential-expressivism of American culture generate in turn a pervasively consumerist view of cultural and religious institutions and symbols. Social historian T. J. Jackson Lears has set forth the progression here by pointing out that "the decline of symbolic structures outside the self has been a central process in the development of a consumer culture joining advertising strategies and a therapeutic ethos."[6] For Lears, consumerism has become in America a comprehensive way of seeing, a whole way of life. As consumerism invades religious conceptions, there occurs a process of "deobjectification" of religious rites and practices, so that these lose their powerful mediating quality and become merely functional aids to the shaping of personal religious consciousness. The result, as George Lindbeck points out, is that today "increasing numbers of people regard all religions as possibly sources of symbols to be used eclectically in articulating, clarifying and organizing the experiences of the inner self."[7]

As formal religious observances lose their traditional mediating, sacramental status and are reconceived functionally, they are prone to being appropriated into the categories of psychology and entertainment. Accordingly, rites and symbols are used to advance self-realization and personal well-being. As they become functionalized and psychologized, religious rites are freely adapted and discarded at will. When Sunday worship is regarded in this way, self-centered voluntarism shapes the practice of church attendance and the expectations that public worship should be therapeutically satisfying leads to disappointment and eventual alienation.

Fragmentation of Culture

The severe fragmentation of modern culture is axiomatic. French writers like Simone Weil have written of *deracinement* (uprootedness), the condition by which individuals come to exist in isolation from others, nature, place, and communal origin. American farmer-philosopher Wendell Berry explains that cultural life is fragmented today because it has lost "the necessary understandings, forms and enactments of the relations among materials and processes, principles and actions, ideals and realities, past and present, present and future, men and women, body and spirit, city and country, civilization and wilderness, growth and decay, life and death."⁸ In other words, nothing coheres.

Among the cultural elements assumed by the Christian tradition of Sunday is an ordered, publicly observed communal life in which the seasons of the year, the hours of the day, the days of the week, leisure time and work time, social and personal interactions are interwoven in a harmonious and dynamic fashion. In the culture in which we now live, public and communal calendars have all but collapsed. Seasons, days, and hours retain merely functional or leisure significance. Personal transitions are privatized as the structures of community fade. The institution of Sunday has been replaced by "the weekend," and national memorials have become shopping days. The traditional rituals and conventions of the American family have been abandoned. It is not surprising that the Christian Sunday in America should be affected by this fragmentation and lose its character as a meaningfully ordered day.

Some will remember the ritual complexity of Sunday in traditional Catholicism. The preceding day was one of preparation involving often house-cleaning, food preparation, and attendance at confession. Sunday itself involved Mass followed by educational, social, or spiritual activities. The day was carefully observed with the family dinner and abstention from servile work. In some places attendance at parish evening devotions was common practice. This scheme depended on an orderly and unified cultural substructure. With the demise of the latter and the advancement of cultural fragmentation, American Catholics now generally observe Sundays in the manner of the culture at large. As a result, Sunday observance has become something extraordinary, intrusive, inconvenient, and easily neglected. Not least, the advent of Saturday evening Masses—a valid pastoral provision in its original conception—has led unwittingly to a further evacuation of the theological and spiritual meaning of Sunday.

Cultural Optimism

The Spanish-American philosopher George Santayana captured a crucial aspect of American self-understanding when he described America as "the land of universal goodwill, confidence in life, inexperience of poisons." The American citizen, he said, is naive about "vanity or wickedness in the ultimate aims of a man, including himself. He thinks life splendid and blameless without stopping to consider how far folly and malice may be inherent in it." The American mode of thought "is confident of a happy and triumphant future."[9]

Henry Steele Commager has commented more recently: "From the beginning most Americans, except Negro slaves, found this world a paradise rather than a purgatory. Whatever they may have said, or sung, they preferred this life to the next, and when they imagined heaven, they thought of it as operating under an American constitution."[10]

Santayana and Commager effectively capture the ethos of the American Dream and its spirituality of optimism, future-orientation, confidence, self-reliance, naivete about evil and sin, and anti-traditionalism. No doubt, the experience of the 1960s and after tempered the American Dream mythology, yet it remains a profoundly formative element in the consciousness of modern Americans.

Accordingly, it is clear that the kind of Christianity that is most notably "American" is that which embodies the features of optimism, self confidence, affirmation of life, and the celebration of progress and individual achievement. The Christianity of the Crystal Cathedral and the spirituality of the New Age movement are among the most notable exponents of optimistic American religion today.

It is not surprising that the Catholic liturgical tradition, with its language of the Cross, sacrifice, repentance, humility, and intercession should encounter some difficulty in such a cultural atmosphere. An optimistic and worldly religious climate is understandably unsympathetic to the Catholic spiritual and liturgical traditions which are marked by a profound consciousness of the transitoriness of the present order and by a conception of worship as a sacramental participation in an eschatological promise surpassing the present world. It is difficult to preach and to recommend the practice of an "eighth day" in a culture quite pleased with the seven it has already.

In the remainder of this essay, I shall take up seven conditions generated primarily within the church itself which have created some difficulties for the viability of the institution of the Christian Sunday. They are: the collapse of mystery; the crisis of ritual competence; the narrowing of liturgical inclusivity; the new pietism; renewed clericalism; the loss of devotional Catholicism; and the neglect of Sunday obligation.

Collapse of Mystery

One of the common complaints made by "conservative" Catholics against the revised liturgy is that it has lost its sense of "mystery." The concern is also increasingly expressed by younger and not-so-conservative Catholics. This assertion covers a multitude and embodies both valid and questionable reactions to the present-day liturgy. The conviction appears essentially to be that the Mass today lacks a sense of importance, depth, reverence, and worthiness.

Such perceptions are not, in my view, valid reactions to the post–Vatican II Order of Mass in itself. They are, however, difficult to refute when directed at the way the liturgy is often celebrated in practice. The characteristic of solemnity, by which I mean the sense of seriousness, weightiness, and significance, is poorly expressed in American Catholic liturgy today. In its place has emerged a pervasive folksiness and casualness, a self-conscious sense of practicality and immediate relevance. A lack of beauty and imagination is a frequent complaint against the church's liturgical life. An ethos of grandeur, majesty and awe have almost completely disappeared in Catholic liturgy in the United States. Even more troublesome is the fact that such conceptions are habitually shunned and discouraged as inauthentic by some American liturgists. No doubt some of the complaints about a lack of "mystery" are held by persons who seem incapable of appropriating the enriching advantages of the revised liturgy. Yet, many who welcome the liturgical changes inspired by the Second Vatican Council make similar complaints that cannot easily be dismissed. In my view, a further deterioration of the complex set of elements which the ordinary Catholic identifies as "mystery" will lead to an ongoing weakening of Sunday observance.

Ritual Competence

Wisely, one of the primary aims of liturgical renewal was the promotion of what the Constitution on the Sacred Liturgy described as "that full, conscious, and active participation in liturgical celebrations which is demanded by the very nature of the liturgy" (CSL, 14). Sound pastoral theory recognizes that people tend to participate in the liturgical life of the church when their sense of spiritual identity and familiarity with it is well developed. Correlatively, worshipers lose interest when they feel alienated or liturgically incompetent. The aim of fuller participation has been achieved in a quite remarkable way in the post–Vatican II liturgy.

In my view, an element that has impeded liturgical competence, however, is the ongoing propensity for change, experimentation, and novelty in American Catholic worship. While some Catholics express satisfaction with sustained creativity in liturgical matters, a more abiding wisdom holds that to be effective, a ritual tradition must be fixed, stable, and repetitive. As sociologist David Martin points out, "rite" depends on "rote," on familiarity and predictability.[11] Otherwise, rite becomes incomprehensible and confusing. While many Catholics are good-humoredly resigned to not knowing "what to expect next" in liturgical celebrations in their parishes, the total effect of habitual change is to create alienation from the liturgy.

The health of Sunday liturgy among American Catholics in the future requires that pastors and liturgical personnel put more faith in the intrinsic power of stable ritual forms and less in the values to be obtained from the kind of liturgical planning that presently consumes so much well-intentioned but questionable energy.

LITURGICAL INCLUSIVITY

By the inclusivity of the liturgy I mean its ability to include and incorporate people of all shades of professional, political, and educational backgrounds, as well as of varying temperaments, emotional types, and personal sensibilities. Anthony Archer, in an engaging study of English Catholicism, has pointed out the notable ability of the "old" liturgy to speak to and incorporate into the English church the Catholic aristocracy, the intellectual and professional classes, as well as the largely Irish working class. The liturgy before its reform had a kind of spaciousness and comprehensiveness that allowed the incorporation of diverse social groupings. According to Archer, the new liturgy has failed in this regard and has become constricted to middle class tastes and concerns and co-opted by a middle class ecclesiastical bureaucracy.[12]

Something similar has arguably occurred in the United States, where the Catholic liturgy been notably adapted to the tastes, sensibilities, manners, and concerns of the middle class, giving rise to what Aidan Kavanagh calls the *embourgeoisement* of the liturgy. This adaptation means that characteristics of political and social liberalism are in evidence today in Catholic worship. In the process, the liturgy has lost its traditional comprehension of Catholic intellectuals and artists, as well as many of the poor who share few of the concerns of the more progressive middle class. At the other end of the social spectrum, conservative groupings in American Catholicism find that the pastoral practice of the liturgy often insults and patronizes them. This relatively recent phenomenon of liturgical exclusiveness needs to be reversed if Sunday worship is to be comprehensive of the actual diversity of American Catholics.

THE NEW PIETISM

Closely related to the issue of universality is the emergence of a new pietism in Catholic pastoral life and liturgy in the United States. By this I mean the emergence of a highly personal, emotive, intimate and self-focused practice of the liturgy. This phenomenon is the result of an understanding of the church as a community of friends and intimates. It conceives the congregation as most appropriately a small group and it tends to assert the primacy of the assembly over the ritual system itself. It often incorporates anti-institutionalism and is anti-hierarchical.

Neo-pietist liturgical assemblies are exclusive in these ways. Firstly, persons not given to emotional and intimate forms of expression and congregational interaction feel embarrassed and threatened and either do not join or leave. Secondly, as sociologist Daniel Olson points out, such congregations are cliquish and do not welcome newcomers. According to Olson, congregations with high intimacy networks have a poor ability to welcome newcomers.[13] Thirdly, because such communities favor worship places that are often neither psychologically nor architecturally public, the newcomer, the reticent and the marginal are discouraged from approaching them. In short, the more pietistic and emotionally restricted that worship styles become, the less accessible Sunday liturgy becomes and the more decline in participation is intensified.

RENEWED CLERICALISM

A particularly destabilizing feature of the new liturgy is the extent to which the structure, style, and "success" of worship today depends on the presidential style of the priest. The clericalism of the postconciliar liturgy in which the priest was the exclusive "actor" in the liturgy has been replaced today by a kind of psychological clericalism whereby the priest's personality and charismatic gifts, rather than the ritual, become the medium for liturgical communication and performance. Instead of the presiding priest serving the rite, the rite becomes the priest's script, which, like an actor, he appropriates, personalizes, and modifies according to inner authority. The tendency today among priests toward excessive personalization, unpredictable intervention, spontaneous commentary, and textual and ritual adaptation has the effect of destabilizing the objective character of the liturgy and turning it into a personal performance. In this process, congregations lose their focus on the objective rite and are psychologically retrained to understand liturgy in a highly clericalist manner. Overall, this phenomenon generates lack of commitment to liturgical participation, a decline in congregational investment, and a tendency for the politics, opinions, and personality of the priest to be a decisive factor in church attendance.

Loss of Devotional Catholicism

In an earlier part of this essay, I suggested that the progressive fragmentation of American culture destroyed the very possibility of retaining the Christian Sunday in its traditional social complexity. The loss of devotional Catholicism generated within the church itself may be seen as a corresponding process contributing to fragmentation. I have in mind the process by which the support for the liturgical life of the church provided by the devotional forms of domestic Catholic religiosity have unraveled and collapsed. In the valid attempt to restore the eucharist to primacy of place in Catholic life, other devotional forms were de-emphasized and even discouraged. But, as Colleen McDannell has shown, one of the functions served by the devotional religion of the Catholic household in the past was the maintenance of a certain balance of power between the parochial and the domestic, the clerical and the laity.[14] Put more benignly, devotional Catholicism served to set up a dynamic relationship between the domestic life of Catholics and the life of the parish officially centered on the eucharist. With the collapse of devotional Catholicism, however, there occurred a cleavage between the domestic and the parochial. Sunday Mass became increasingly isolated from the Catholic household. The eucharist no longer found symbolic reflection in domestic life, and the energy to participate in the

Mass and the sacraments was no longer generated by the symbolic structures of Catholic daily life, but now had to be abstractly generated.

Neglect of Sunday Obligation

While ecclesiastical law requires all Catholics over the age of seven to attend Sunday Mass, many liturgists, canonists, and pastors have questioned the value of such an obligation, preferring instead the inculcation of personal responsibility to participate in the church's liturgy. While such a position has commendable intentions, it can, in my view, easily create a loosening of the ordinary Catholic's sense of the profound and intrinsic connection between daily Catholic faith and participation in the Sunday eucharist. Laws are, after all, complex cultural agents and they communicate and advance in a powerful way virtues that cannot be communicated in any other way. The extent to which the pastoral and catechetical down-playing of the Sunday Mass obligation has weakened Mass-going is, of course, very difficult to calculate. It is, however, quoted by Catholics as at least one of the reasons they no longer attend Mass. While a merely legalistic commitment to Sunday observance is, of course, very inadequate, pastors, catechists, and liturgists ought, in my view, think carefully about the instructive and informative value of the Sunday obligation and about the way it symbolizes the weighty and pressing connection between daily faith and the Sunday eucharist. In the long run, the pastoral relativization of the Sunday obligation will only serve to undermine further the Catholic commitment to Sunday observance.

Conclusion

The purpose of this essay is not to celebrate and affirm the numerous benefits of liturgical reform or of the many ways in which Catholic life has been advanced by the revised liturgy and its pastoral implementation. This essay is an analysis of problems and failures—and, therefore, represents only one side of the story of Sunday in modern North America. The extent to which the analysis provided here is correct is for the reader to decide. However, few will disagree that Sunday worship among Catholics is today beset by serious problems. The way forward begins at least in part in an analytic probing of the unpleasant.

1. Alexis de Tocqueville, *Democracy in America*, trans. and ed. Harvey C. Mansfield and Debra Winthrop (Chicago: University of Chicago Press, 2000) 104, 105.

2. Robert N. Bellah, et al., *Habits of the Heart: Individualism and Commitment in American Life* (New York: Harper and Row, 1985) 221.

3. George A. Lindbeck, *The Nature of Doctrine: Religion and Theology in a Postliberal Age* (Philadelphia: The Westminster Press, 1984) 22.

4. Bellah, *Habits of the Heart*, 221.

5. Nathan Mitchell, "The Sense of the Sacred," *Parish: A Place for Worship*, ed. Mark Searle (Collegeville, MN: The Liturgical Press, 1981) 74, 72, 69, 71.

6. T. J. Jackson Lears, "From Salvation to Self-Realization: Advertising and Therapeutic Roots of the Consumer Culture, 1880–1980," *The Culture of Consumption: Critical Essays in American History, 1880–1980*, ed. Richard R. Fox and T. J. Jackson Lears (New York: Pantheon Books, 1983) 21.

7. Lindbeck, *The Nature of Doctrine*, 22.

8. Wendell Berry, *The Unsettling of America: Culture and Agriculture* (San Francisco: Sierra Club Books, 1986) 21.

9. George Santayana, *Character and Opinion in the United States* (New York: W. W. Norton, 1964) 144, 213.

10. Henry Steele Commanger, *The American Mind: An Interpretation of American Thought and Character Since the 1800s* (New Haven: Yale University Press, 1950) 162.

11. See David Martin, *The Breaking of the Image: A Sociology of Christian Theory and Practice* (Oxford: Basil Blackwell, 1985) esp. 81–102.

12. See Anthony Archer, *The Two Catholic Churches: A Study in Oppression* (London: SCM Press, 1986).

13. Daniel V. A. Olson, "Church Friendships: Boon or Barrier to Church Growth?" *Journal for the Scientific Study of Religion* 28 (1989) 432–47.

14. Colleen McDannell, *The Christian Home in Victorian America, 1840–1900* (Bloomington, IN: Indiana University Press, 1986).

Part III

The Arts and Liturgy

Chapter 6

Paradigms in American Catholic Liturgical Music

Catholic liturgical music in the United States today appears to be outgrowing much of the divisiveness, controversy, and acrimony that has beset it in recent decades. Soon after the promulgation of the Constitution on the Sacred Liturgy in 1963, serious and long-lasting cleavages began to appear among church musicians and commentators on the role of music in the liturgy. Rembert Weakland wrote at the time that "Church musicians throughout the country are much divided among themselves on what should be done, on what is good 'Church' music and what is not, and on the path that future Church music should take."[1]

Following the Fifth International Church Music Congress in Chicago and Milwaukee in 1966, the deepening divisions were institutionalized.[2] The Church Music Association of America chose to affiliate with the Consocietas Internationalis Musicae Sacrae, leading to the disaffection of much of its membership and their consequent affiliation with the more progressive European-based Universa Laus and a decade later with the National Association of Pastoral Musicians in the United States. An attempt to heal the emerging divisions took place at a crucial gathering in Kansas City later that year, but to no lasting avail.[3]

Sacred Music, the publication of the Church Music Association of America, has spoken in retrospect of what happened in the mid-1960s as "a revolution" and it saw itself "at war" with the more "progressive" trends in church music associated with Rembert Weakland, Frederick McManus, and Godfrey Diekmann in the United States and Joseph Gelineau, Bernard Huijbers, and the music editors of *Concilium* in

Europe.[4] With similar vehemence, the more "progressive" voices and platforms expressed a lack of sympathy for the elements of "traditionalism" in Catholic liturgical music. Though the rhetorical exchanges have muted somewhat in recent years, the growing diversity in theory and practice has added complexity to the debate.[5] Yet liturgical music is still able to serve as a lightening rod for the wide range of emotions and sensibilities surrounding the renewal of the church that exist in the American Catholic community today. This was signified by the very large number of reviews accorded the 1990 publication of *Why Catholics Can't Sing* by Thomas Day and the heated debates the book occasioned—even in journals and magazines not usually interested in liturgy or music.[6]

This essay represents an attempt to bring some conceptual organization to the diverse attitudes and practices that exist in the area of Catholic church music in the United States today. To this end, I suggest the coexistence of six principal paradigms to explain variously the diversity and pluralism in musical theories and styles, the absence of conceptual and practical consensus in the field, and the contrasting agendas that are a notable aspect of the liturgical life of the American church.[7] These paradigms are the neo-Caecilian, the folk/popular, the ethnic, the ritual-functional, the modern classical, and the ecumenical/eclectic.

By a paradigm, I mean simply a way of seeing, a way of looking at and organizing complex data into a manageable and coherent whole.[8] The paradigms I propose should not be seen as mutually exclusive or restrictive, but rather as representing a set of differing commitments, allegiances, and concerns interacting in a mutually aware manner, sometimes creatively, sometimes conflictually. An individual or group may operate within more than one paradigm at the same time. The fact that paradigms are not rigidly self-contained or mutually exclusive is evidenced by the fact that while most practicing musicians and liturgical music scholars operate primarily within one paradigm, they may operate at least partially in others and can even be in the process of paradigm shifts.

A methodology of paradigms must be invoked carefully if it is not to encourage entrenched mindsets or stagnate discussion. Used properly, it can bring tentative clarity to complex and inconclusive data. As Avery Dulles points out, "Each paradigm brings with it its own favorite set of images, its own rhetoric, its own values, certitudes, commitments and priorities. It even brings with it a particular set of preferred problems."[9] Paradigms operate as exploratory and relevatory devices. It is not surprising that, in a time of considerable change and development, the methodology of paradigm construction and analysis is widely used in theology.[10] It has also become a familiar feature of present-day liturgical and sacramental theology.[11]

Neo-Caecilianism and the Restoration Agenda

The neo-Caecilian paradigm is named by reference to the neo-Caecilian movement in Germany, which began in the second half of the nineteenth century in an attempt to reform and improve the quality of church music. Spearheaded by Francis Xavier Witt (1839–1880), the movement had as its ideal the restoration of Gregorian chant and the unaccompanied polyphonic works of the Renaissance.[12] The reforms were enacted against a *status quo* characterized by excessive attachment to operatic styles and a musical ethos at odds with the authentic character of the liturgy.[13] Of this period, Joseph A. Jungmann commented that music had "spread its gorgeous mantle over the whole Mass, so that the other details of the rite scarcely had any significance."[14] In the Baroque era, "the liturgy was not only submerged under this ever-growing art but actually suppressed, so that even at this time there were festive occasions which might best be described as 'church concerts with liturgical accompaniment.'"[15]

Through the rediscovery of the works of the Renaissance and the advancement of scholarship on Gregorian chant, what Jungmann calls "a Catholic restoration" intent on renewing the integrity of rite and sacred text was initiated. The Caecilian movement became the main promoter and agent of this restoration.[16] This movement, linked in inspiration with the work of Prosper Guéranger and the Benedictine monks of Solesmes in restoring Gregorian chant, received official acceptance in Pius X's *motu proprio* on sacred music in 1903 entitled *Tra le sollecitudini*, which restored chant and polyphony to primacy in the church's worship. Pius X deplored "the sad influence exercised on sacred art by profane and theatrical art,"[17] recognized Gregorian chant as "the supreme model for sacred music,"[18] and accorded a special place to "the classic polyphony, especially of the Roman school, which reached its greatest perfection in the fifteenth century, owing to the works of Pierluigi da Palestrina."[19]

The aims of this restoration movement were advanced in the United States through the American Caecilian Society founded by John B. Singenberger and Monsignor Joseph Salzmann in Milwaukee in 1873. The work of this society was carried on largely through the publication *Caecilia* and a series of national conventions. In the late 1950s, the agenda of this movement was taken over by the Society of Saint Caecilia and later in part by the Church Music Association of America and its publication *Sacred Music*.

In speaking of a neo-Caecilian movement in the Catholic church in the United States today, we are referring to a *present-day* way of regarding church music that approvingly invokes the conceptual framework of the original Caecilian movement and regards the aims of this movement as having continuing validity. Accordingly, it tends to read the Second Vatican Council in somewhat preconciliar terms and it is generally uneasy with musical developments in the church since the Second Vatican Council.

The principal commitment in the neo-Caecilian paradigm is toward the maintenance of the heritage of Gregorian chant, Renaissance polyphony, and the liturgical masterpieces of the Classical and Romantic periods. This commitment is wedded to a strong disposition toward Latin as the church's primary liturgical language; thus it finds the loss of the Latin heritage a matter of the gravest concern. It abhors what it regards as the corruption of church music which has occurred in recent decades and it regards itself as part of the long tradition of defending church music from destructive secular influences. The neo-Caecilian approach promotes a strongly contemplative and receptive understanding of active participation in worship and, accordingly, maintains a major emphasis on the integral role of choral music in the liturgy.[20] The advancement of the unity and integrity of the Roman liturgy is a major priority of this outlook; thus it looks askance at many proposed programs of musical inculturation.

This paradigm looks for its formal present-day grounding in the following affirmations of the Constitution on the Sacred Liturgy of the Second Vatican Council: "The musical tradition of the universal Church is a treasure of inestimable value, greater even than that of any other art";[21] "The treasury of sacred music is to be preserved and cultivated with great care";[22] "The Church recognizes Gregorian chant as being specially suited to the Roman liturgy. Therefore, other things being equal, it should be given pride of place in liturgical services";[23] "Other kinds of sacred music, especially polyphony, are by no means excluded from liturgical celebrations so long as they accord with the spirit of the liturgical action."[24]

To more or lesser degrees, this paradigm operates in the United States today (in descending degrees of severity) in Lefebvrite or separatist Catholic groups, in parishes or institutions promoting the so-called Tridentine Mass, and in those situations where preference is shown for the 1969 Order of Mass celebrated in Latin. Exponents of the neo-Caecilian paradigm do not by any means exclude congregational singing or modern compositions with vernacular texts. In general, however, the preference is in favor of the pre-1960s world of church music and those admonitions of the Second Vatican Council are seemingly consistent with such a preference.

It seems reasonable to suggest that the neo-Caecilian paradigm is significantly operative in the ongoing work of the Church Music Association of America and its publication *Sacred Music*, which maintains friendly association with European neo-Caecilian publications like Una Voce in France and Bollettino Ceciliano in Italy. The association maintains close ties with the Latin Liturgy Association of America and with various "conservative" organizations concerned about the general direction of renewal in the church. Editorially, *Sacred Music* takes a very critical, even dismal, view of the condition of church music since the Second Vatican Council, regarding the current state as "an impoverishment" and a "disintegration" of the Roman liturgy.[25] Perhaps the best known exponent and practitioner of the neo-Caecilian paradigm in the United States today is Monsignor Richard J. Schuler, pastor at St. Agnes Church in St. Paul, Minnesota.[26] Other notable figures more or less supportive of this perspective are Monsignors Francis P. Schmitt and Robert A. Skeris.[27] On the international level, the Consociatio Internationalis Musicae Sacrae is thought by many to be the principal organizational focus of neo-Caecilian sympathies.

THE FOLK MOVEMENT AND POPULAR CULTURE

The second paradigm, which stands at some distance from the first, may be described as the folk/popular. Lawrence Madden views the emergence of music in this style as the result of a confluence of three disparate movements in the 1960s: the folk music revival associated with the civil rights era and the peace movement; the official ecclesiastical allowance of instruments other than the organ into the liturgy; and the new openness to modern culture expressed in the Pastoral Constitution on the Church in the Modern World promulgated by the Second Vatican Council.[28] To these I would add two other factors: the burgeoning popular music industry of the 1960s which generated both an explosion in musical composition and rapid obsolescence in musical tastes; and the advent of a youth culture with its own particular symbol system and artistic sensibility.

The aims of church music composed in the folk/popular style were simplicity of form, melodic attractiveness, ease of performance, congregational accessibility, and a celebratory and festive character. This musical style aimed to establish intimacy and personalism in place of the perceived formality and institutionalism of the received liturgical tradition. This went hand in hand with a strong emphasis on spontaneity, emotional warmth, and spiritual immediacy.[29] A definite desire to connect liturgical expression with the popular culture of the day was clearly operative.

As mentioned already, the protocol of the Second Vatican Council for the development of a folk/popular idiom is found generally in the spirit of openness to new cultural expressions set out in chapter two of the Pastoral Constitution on the Church in the Modern world, which recognizes the appropriateness of the use of the cultural resources of the modern era to advance the liturgical life of the church.[30] The folk/popular paradigm also looked to article 19 in the Constitution on the Sacred Liturgy which declares: "With zeal and patience pastors of souls must promote the liturgical instruction of the faithful and also their active participation, both internal and external, taking into account their age, condition, way of life and standard of religious culture."[31] The paradigm saw itself in those sections of the Constitution on the Sacred Liturgy which encourages congregational singing, especially in the following: "Religious singing by the faithful is to be intelligently fostered so that in devotions and sacred exercises as well as in liturgical services, the voices of the faithful may be heard."[32]

Together, the various influences created a style of church music that was novel and striking in character. As Lawrence Madden puts it, "Encouraged by this new spirit of openness, church musicians soon introduced the 'folk' song and 'folk' instruments into the church's worship. As a result, either for the first time or for the first time outside 'Benediction' services, congregational song was raising the roof in many Roman Catholic parishes—at the 'folk' Mass."[33]

The history of the folk/popular idiom in Catholic liturgy in the United States has generally followed four phases.[34] The first phase began in the late 1960s when composers Ray Repp, James Thiem, Joe Wise, Miriam Therese Winter, and others produced what might be called "liturgical folk songs." These combined simple melodies of a popular and attractive style with lyrics expressing general religious themes. The second phase emerged in the 1970s with the advent of the Dameans (Mike Balhoff, Gary Daigle, and Darryl Ducote) and the St. Louis Jesuits (Roc O'Connor, Dan Schutte, Bob Dufford, and John Foley). The composers of this period, many of whose works found their way into the popular *Glory and Praise* collections published in 1977 and after, sought to promote in musical composition a greater attention to liturgical and biblical texts. The third phase was represented by Marty Haugen, David Haas, Michael Joncas, and James Chepponis in the 1980s. The musical style of these composers exhibited much greater knowledge of the dynamics of congregational singing and a more refined attention to textual integrity and ritual context. A fourth phase seems to belong to the composers associated with Oregon Catholic Press, including Owen Alstott, Randall DeBruyn, Christopher Walker, and Bernadette Farrell. It is noteworthy that a number of the leaders of the fourth phase are from England, signifying that the folk/popular idiom has become thoroughly international and is now a familiar part of the liturgical life of the Catholic church throughout the English-speaking world.[35]

The composers in the later phases evidence a level of compositional sophistication beyond that found in the earlier expressions of the folk/popular idiom. They also represent a merging of the folk/popular type with the more "traditional" styles of church music.[36] Thus, as Virgil Funk suggests, it is unlikely that new clearly definable waves in this style will occur in the future with the same rapidity as in recent decades; indeed, a certain kind of "settling in" may be expected.[37] More recently, the guitar (the primary instrument of the earlier folk/popular idiom) has been supplemented or even replaced by ensembles that include bass, piano, synthesizer, and various wind instruments. The organ has even been restored in this idiom because of its perceived strength in providing congregational support.[38]

While no national church music organization or publication in the United States, with the possible exception of *Modern Liturgy,* operates exclusively in the folk/popular style, the National Association of Pastoral Musicians and its magazine *Pastoral Music* accords the idiom considerable practical attention and generally positive, if not uncritical, evaluation.[39] The principal resources associated with folk/popular practice include the *Assemblybook,* produced by North American Liturgy Resources; *Gather,* published by G.I.A. Publications; the *Glory and Praise* collection, published by North American Liturgy Resources and G.I.A. Publications; and *Journeysongs,* issued by Oregon Catholic Press.

THE DEVELOPMENT OF ETHNIC EXPRESSION

While the folk/popular idiom emerged in the 1960s in the United States within the general context of postconciliar openness to the modern world, the use of distinctively ethnic music in the liturgy has its roots outside "mainstream" North American popular culture in ethnic communities with vital and distinctive musical traditions, notably those of Black and Hispanic Americans. While the folk/popular paradigm is, as we suggested, beginning to diversify, the ethnic traditions of liturgical music in the United States are still, for the most part, in their early stages of development. The ethnic paradigm stands in some tension with the folk/popular in that it regards the latter as an expression of the hegemonous character of mainstream North American culture vis-à-vis ethnic cultures.

The principal protocol of the Second Vatican Council invoked for the development of ethnic expressions in Catholic liturgical music in the United States is found in article 119 of the Constitution on the Sacred Liturgy which states: "In certain countries, especially in mission lands, there are people who have their own musical tradition, and this plays a great part in their religious and social life. For this reason their music should be held in proper esteem and a suitable place is to be given to it, not only in forming their religious sense but also in adapting worship to their native genius, as indicated in articles 39 and 40."[40] The same article continues: "Therefore, in the musical training of missionaries, great care should be taken to see that they become competent in promoting the traditional music of those peoples both in the schools and in sacred services, as far as may be practicable."[41]

The principles articulated here took on considerable importance as Catholic ethnic communities with roots in Latin America, Africa, and Asia began to assert a distinctive cultural identity for themselves within the church in the United States. The emerging multicultural consciousness of the 1980s, as well as more sustained attention to conciliar principles of cultural adaptation, have provided additional impetus to the advancement of diverse ethnic music traditions and to multicultural liturgical expressions.[42]

While attempts were apparent as far back as the 1940s to develop a Black Catholic musical tradition, it was only in the 1960s with Clarence Joseph Rivers and his American Mass Program that Black Catholic music in the United States came into its own. The body of such music has been considerably expanded since then by composers like Grayson Warren Brown, Leon C. Roberts, Edward V. Bonnemere, and Mary Lou Williams.[43] In 1983, the National Black Catholic Clergy Caucus authorized work on an African American hymnal, which was published in 1987 with the title *Lead Me, Guide Me*.[44] The coordinator of the project was Cleveland auxiliary bishop James P. Lyke (later archbishop of Atlanta). The project involved many of the leading organizations dedicated to the advancement of Black American liturgical life, including the Institute for Black Catholic Studies at Xavier University in New Orleans, the National Association of Black Catholic Musicians, the National Office for Black Catholics, the subcommittee on Black liturgy of the Bishops' Committee on the Liturgy, as well as prominent figures such as J-Glenn Murray and Thea Bowman. The hymnal draws on the heritage of Black spirituals and hymns as well as on modern compositions inspired by the Black idiomatic repertoire. The music of this tradition, strongly rhythmic in character, is characteristically emotional, energetic, and "soulful."[45] The project to create a distinctive liturgical–musical practice in the Black tradition continues within a framework of ongoing discussion about the general liturgical and spiritual life of Black Catholics in the United States.[46]

Hispanic Americans represent the other American Catholic ethnic group which has produced a significant body of liturgical music inspired by popular cultural traditions. More than most American language groups, Hispanics represent considerable cultural diversity, coming as they do from Mexico, Puerto Rico, Cuba, Central and South America. Among the earliest expressions of Hispanic American music after the Second Vatican Council was the "Mariachi Mass" based stylistically on the exuberant music of popular family and community celebrations and accompanied typically by guitars, vihuelas, violins, bass guitars, and trumpets. In general, a style of Hispanic liturgical music has emerged which is characteristically warm, dance-like, celebrative, and festive.[47]

The more notable efforts on behalf of Hispanic American liturgy and music have been spearheaded by the Mexican American Cultural Center in San Antonio, Texas, which was designated by the United States Catholic Conference an official research center for the advancement of Hispanic liturgy. The center has worked assiduously to integrate the official forms of the Roman liturgy and the extensive repertoire of Hispanic devotions and festivals, including the Quinceaneras, the Posadas, and the celebration of Our Lady of Guadalupe. The Institute of Hispanic Liturgy and the United States Catholic Conference Secretariat for Hispanic Affairs are also leaders in this area. Considerable discussion of Hispanic American liturgy was generated by the process which led to the National Pastoral Plan for Hispanic Ministry published in 1987.[48] In 1989, Oregon Catholic Press published an Hispanic Catholic hymnal, *Flor y Canto,* which has made available to the wider Spanish-speaking community the extensive musical repertoire composed in recent years by well-known figures such as Carlos Rosas, Cesareo Gabarain, and Mary Frances Reza.[49]

Some attempts have been made to develop a body of ethnic music for other American Catholic communities, including a "Polka Mass" for Eastern Europeans and compositions using Irish folk tunes for Irish Americans.[50] In general, however, the ethnic paradigm operates mostly within Black and Hispanic Catholic communities. It often reflects the ongoing cultural crises and challenges that beset these communities.[51] For this reason, themes of justice, freedom, communal identity, and prophetic critique of the mainstream culture suffuse ethnic Catholic music and liturgy in a notable way.[52]

FUNCTIONALISM AND SCHOLARLY CONSTRAINT

The fourth paradigm, the ritual-functional, is so named because the principal concern among its exponents is the manner in which music functions to serve ritual texts and actions.[53] The fundamental protocol of the Second Vatican Council for this paradigm is found in the assertion of article 112 of the Constitution on the Sacred Liturgy that "sacred music is to be considered more holy, the more closely connected it is with the liturgical action."[54] The same article calls to mind "the ministerial function exercised by sacred music in the service of the Lord."[55] Article 116 of the Constitution sets forth the principle that the various kinds of sacred music are acceptable "so long as they accord with the spirit of the liturgical action as laid down in article 30."[56] This paradigm is particularly attentive to article 34 which states: "The rites should be distinguished by a noble simplicity. They should be short, clear and free from useless repetitions."[57]

A primary concern of theorists and practitioners in this paradigm is that music be regarded and performed in the closest possible relationship to rite so that the cleavage between the rite and music that is a reoccurring problem in liturgical history be assiduously avoided. The paradigm embodies the conviction that text and action in the liturgy must severely control and discipline the musical and artistic elements. The task of composers, accordingly, is not primarily the setting of texts for their general poetic and spiritual expressivity but, more focally, for their ritual and performative facility.[58]

The principal exponents of the ritual-functional paradigm are liturgists, liturgical theologians, and musicians whose primary training is in the field of liturgical scholarship. For this reason, the most scholarly work in the area of liturgical music theory today probably comes from the ritual-functional school. Among the more notable early (European) scholars were Joseph Gelineau, Lucien Deiss, and Bernard Huijbers. After initial training in music, Gelineau completed a doctoral degree in theology with a dissertation entitled *The Liturgical Forms of the Psalms*. His extensive study of the music of ancient cultures was inspired by a search for fundamental and universal musical structures and his theoretical conclusions led him to produce the well-known body of chant settings that bears his name. Gelineau's theory of liturgical music is set out in his book *Voices and Instruments in Christian Worship*,[59] a work that remains a classic analysis of the relationship between music, rite, and word, as well as of the various musical forms and genres of the liturgy.

Lucien Deiss, who was trained both as a scripture scholar and a musician, has also treated extensively the ministerial function of liturgical music and, like Gelineau, has analyzed in considerable detail the various musical forms of the liturgy.[60] Deiss has also produced a body of music characterized by commitment both to simple formulaic structure and attractive lyricism. He is probably the most popular composer in this genre and his compositions are often assumed into the folk/popular paradigm.

Bernard Huijbers, a leading composer of modern liturgical music in Holland, has taken up concerns about ritual-functionalism in his research into basic musical forms and the "elementary music" of early European cultures. By elementary music, he means "music in which *the musical elements in themselves are sufficient, used in their simplest form and simplest combinations, and not multiplied, varied or played off against each other.*"[61] From this Huijbers has devised his definition of ritual music, by which he means "music where quality is determined by and subordinated to its integration into the liturgical action."[62] He is generally more radical than Gelineau and Deiss in his outlook and he demonstrates a notable antipathy toward the "sacral" elements of the Catholic liturgical-musical tradition.

The European organization Universa Laus, with which Gelineau and Huijbers were prominently associated from its inception, has been notable among liturgical music groups for whom, in Gelineau's words, the "function-form-meaning" question has been a preoccupation.[63] From the deliberations and discussions of this organization has come the conviction that the most appropriate designation for music in the liturgy is not "liturgical music" or "church music" but "Christian ritual music."[64]

North American liturgists who have been operating within the ritual-functional paradigm include Edward Foley, Mary McGann, and the late Mark Searle. Foley has done extensive work on the ritual dynamics of music in the liturgy, extending his investigations into ethnomusicology, psychobiology, and the anthropology of music.[65] McGann and Foley have carried on noteworthy research on the relationship between rite and music in the eucharistic prayer.[66] Mark Searle's concerns about musical function in the liturgy were focused more generally on the ritual and theological restraints that must operate on musical composition and performance, on the importance of congregational ownership of liturgical music, on the necessity of a fixed repertoire, and on the unifying power of a stable "canon" of ritual music.[67]

Among organizations in which the ritual-functional paradigm is predominantly operative are the North American Academy of Liturgy, the International Commission on English in the Liturgy, and the Milwaukee-based Symposia on Liturgy and Music held under the patronage of Archbishop Rembert Weakland.[68] Published musical resources inspired by the ritual-functional paradigm include much of the service music presented in the various editions of *Worship* and in the music publications of the International Commission on English in the Liturgy. The presidential chants provided in the sacramentary used in the United States clearly belong within the ritual-functional category.[69] Monastic liturgical music represents the most notable expression of sustained practice in this paradigm.

THE IDEALS OF MODERN CLASSICISM

The fifth paradigm is the modern classical. I use the term *classical* here in both the popular musical and the technical theological senses rather than in the precise historical sense employed by musicology. In the popular sense, "classical" liturgical music refers to Gregorian chant and the "art music" of European Catholicism. This embraces Renaissance polyphony and the choral music of the baroque, romantic, classical, and modern eras. In the theological sense, my usage has reference to the term *classic* as employed by University of Chicago theologian David Tracy: a text, symbol, event, or work of art that is central to a religious or cultural tradition.[70]

The "classics" of Roman Catholic music may be said to have been identified by Pius X when Gregorian chant and Renaissance polyphony were accorded a special place in Roman Catholic liturgical tradition. This classical selection was reaffirmed in article 116 of the Constitution on the Sacred Liturgy of Vatican II, which stated that Gregorian chant is "specially suited to the Roman liturgy" and that the tradition of polyphony continues to have a valid place in liturgical celebrations.[71] Importantly, however, the modern classical paradigm aspires, in Tracy's language, to "a nonclassicist notion of the classic," that is to a recognition that a classic production, while remaining a permanent and normative feature of a religious tradition, gives rise to and inspires new interpretations and forms.[72] Accordingly, the modern classical paradigm recognizes the "classic" character of Gregorian chant and Renaissance polyphony as *the basis for new developments and expressions*. While the neo-Caecilian paradigm accords Gregorian chant, Renaissance polyphony, and the traditional repertoire an absolute and virtually exclusive status, the modern classical recognizes that these embody a normative set of musical dynamics to be appropriated in a modern idiom. This outlook also seeks to maintain and develop the "classical" practice of the tradition which includes excellence in composition and performance, a high regard for the choral dimensions of the liturgy, and the critical need for ecclesiastical institutions supportive of the advancement of liturgical-musical culture. This paradigm, unlike the neo-Caecilian, has both conservative *and creative* dimensions.[73]

The modern classical paradigm finds its particular protocol in article 121 of the Constitution on the Sacred Liturgy which states:

> Composers, animated by the Christian spirit, should accept that it pertains to their vocation to cultivate sacred music and *increase its store of treasures*. Let them produce compositions which have the qualities proper to genuine sacred music and which can be sung not only by large choirs but also by smaller choirs and which make possible the active participation of the whole congregation.[74]

This paradigm is attentive to the value of a conscious continuity between the inherited tradition of church music and the requirements of modern liturgical renewal. It takes seriously the principle of article 23 of the Constitution on the Sacred Liturgy that "care must be taken that any new forms adapted should in some way grow organically from forms already existing,"[75] a principle spelled out more fully in article 59 of *Musicam Sacram:*

> Musicians will enter on this new work with the desire to continue that tradition which has furnished the Church, in her divine worship, with a truly abundant heritage. Let them examine the works of the past, their types and characteristics, but let them also pay careful attention to the new laws and requirements of the liturgy, so that "new forms may in some way grow organically from forms that already exist" [Constitution on the Sacred Liturgy, article 23], and the new work will form a new part in the musical heritage of the Church, not unworthy of the past.[76]

The modern classical paradigm in liturgical music is, to borrow a term from David Tracy, revisionist in outlook: it critically correlates the "classical" tradition of Catholic music and the developments of modern musical culture, but never abandons the dialectic between the two.[77] While holding the "classics" of Gregorian chant and Renaissance polyphony in high regard, the modern classical composer is committed unhesitantly to the musical world of the late twentieth century and to the liturgical renewal of the church set in place by the Second Vatican Council.

This perspective has been spelled out in a notable way by Cardinal Joseph Ratzinger, for whom Gregorian chant and Palestrina provide "signposts" for postconciliar liturgical music. For the cardinal, however, this "does not imply that all church music must be an imitation of such music."[78] Indeed, "correctly understood, the reference to Gregorian chant and Palestrina simply means that we find here a standard which provides orientation. But the results of creatively applying and transforming such orientation cannot of course be determined in advance."[79] For new creative possibilities in this regard, Ratzinger points to Africa, Asia, and Latin America, which appear to be "on the threshold of a new florescence of the faith which could also give rise to new cultural forms."[80]

In line with this outlook, musicologist Peter Jeffery advocates a renewal and reappropriation of the Catholic chant tradition not as a nostalgic or preservationist exercise but on the basis of the inner flexibility and dynamism of chant which allows it to be responsive to the modern vernacular needs of the liturgy.[81] This task has been taken up with various degrees of success by Mary Berry, Cecile Gerkin, and by American Episcopalians Mason Martens and Peter Hallock.

The most notable North American liturgical composers in the modern classical idiom are Richard Proulx, Theodore Marier, Gerald Near, Leo Nestor, and Jerome Coller. Among these there is considerable diversity—some operating on the "modern" end and others on the "classical" end of the paradigmatic spectrum. All, however, operate with a high theoretical and practical respect for the canons and achievements of Western music, even as they compose in modern styles. All have appropriated the prescriptions and developments of postconciliar liturgical reform and, thus, do not share the neo-Caecilian outlook.

The paradigm finds strong institutional expression in the Conference of Roman Catholic Cathedral Musicians, as well as in the music departments of many American colleges and universities. In practice, it is apparent in the more distinguished Catholic cathedrals in the United States, in which a concern for both the preservation of the heritage and the organic development of the church's musical tradition is operative. The paradigm finds sympathy in the National Association of Pastoral Musicians Friends of Chant.

The Influences of Ecumenism and Eclecticism

The ecumenical/eclectic paradigm differs from those already described in that it is the most fluid, is the least clearly definable, and ranges freely over the other five, picking and choosing from them rather than taking a distinctive stance alongside them. Nevertheless, it represents an outlook that is operative in the world of Catholic liturgical music in the United States today. The ecumenical/eclectic paradigm habitually practices and justifies the incorporation into the liturgy of music of any style, period, tradition, and source that it deems serviceable to particular congregational needs. By character, it has its grounding not in any particular prescription or principle of the Second Vatican Council but more generally in two other sources: the modern ecumenical movement and North American cultural eclecticism.

One of the principal achievements of the ecumenical movement was the new respect on the part of Roman Catholicism for the liturgical and spiritual traditions of the other Christian churches and ecclesial communities. This new openness in the mid-1960s generally coincided with the critical necessity in Roman Catholicism for ready-made music in the vernacular, a need created by the reforms of the Second Vatican Council and the movement away from the use of Latin. This led to a wholesale borrowing of Protestant hymnody for use in Catholic liturgy and, to a lesser extent, the use of service music from the Lutheran and Anglican liturgical traditions.[82] By the same process, the music of the Taize community in France has become widely popular in Catholic quarters.[83] Black spirituals have become a familiar part, not only of Black Catholic, but of mainstream Catholic worship in the United States.

The process of liturgical borrowing from non-Catholic sources was facilitated by the characteristic eclecticism of modern American culture. This pattern of eclecticism is to be distinguished from the multiculturalism represented in the coexistence of different ethnic or national communities embodying distinctive liturgical and musical traditions, although the latter are certainly not immune from eclectic tendencies. Thoroughgoing eclecticism refers to the process by which mainstream North American cultural expression borrows freely, widely and with some superficiality from diverse cultural or artistic sources. Cultural eclecticism is systemically enabled by mass communication technology which detaches musical performance from its traditional localization and temporalization within particular communities and makes it available to diverse populations and communities through recordings, radio and television.[84] An eclectic outlook is generated by the greater variety of music available today, by discontinuous media programming, and by the juxtaposition of many musical excerpts and styles in popular experience. This paradigm is probably more deeply influenced by the modern entertainment ethos than are any of the others. The theorists and practitioners of the ecumenical/eclectic paradigm do not hesitate to engage the needs and sensibilities of people raised in a consumer culture. Thus they generally favor a more dramatic and sensory style of music in the liturgy. What Virgil Funk describes as the "dramatic" style in liturgical music is verified in the musical practice of this paradigm.[85]

Typically, the ecumenical/eclectic paradigm finds concrete expression in liturgies in which a Protestant hymn, a Black spiritual, a piece of Gregorian chant, and a polyphonic Latin motet are used side by side. This occurs in culturally homogenous congregations in which the need to respond to various tastes is a high pastoral priority. It also finds expression in some kinds of multicultural celebrations in which various ethnic groups come together and the need to symbolize their cultural diversity within a mainstream North American framework is accorded importance.

This paradigm is generally less concerned about liturgical and musical principles or about theoretical considerations of a theological or liturgical kind than about the pastoral imperative to respond effectively to the spiritual needs of particular communities. This approach has been promoted over the years to more or lesser degrees in the popular writings and lectures of Joseph Champlin, John Gallen, and James Empereur. While no liturgical music organization espouses this approach exclusively or primarily, it finds occasional expression in the forums of the National Association of Pastoral Musicians. Examples of wholesale ecumenical borrowing from Protestant sources are rare. One example was the practice at St. Mary's Cathedral in Minneapolis in the 1980s in which an Anglican musical style was assumed into the Roman liturgy. The most notable expression of a full-fledged ecumenical/eclectic style in recent decades has been that of the Cathedral of St. Francis deSales in Oakland, California, in which the character of the liturgy changed considerably from Sunday to Sunday and a notable freedom to incorporate (without much evident restriction) music from a wide variety of secular and ecclesiastical sources was operative.

By definition, composers do not produce work in an ecumenical/eclectic style (since such compositions would tend to be internally incoherent). However, Alexander Peloquin has over the decades produced work displaying diverse stylistic characteristics within single compositions and, in general, he has experimented quite freely with stylistic identity. For obvious reasons, there are few specifically designed resources for ecumenical/eclectic liturgical music practice.

Conclusion

At the outset, I stated the value for theology and liturgical studies of a methodology of paradigm construction in organizing complex data into coherent and understandable frameworks. This approach can be useful in bringing conceptual order to the specific world of Catholic liturgical music in the United States. As will be evident from my analysis, each paradigm has strengths and weaknesses; each highlights theoretical and practical commitments that are worthy of attention and advancement; not least, each paradigm can claim foundation in and be legitimized in one way or another by reference to the Constitution on the Sacred Liturgy, as well as to other official liturgical documents. These factors warn, therefore, against simple attempts to play the various paradigms off against each other, of selecting one as absolute, and dismissing the others.

Yet, a process of arbitration cannot and should not be avoided completely. The standard procedure in paradigm theory is to ask eventually which paradigm is the most adequate to the data, and thus most completely incorporates the legitimate concerns and insights of the others. Yet, arbitrating between the various paradigms in liturgical music theory and practice is no easy matter.[86] Of necessity, it requires a standpoint from which to evaluate, judge, and draw conclusions. One standpoint is, of course, provided by the Constitution on the Sacred Liturgy. Yet, there exists today among liturgists considerable discussion of the normative status of that document. It is, for instance, possible to read the Constitution with a preconciliar hermeneutic so that it is interpreted in the light of such documents as *Tra le sollecitudini* (1903) and *De Musica Sacra* (1958).[87] Such an approach would tend to argue for the greater validity of the neo-Caecilian paradigm. It is also possible to read the Constitution within a postconciliar hermeneutical framework, so that the document is effectively relativized by postconciliar insight and greater authority is accorded, for example, to *Music in Catholic Worship* or even to unofficial statements on church music, such as those of Universa Laus. Yet again, the Constitution can be read in a strictly conciliar manner, so that its principles and prescriptions are taken to be of continuing normativity for Catholic liturgical music.[88]

There is the further question of whether or not one paradigm can be proposed—even in the United States—as a general model, especially in view of what many describe today as a pluralistic world and a multicultural church. Must the Constitution on the Sacred Liturgy of necessity be regarded as Eurocentric and thus limited to Latin (even Western European) Catholicism? Does the prescriptive advent of a "world church" replacing the more uniform style of Roman Catholicism mean that hitherto authoritative ecclesiastical statements on liturgy, as well as other matters, are now of more limited significance?[89] These questions are further complicated by the aversion in some kinds of culture theory to the proposition and advancement of generally applicable criteria.

The task of arbitrating between the paradigms presented here is an immensely complex one and is beyond the scope of this essay. The important and crucial questions raised represent a second moment to the description—my principal intention here—of the complicated, sometimes conflictual, but rarely uninteresting world of Catholic liturgical music in the United States.

---

1. Rembert C. Weakland, "The Church Music Association of America," *Sacred Music* 92 (1965) 2.

2. See *Sacred Music and Liturgy Reform After Vatican II.* Proceedings of the Fifth International Church Music Congress, Chicago–Milwaukee, August 21–28, 1966, ed. Johannes Overath (Rome: Consocietas Internationalis Musicae Sacrae, 1969).

3. The proceedings of this conference were published under the title *Harmony and Discord.* An Open Forum on Church Music, conducted by the Liturgical Conference and the Church Music Association of America, November 29—December 1, 1966 (Washington, DC: The Liturgical Conference, 1966).

4. See "Revolution in the Church," *Sacred Music* 114 (1987:1) 4–6; also "The Battle," Sacred Music 107 (1980:4) 25; "Growth or Revolution?" Sacred Music 118 (1991:4) 3–4.

5. A useful overview of the controversies is found in the chapter entitled "Catholic Church Music: An American Perspective," in Miriam Therese Winter, *Why Sing? Toward a Theology of Catholic Church Music* (Washington, DC: The Pastoral Press, 1984) 3–27. See also William A. Bauman, "Church Music in America: Vatican II to '82," *Pastoral Music* 7 (1983:3) 30–33. The simmering feuds of the early postconciliar era reappeared more recently in the account of conciliar reform provided in Annibale Bugnini, *The Reform of the Liturgy, 1948–1975*, trans. Matthew J. O'Connell (Collegeville, MN: The Liturgical Conference, 1990).

6. Thomas Day, *Why Catholics Can't Sing: The Culture of Catholicism and the Triumph of Bad Taste* (New York: The Crossroad Publishing Company, 1990).

7. While my immediate interest is in looking at Catholic church music in the United States, readers in other parts of the English-speaking world will probably find parallels in their situations.

8. See Margaret Masterman, "The Nature of Paradigm," in *Criticism and the Growth of Knowledge*. Proceedings of the International Colloquium in the Philosophy of Science, London, 1965, vol. 4, ed. Imre Lakatos and Alan Musgrove (Cambridge: The University Press, 1970) 76–79.

9. Avery Dulles, *Models of the Church* (Garden City, NY: Doubleday, 1974) 29.

10. On the theological use of models and paradigms, see Ian T. Ramsay, *Models and Mystery* (London: Oxford University, 1964); Ewart Cousins, "Models and the Future of Theology," *Continuum* 76 (1969) 78–92; R. P. Scharlemann, "Theological Models and Their Construction," *The Journal of Theology* 53 (1973) 65–82; Hans Küng and David Tracy, *Paradigm Change in Theology: A Symposium for the Future*, trans. Margaret Köhl (New York: Crossroad, 1989).

11. See Piet Fransen, "Sacraments as Celebrations," *The Irish Theological Quarterly* 43 (1976:3), 151–70; George S. Worgul, *From Magic to Metaphor: A Validation of the Christian Sacraments* (New York: Paulist Press, 1980) esp. 201–22; John N. Schanz, Introduction to the Sacraments (New York: Pueblo Publishing Co., 1983) esp. 130–74; James Empereur, *Models of Liturgical Theology*. Alcuin/Grow Liturgical Study 4 (Bramcote, Nottingham: Grove Books, Ltd., 1987); idem, *Worship: Exploring the Sacred* (Washington, DC: The Pastoral Press, 1987); Geoffrey Wainwright, "Christian Worship and Western Culture," *Studia Liturgica* 12 (1977) 20–33. In relation to church music, see Virgil C. Funk, "Reflections on the Issues of Enculturation, Style and the Sacred/Secular Debate," *Proceedings of the Annual Meeting of the North American Academy of Liturgy*, Nashville, TN, January 2–5, 1989, 56–60. For an identification of "approaches," "challenges" and "streams" in the development

of modern church music, see Michael Joncas, "Roman Catholic Liturgical Composition in the United States," *Liturgy* 9 (1990:1) 43–53.

12. See the essay by F. J. Moleck entitled "Caecilian Movement," in the *New Catholic Encyclopedia,* vol. 2 (New York: McGraw-Hill, 1967) 1041–42. See also Karl Gustav Fellerer, The History of Catholic Church Music, trans. Francis A. Brunner (Baltimore: Helicon, 1961) 180–220; J. Vincent Higginson, "The American Caecilian Society," *Catholic Choirmaster* 28 (1942) 107–109.

13. The struggle between liturgically appropriate music and that considered unworthy in the liturgy has a long history. See Robert F. Hayburn, *Papal Legislation on Sacred Music, 95 A.D. to 1977 A.D.* (Collegeville, MN: The Liturgical Press, 1979).

14. Joseph A. Jungmann, *The Mass of the Roman Rite: Its Origins and Development,* trans. Francis A. Brunner (New York: Benziger Brothers, 1951) 148.

15. ___, 149. Regarding the reforming trends of the time, see R. G. Pauly, "The Reforms of Church Music Under Joseph II," *Music Quarterly* 43 (1957) 372–82.

16. Jungmann, *The Mass of the Roman Rite,* 156ff.

17. Text in R. Kevin Seasoltz, *The New Liturgy: A Documentation,* 1902–1965 (New York: Herder and Herder, 1965) 3.

18. ___, 5.

19. ___, 6.

20. This theme is variously explored in Overath, ed., *Sacred Music and Liturgy Reform After Vatican II,* especially in the essay by Colman E. O'Neill, "The Theological Meaning of *Actuosa Participatio* in the Liturgy," 89–108.

21. Text in Austin Flannery, ed., *Vatican Council II: The Conciliar and Post-Conciliar Documents* (Collegeville, MN: The Liturgical Press, 1975) 31.

22. ___, 32.

23. ___.

24. ___, 33. For simplicity of analysis, I am restricting myself for the most part to the Constitution on the Sacred Liturgy since this remains the charter document for modern liturgical renewal. The argument here would be considerably amplified by reference to other official documentation on church music, especially the 1967 instruction *Musicam Sacram* (text in Flannery, ed., *Vatican Council II,* 80–97) and *Music and Catholic Worship,* Bishops' Committee on the Liturgy (Washington, DC: United States Catholic Conference, 1972).

25. See editorial, "An Impoverishment?" *Sacred Music* 108 (1981:1) 3–4.

26. See Richard J. Schuler, "Saint Agnes, Sunday Morning," *Sacred Music* 114 (1987:3) 15–16. More generally, see Robert A. Skeris, ed., *Cum Angelis Canere:*

Essays on Sacred Music and Pastoral Liturgy in Honor of Richard J. Schuler (St. Paul, MN: Catholic Church Music Associates, 1990).

27. See Francis P. Schmitt, *Church Music Transgressed: Reflections on "Reform"* (New York: Seabury Press, 1977); Robert A. Skeris, *Divini Cultus Studium: Studies in the Theology of Worship and of Its Music* (Altötting: Verlag Alfred Coppenrath, 1990); *Chroma Theou: On the Origins and Theological Interpretation of the Musical Imagery Used by the Ecclesiastical Writers of the First Three Centuries* (Altötting: Verlag Alfred Coppenrath, 1976); *Crux et Cithara: Selected Essays on Liturgy and Sacred Music Translated and Edited on the Occasion of the Seventieth Birthday of Johannes Overath* (Münster: Verlag Alfred Coppenrath, 1983). The work of Skeris exhibits a strong scholarly quality and may not be described without qualification as neo-Caecilian. However, Skeris provides considerable expression of neo-Caecilian sympathies in his more popular articles. See, for instance, "Liturgical Music and the Restoration of the Sacred," *Sacred Music* 118 (1991:2) 2–13. Skeris also serves on the Board of Directors of the Church Music Association of America. A more thorough-going expression of the neo-Caecilian position is found in Lawrence A. Stich, "The Plight of the Papist Musician," *Homiletic and Pastoral Review* 85 (1985) 10–20.

28. Lawrence J. Madden, "Is the Folk Mass America's Only Contribution to Liturgy?" *Pastoral Music* 14 (1990:4) 53. Article 120 of the Constitution on the Sacred Liturgy declares that while the pipe organ is held in high esteem, "other instruments also may be admitted for use in divine worship, in the judgment and with the consent of the competent territorial authority" (Flannery, ed., *Vatican Council II*, 33).

29. On the folk/popular style, see Ed Gutfreund, *With Lyre, Harp and a Flatpick* (Cincinnati: North American Liturgy Resources, 1973); Kent Schneider, *The Creative Musician in the Church* (West Lafayette, Ind.: Center for Contemporary Celebration, 1976); Timothy Schoenbachler, *Folk Music in Transition: The Pastoral Challenge* (Phoenix: Pastoral Arts Associates, 1979).

30. See especially art. 58; Flannery, ed., *Vatican Council II,* 962.

31. Flannery, ed., *Vatican Council II,* 9.

32. Art. 118; Flannery, ed., *Vatican Council II;* see arts. 28, 30, 113, and 114.

33. Madden, "Is the Folk Mass America's Only Contribution to the Liturgy?" 54.

34. Here I am adapting a scheme proposed by Virgil C. Funk. See the essay entitled, "The Future of Church Music," in Virgil C. Funk, ed., *Sung Liturgy: Toward 2,000 A.D.* (Washington, DC: The Pastoral Press, 1991) 98.

35. This development serves as a reminder that this paradigm has from the beginning been weighted more toward the "popular" than the "folk," more by the popular culture of the English-speaking world than by distinctive folk music traditions.

36. The liturgical compositions of Henry Bryan Hays, a "classical" composer, represent probably the most remarkable attempt to compose in a manner at once deeply rooted in the American folk tradition and strikingly modern in harmonic structure and character. See Henry Bryan Hayes, *Swayed Pines Songbook* (Collegeville, MN: The Liturgical Press, 1981).

37. Funk, "The Future of Church Music," 98–99.

38. See Marty Haugen, "Leadership Skills and Instrumentation," *Liturgy* 6/3 (1987) 69–73.

39. Evaluations of folk/popular liturgical music practice are found in the essays of Ken Meltz, James Chepponis, Marty Haugen, David Haas, and James Lopresti in the April–May 1984 issue of *Pastoral Music,* vol. 8, no. 4, entitled *Contemporary "Folk" Groups: A Changing Scene.*

40. Flannery, ed., *Vatican Council II,* 33. See articles 39 and 40 of the Constitution on the Sacred Liturgy regarding the ecclesiastical process by which adaptations may be made. See, more recently, *Inculturation and the Roman Liturgy.* Instruction of The Congregation for Divine Worship and the Discipline of the Sacraments (Washington, DC: United States Catholic Conference Publishing Services, 1994).

41. Flannery, ed., *Vatican Council II,* 33.

42. Articles 37 to 40 of the Constitution on the Sacred Liturgy represent what Anscar Chupungco calls "the Magna Carta of Liturgical Adaptation." See Anscar J. Chupungco, *Cultural Adaptation of the Liturgy* (New York: Paulist Press, 1982) 42ff. See also Mark R. Francis, *Liturgy in a Multicultural Community.* American Essays in Liturgy (Collegeville, MN: The Liturgical Press, 1991); the Guidelines for Multilingual Masses produced in 1987 by the Federation of Diocesan Liturgical Commissions (PO Box 29039, Washington, DC 20017).

43. A brief history of Black Catholic music is provided in Clarence J. Rivers, "Should a White Parish Sing Black Music?" *Pastoral Music* 1 (1977:5) 7–13. See also by Rivers, *Soulfull Worship* (Washington, DC: National Office for Black Catholics, 1974); *The Spirit in Worship* (Cincinnati, OH: Stimuli, Inc., 1978); also Ronald L. Sharps, "Do Black Parishes Sing More?" *Pastoral Music* 8 (1984:3) 22–26.

44. *Lead Me, Guide Me: The African American Catholic Hymnal* (Chicago: G.I.A. Publications, 1987).

45. A useful description of the characteristics of Black Catholic liturgical music is provided in the preface to *Lead Me, Guide Me* written by Thea Bowman entitled, "The Gift of African American Sacred Song" (no pagination given); and in the subsequent essay in the hymnal by J-Glenn Murray entitled "The Liturgy of the Roman Rite and African American Worship." See also the essay by Grayson W. Brown entitled "Music in the Black Spiritual Tradition," in *This*

Far by Faith: American Black Worship and its African Roots (Published jointly by the National Office for Black Catholics and The Liturgical Conference, both in Washington, DC, 1977) 88–93; also Johannes Riedel, "Folk, Rock and Black Music in the Church of Today," *Worship* 44 (1970) 514–27.

46. See the various essays in *This Far by Faith;* also *In Spirit and Truth: Black Catholic Reflections on the Order of the Mass,* Secretariat, Bishops' Committee on the Liturgy (Washington, DC: United States Catholic Conference, 1988); *Plenty Good Room: The Spirit and Truth of African American Catholic Worship,* Secretariat for the Liturgy and Secretariat for Black Catholics (Washington, DC: United States Catholic Conference, 1990); Wilton D. Gregory, "Children of the Same Mother: Catholic Worship and African-Americans." Address to the Symposium for Ministers in the African-American Community, Atlanta, GA, 2 May 1990; James P. Lyke, "Liturgical Expression in the Black Community," Worship 57 (1983) 14–26.

47. A brief history of the early work of developing Hispanic American liturgy and music is presented in Carlos Rosas, "Mexican Americans Sing Because They Feel Like Singing," *Pastoral Music 1* (1977:5) 14–17. See also Ricardo Ramirez, *Fiesta, Worship and Family* (San Antonio, TX: Mexican American Cultural Center, 1981); idem, "Reflections on the Hispanicization of Liturgy," *Worship* 57 (1983) 26–34; idem, "Liturgy from the Mexican-American Perspective," *Worship* 51 (1977) 293–98; Robert Escamilla, "Worship in the Context of the Hispanic Culture," *Worship* 52 (1977) 290–93; Celeste Burgos and Ken Meltz, "'How Shall We Sing the Lord's Song in a Foreign Land?'" *Faith and Form* 22 (1989) 16–18; Rosa Maria Icaza, "Spirituality of the Mexican American People," *Worship* 63 (1989) 232–46. More generally, see Manuel Peña, *The Texas-Mexican Conjunto: History of a Working-Class Music* (Austin, TX: University of Texas Press, 1985).

48. See the National Conference of Catholic Bishops' *National Plan for Hispanic Ministry* (Washington, DC: United States Catholic Conference, 1988); also *The Hispanic Presence: Challenge and Commitment. A Pastoral Letter on Hispanic Ministry* (Washington, DC: United States Catholic Conference, 1984).

49. *Flor y Canto* (Portland, OR: Oregon Catholic Press Publications, 1989). Regarding other publications in this genre, see Mike Boehm, "Musical Resources for the Hispanic Community," *Pastoral Music* 10 (1986:3) 24–25.

50. See, for instance, Regina Koscielska, "Polka Mass: Ethnic Liturgy?" *Pastoral Music* 8 (1984:3) 27–29.

51. See M. Francis Mannion, "Evangelization and American Ethnicity," *Proceedings of the Seventeenth Convention of the Fellowship of Catholic Scholars,* Corpus Christi, TX, 25–27 September 1994, 145–92.

52. See also the various essays in *Music and the Experience of God* (*Concilium* 202), ed. David Power, Mary Collins and Melonee Burnum (Edinburgh: T. and T. Clark, Ltd., 1989).

53. The fundamental outlook here resonates with the "functionalist" outlook in modern architecture and the operative principles of architectural theorists such as Louis H. Sullivan, who proposed the axiom, "form follows function." See generally, Le Corbusier, *Towards a New Architecture,* trans. F. Etchells (London: J. Rodker, 1931); Walter Gropius, *Apollo in the Democracy: The Cultural Obligation of the Architect* (New York: McGraw Hill, 1968).

54. Flannery, ed., *Vatican Council II,* 32.

55. ___, 31.

56. ___, 33.

57. Flannery, ed., *Vatican Council II,* 12.

58. The importance of attending to and respecting the diversity of verbal and ritual forms in the liturgy within which music must operate is heavily underscored. Article 30 of the Constitution on the Sacred Liturgy underlines this diversity when it states: "To promote active participation, the people should be encouraged to take part by means of acclamations, responses, psalms, antiphons, hymns as well as by actions, gestures and bodily attitudes" (Flannery, ed., *Vatican Council II,* 11).

59. Joseph Gelineau, *Voices and Instruments in Christian Worship,* trans. Clifford Howell (Collegeville, MN: The Liturgical Press, 1964). See also Charles S. Pottie, *A More Profound Alleluia! Gelineau and Routley on Music in Worship* (Washington, DC: The Pastoral Press, 1984). Pottie makes the important point that, for Gelineau, functionalism is not mere utilitarianism but includes the symbolic and artistic features of music. See esp. 26–43.

60. Lucien Deiss, *Spirit and Song of the New Liturgy,* trans. Lyla L. Haggard and Michael L. Mazzarese (Cincinnati, OH: World Library Publications, 1970).

61. Bernard Huijbers, *The Performing Audience: Six and a Half Essays on Music and Song in Liturgy,* trans. Ray Noll, et al. (Cincinnati, OH: North American Liturgy Resources, second edition, 1974) 20 (emphasis in the original).

62. Huijbers, *The Performing Audience,* 125.

63. See the "conclusions" by Joseph Gelineau in *Growing in Church Music.* Proceedings of a Meeting on "Why Church Music?" conducted by the Society of St. Gregory (England) and Universa Laus, Strawberry Hill, London, England, 1978 (Washington, DC: Universa Laus English Edition, 1979) 58. Prominent early names associated with Universa Laus include Helmut Hucke (the music editor of *Concilium* in its first years) and the Italians Eugenio Costa and Gino Stefani.

64. See Claude Duchesneau and Michel Venthey, *Music and Liturgy. The Universa Laus Document and Commentary*, trans. Paul Inwood (Washington, DC: The Pastoral Press, 1992). See also the commentary by Eugenio Costa, "Music at the Crossroads: Liturgy and Culture," in Funk, ed., *Sung Liturgy*, 65–76.

65. Edward Foley, *Music in Ritual: A Pre-Theological Investigation*. American Essays in Liturgy I (Washington, DC: The Pastoral Press, 1984). See also by Foley, "Meaning, Musical Forms, and Faith," *Pastoral Music* 7 (1983:5) 11–15; "Ethnomusicology Can't Solve All of Our Problems, But . . . " *Pastoral Music* 14 (1990:6) 37–41; "Liturgical Music: A Bibliographic Introduction to the Field," Liturgical Ministry 3 (1994) 130–43.

66. Edward Foley and Mary McGann, *Music and the Eucharistic Prayer*. American Essays in Liturgy 8 (Washington, DC: Pastoral Press, 1988).

67. See, for instance, Mark Searle, "Ritual and Music: A Theology of Liturgy and Implications for Music," *Assembly* 12 (1986:3) 314–17; "Ritual Constraints on Liturgical Music." Address to the 1985 Milwaukee Symposium of Church Composers (unpublished).

68. See the reports of the Music Study Group in the various volumes of the *Proceedings* of the Annual Meeting of the North American Academy of Liturgy; also *The Milwaukee Symposia For Church Composers: A Ten-Year Report* (Washington, DC: The National Association of Pastoral Musicians, 1992).

69. *Resource Collection of Hymns and Service Music for the Liturgy*, International Commission on English in the Liturgy (Chicago: G.I.A. Publications, 1981); *ICEL Lectionary Music*, International Commission on English in the Liturgy (Chicago: G.I.A. Publications, 1982). A brief statement of ICEL's approach to liturgical music is found in Peter C. Finn, "Sung Liturgy as the Norm: ICEL's Music Program," *Pastoral Music* 15 (1991:3) 53–55. See also the references to music in Peter C. Finn and James Schellman, eds., *Shaping English Liturgy: Studies in Honor of Archbishop Denis Hurley* (Washington, DC: The Pastoral Press, 1990). On the sacramentary chants, see Edward McKenna, "Use of Music in the Roman Sacramentary," *Worship* 65 (1991) 65–68.

70. See David Tracy, *The Analogical Imagination: Christian Theology and the Culture of Pluralism* (New York: Crossroad, 1981) esp. 99–153.

71. Flannery, ed., *Vatican Council II*, 32–33. Article 117 called for the completion of the typical edition of Gregorian chant, a project still underway at the time of the Second Vatican Council.

72. Tracy, *The Analogical Imagination*, 100; see 107ff. The terms *classicism* and *classicist* generally suggest a fundamentalist outlook in regard to "classic" works. This attitude ascribes a rigid authority to "classics" and insists on a narrow framework of interpretation. On classicism and the liturgy, see the contrasting approaches in Stephen Happel, "Classicist Culture and the Nature

of Worship," *The Heythrop Journal* 21 (1980:3) 288–302; and M. Francis Mannion, "[Part V] The Roman Liturgy and Cultural Adaptation," *Liturgy OCSO* 24 (1990:3) 12–26.

73. A parallel may be identified in the New Classical movement in modern architecture which eschews mere historic reproduction, yet is strongly inspired by the classical architectural vocabulary. See Thomas Gordon Smith, *Classical Architecture: Rule and Invention* (Layton, UT: Gibbs M. Smith, Inc., 1988).

74. Flannery, ed., *Vatican Council II,* 33–34 (emphasis added).

75. ___, 10.

76. ___, 95.

77. See David Tracy, *Blessed Rage for Order: The New Pluralism in Theology* (New York: The Seabury Press, 1975) esp. 32ff.

78. Joseph Cardinal Ratzinger, "Liturgy and Church Music," in Skeris, ed., *Divini Cultus Studium,* 196 (published also in *Communio* 13 [1986] 377–91). See also by Ratzinger, the essay entitled "Music and Liturgy," in *The Spirit of the Liturgy,* trans. John Saward (San Francisco: Ignatius Press, 2000), 136–56; the essay entitled, "On the Theological Basis of Church Music," in *The Feast of Faith: Approaches to a Theology of the Liturgy* (San Francisco: Ignatius Press, 1986) 97–126; "Theological Problems of Church Music," in Skeris, *Crux et Cithara,* 214–30. More generally, see Aidan Nichols, *The Theology of Joseph Ratzinger: An Introductory Study* (Edinburgh: T. and T. Clark, 1988) esp. 207–24.

79. Ratzinger, "Liturgy and Church Music," 196.

80. ___, 196. I disagree with Michael Joncas when he describes the cardinal's position on church music as "classicist." See Michael Joncas, "Whose Culture? Whose Tradition? Educational Challenges," *Pastoral Music* 14 (1990:6) 32, note 9. In my judgment, the "classicist" position in church music is verified in neo-Caecilianism (to which the cardinal does not subscribe) and precludes the kind of cultural openness Ratzinger's writings espouse, even if in an undeveloped manner.

81. Peter Jeffery, "Chant East and West: Toward a Renewal of Tradition," Power et al., eds., *Music and the Experience of God,* 20–29.

82. Protestant influences have been institutionalized somewhat in Catholic worship in the United States in the establishment of a "Hymn of the Day" in the third edition of the G.I.A. hymnal *Worship.* See generally Kevin W. Irwin, *Context and Text: Method in Liturgical Theology* (Collegeville, MN: The Liturgical Press, 1994) 236–39.

83. See Brother Robert, "Taize Music . . . A History," *Pastoral Music* 11 (1987:3) 19–22; Gordon Truitt, "Lessons from Taize," *Liturgy* 6/3, 85–86.

84. On this, see Edward Foley, "Let Us Pray. In God We Trust . . . " *Pastoral Music* 10 (1985:1) esp. 24–25.

85. Virgil F. Funk, "Reflections on the Issues of Enculturation, Style and the Sacred-Secular Debate," *Proceedings of the Annual Meeting of the North American Academy of Liturgy,* Nashville, TN, 2–5 January 1989, 56–60; also idem., "Do It With Style," *Pastoral Music* 14 (1990:4) 25–28. See also Edward Foley, "Theater, Concert, or Liturgy: What Difference Does It Make?" in Funk, ed., *Sung Liturgy,* 77–93. More generally, see the reflections by Eileen Elizabeth Freeman, "Pochohontas Never Sang Gregorian Chant," *Pastoral Music* 1 (1977:3) 16–19.

86. Criteria might include some or all of the following: continuity with Catholic musical tradition; openness to new cultural developments; responsiveness to the requirements of congregational participation; regard for the choral dimensions of the liturgy; respect for textual and ritual integrity; and—perhaps most elusive yet unavoidable—appropriate artistic and spiritual quality.

87. Texts in Seasoltz, *The New Liturgy,* 3–10; 255–82.

88. On this general matter, see the chapter entitled "The Continuing Challenge of the Second Vatican Council: The Hermeneutics of the Conciliar Statements," in Walter Kasper, *Theology and Church,* trans. Margaret Köhl (New York: Crossroad, 1989) 166–76.

89. See the chapter entitled "Basic Theological Interpretation of the Second Vatican Council," in Karl Rahner, *Theological Investigations,* vol. 20, trans. Edward Quinn (New York: Crossroad, 1981) 77–89.

Chapter 7

Toward a New Era in Liturgical Architecture

The fundamental conviction of this essay is that, at both conceptual and practical levels, Catholic liturgical architecture is today beset by critical problems requiring substantive solutions. It is no secret that popular criticism of modern church styles abound, while the fascination with traditional forms of architecture continues to be evident. In professional ecclesiastical circles, considerable theological disagreement attends discussion of the nature and function of art and architecture in Catholic worship.

In the wider field of architecture, the modern—or more accurately the modernist—movement is under increasing criticism and the once rather unified world of twentieth-century architecture is giving way to a whole new set of experiments and schools of thought which may be widely described as "postmodernist." The coalescence of crises in Catholic liturgical architecture and in the general field of architecture may be providential. We should look for creative and positive results from the intersection of common concerns and visions.

It is becoming apparent, then, that church architecture—like architecture in general—is entering a new era. This new era in liturgical architecture will be neither an anti-modern return to "tradition" nor a logical development of modern trends. Clearly no consensus as yet exists on the direction in which Catholic architecture ought to develop. New points of view have yet to crystallize into anything approaching a coherent perspective.[1] Various sorts of extremes and reactionary solutions need to be guarded against, however. History offers us no simple model or ideal to which to return, even as it does provide ample inspiration for appropriation in new idioms.

In this presentation, I shall offer ten theses which I regard as desirable in any conceptualization of the future of Catholic liturgical art and architecture. The various theses are interconnected and each more or less builds on some aspect or other of the previous ones. It will be evident that each of the theses stands in some measure as a challenge or corrective to much that has obtained in the area of church architecture in this century, but especially over the past thirty years. My concern here is more with theory and principle than with practical design matters—and given my lack of competence in the latter area, it should not be otherwise. What I have to say here represents only one perspective—and one limited by my experience of service to the church in the United States. I offer it as part of a necessary conversation that has already begun and must be advanced thoughtfully and constructively.

THESIS ONE: SACRAMENTAL ROLE

Architecture plays neither a sacral nor a merely functional role—but rather a sacramental role—in Catholic worship; the place of worship is neither temple nor "meeting house," but sacramental building. The building in which Catholic Christians worship is not simply a cover for the community at prayer, a shelter for liturgical action, or a "tent" for the assembled people of God. The building does not function merely as a "skin" for liturgical worship. While liturgical architecture has an indisputably functional element, this functionality operates within a framework that is constitutively sacramental. To say that liturgical architecture is sacramental is to affirm that architecture participates integrally in the sacramental order of the church. Architecture enters intrinsically into the action of the liturgy. Material place symbolically amplifies the liturgical action, and the liturgy, in turn, draws into itself the spatial and the material.[2]

On the one hand, then, church buildings are not merely functional meeting houses, that is, places of no constitutive significance or without mediating role vis-á-vis divine presence and action in the world. To hold that a church building is simply a functional dwelling is to imply that divine presence is operative no more in a liturgical building than anywhere else. Catholicism may not embrace such a perspective and be true to its received tradition. Neither historic nor modern rites for the dedication of churches allow for a functional theology of the Catholic place of worship.[3]

Liturgical buildings, on the other hand, should not be conceived of as sacral places, that is, places that limit, contain or bind divine presence and action. God does not dwell exclusively in church buildings. The conception of churches as temples in the sense understood in the history of religions is theologically foreign to Catholic Christian worship. The temple, typically and ideally, has been understood as the *exclusive* earthly dwelling place of the divine. A Christian church building cannot be conceived of in this way.[4]

The Catholic cathedral, basilica or church, then, is neither mere meeting house (about which assertions of extraordinary divine presence are denied) nor temple (in which God's earthly presence is thought to be exclusively located). It is a sacramental building. This means that God is indeed intensely present in the sacramental place of worship, but this presence is of a character that mediates, reveals, and celebrates the holiness and action of God in creation, history, and culture. The sacramental church building becomes, in a sense, a lens through which is revealed God's omnipresence. As Cardinal John Henry Newman so expressively pointed out, the church building prefigures the end to which all creation is called.[5]

My purpose in describing a liturgical building precisely as *sacramental* is to seek to overcome the polarity between those who, on one hand, argue that church buildings are merely functional—and thus no more God's dwelling place than any other building or place—and those who seek to safeguard the belief that God dwells in a special way in the church building, but who easily resort to a temple theology in the process.[6] The debates of the past thirty years between the "sacralists" and the "functionalists" need to be left behind as the church articulates a more adequate understanding of the sacramental character of its places of worship.[7]

Thesis Two: A Harmonius Relation

The holiness of the Christian assembly and the holiness of the liturgical building are not oppositional, but harmoniously related and mutually constitutive; the church building is both domus Dei and domus ecclesiae.
This thesis builds on the one just outlined. Conceptual oppositions between the holiness of the worshiping assembly and the holiness of the place of worship are commonplace today. They are constantly repeated in discussions and publications—and for the most part

without much critical examination. Which comes first: the church building or the people of God? Which may be called holy: the people or the building? Does the holiness of one proceed from that of the other? Which of the two takes theological precedence? In my opinion, these questions espouse a way of thinking that is fundamentally inadequate, both from the point of view of an adequate liturgical theology and of a developed architectural anthropology.

The presently dominant way of answering the questions I have just stated is highly problematic. The standard answer is that it is the people who are holy—and that from the holiness of the people is derived the holiness of the building. Some respond to this position, on supposedly traditional grounds, that since the church building is a sacred, consecrated place, the holiness of the people derives from the holy place. To enter a holy place is to be sanctified and to be affected by its holy status.[8]

I would argue that the more adequate position is that the holiness of the church building and the holiness of the people of God are mutually generative and interactively constitutive. On the one hand, a church building is holy because it participates in the objective sanctifying and redeeming action of God at work in the sacramental liturgy. On the other hand, a church building is holy because of the holiness of the baptized community which inhabits it and worships within it. Christian commentators have not hesitated to speak of the holiness of the people in architectural terms, suggesting that the liturgical building operates as a model of human holiness.[9] Yet the place of worship itself is sanctified by the living Body of Christ.

A more adequate perspective than is usually operative would hold together the various features of this question. It would enshrine the recognition that the liturgical building sanctifies the people; and that the people sanctify the place of worship. People and building are irreducibly holy, each according to its particular mode of participation in the sacramental order of the church.[10]

It follows, then, that there is no necessary opposition between the holiness of God's people and the holiness of the liturgical building. Post-Tridentine overemphasis on the holiness of the place of worship—to the neglect of the holiness of the people—is not appropriately balanced by a post–Vatican II insistence on the holiness of the congregation accompanied by a denial that there is anything intrinsically holy about a place of worship. Assertions of the holiness of the church building, on one hand, and the holiness of God's people, on the other, are by themselves partial; together they form the whole theological truth. Liturgical buildings are both *domus Dei* (house of God) and *domus ecclesiae* (house of the church). For this reason, both the people of God and liturgical buildings may be appropriately spoken of as "church." The modern tendency to set up dualisms and oppositions in this matter is artificial and unnecessary.[11] This trend needs to be left behind and a more holistic and integrated outlook espoused as the church advances toward a more adequate liturgical-architectural theory and practice.[12]

THESIS THREE: RITUAL FORM, WORSHIPING CONGREGATION, ORDAINED MINISTRY

Adequate liturgical-architectural theory and practice enshrine the recognition that the primary elements of liturgical events are ritual form; worshiping congregation; and ordained ministry. It is an axiom today, at least in the United States, that the worshiping assembly is the primary symbol of Christian liturgy. This theme appears with notable regularity in discussions about the artistic and architectural features of worship. The origin of this principle, as far as I have been able to trace, is the document *Environment and Art in Catholic Worship,* produced by the United States Bishops' Committee on the Liturgy in 1978.[13] The intent of this assertion is to highlight the dignity and centrality of the people of God at worship and, for this reason, it may be welcomed. As an objective principle, the axiom needs, however, to be questioned, both because it is conceptually confusing and serves to distort an adequate Catholic understanding of the manner in which the liturgy is operationally structured.[14]

It is, I suggest, theoretically confusing to speak of the people at worship as "symbols." To be useful, words need to have some stability: people are people and symbols are symbols. For this reason, it is justifiable to state that the primary symbol of the liturgy is the symbol system itself, the sacramental rites. While the worshiping people, in engaging and enacting the liturgical rites, become themselves in a certain way symbolic (for instance, of the eschatological community), this occurs in a manner that is dependent on the ritual symbols. To assert simply that the assembled congregation is the primary symbol is to collapse both the necessary distinction and relationship between the people and the liturgical symbol system.[15]

In saying this, I am not for a moment playing down the importance of the assembly. Rather, I am suggesting the need for a more adequate way of speaking about the relationship between the various elements of the liturgy. Let me spell out my thesis here in a positive fashion. The event of Catholic liturgical worship is, I would hold, composed irreducibly of three elements: the worshiping congregation, the ritual symbolic form, and the ordained ministry. None of these elements may be taken to be the unqualified principle, origin, or source of the others. In a liturgical event, the ritual form, the ordained minister, and the worshiping congregation properly exist in an integrated and mutually intended relationship. There occurs, to invoke an Eastern term, a "synergy" of the three elements.

There is, then, not one primary element in the liturgy; there are three primary elements. The ascendency of any of the three generates one or other of the recurring deviations of Christian liturgical history: ritualism, clericalism, or congregationalism. To hold that the assembly is the primary symbol or element is to offend both conceptually and practically against the harmonious and synergistic interrelationship that should exist among people, rite, and ordained ministry.

What are the liturgical consequences of the assertion of the symbolic primacy of the assembly? Principally, that the sacramental ritual is downplayed in theological and practical importance. If the sacramental rites are not primary, then they must be secondary. The liturgical symbol system, consequently, is no longer regarded as the revered medium of God's presence and action, but as the subjective creation and self-expression of the worshiping community. The result is that liturgical forms lose their proper autonomy and objectivity and are radically disempowered.

Why is this issue significant for liturgical art and architecture? I would answer that when the sacramental ritual is conceptually deprived of its distinctive status and is regarded as secondary and derivative, the consequences are that the art and architecture of the liturgy are accorded a role that is marginal or derivative. Liturgical art and architecture lose the theological weight that has been traditionally ascribed to them. It is no accident that the Protestant congregational churches have historically set art and architecture in a rather secondary and subservient role in public worship.[16] Catholicism will be led inevitably in the same direction if it fails to renew its theological conception of the complex structure of the liturgy and of the place of the material and the aesthetic in the theological order of worship.[17]

Thesis Four: Iconographic Tradition vs. Iconoclasm

Catholic worship requires a renewal of its iconographic tradition; modern iconoclasm generates a narrowing and an impoverishment of Christian vision and ecclesial self-understanding. Catholic orthodoxy (that is, right belief formed through right worship) is profoundly connected today as in the past to matters of visual representation in liturgy. We need only reflect on the early iconoclastic controversies and the history of the Protestant Reformation to remind us of the theological complexities involved here.[18] The whole range of liturgical images and iconography in Catholicism has never been regarded as merely decorative in function, but as having some significant theological dimensions. It has been recognized, at least implicitly, that visual representations serve to establish, situate, and orient the worshiping community in relation to the trinitarian life of God and the communion of saints and angels, as well as to call to mind the great events of biblical revelation. While the Christian East certainly has had a far more stable and conscious grasp of this truth over the centuries than has the West, the Latin tradition has from the beginning depended on the iconographic as at least a tacit programmatic feature of worship.[19]

Representations within the liturgical assembly of Christ, Mary, the saints, and angels, as well as imaginative anticipations of the life of eternity, are critical to sustaining a strong and compelling vision of the Christian reality. These aspects of faith cannot be adequately expressed, engaged, or advanced by the verbal alone. The saying that a picture is worth a thousand words is eminently true of the liturgy.

Without adequate trinitarian, christological, eschatological, and cosmic frames of reference visually embodied in places of worship, liturgy easily and quickly degenerates into self-referentiality, narcissism, and introversion. Christian vision shrinks and narrows and hope becomes vague and abstract. If Christ, Mary, the saints, and angels are not visibly represented in liturgical environments, it is easy for them to be subtracted from Christian consciousness.[20] The iconographic in worship serves, then, to manifest the truth that the worshiping community does not live in and from itself. Today more than ever, Catholic worshiping assemblies require vital liturgical statements that liturgy is never the product of isolated communities in self-expressive modality, but always the action of the whole Body of Christ. The horizon of the liturgy is the kingdom of God; its ontological source is God the Trinity; its foundational agent is Christ the Lord; and its celebrating community is that of all redeemed humanity.[21]

While it could be said that the iconographic is not essential to Catholic liturgy, as, for instance, Cistercian architectural history seems to indicate, it may be argued that the impoverished spirituality of modernity requires its critical renewal for the future.[22] The rebirth of the iconographic, I would argue, is one of the principal challenges facing Catholic art and architecture as it enters a new era.[23] Western Catholicism would do well to look to the Christian East both for theological and programmatic inspiration in this matter.[24] Architects and artists would also be usefully (if not uncritically) inspired in a more general way by those eras in which notable liturgical expressivity in the arts was strongly operative, in particular the early Christian, the Renaissance, and the baroque eras.[25]

Thesis Five: Artistic Expressivity Is Crucial

A rich architectural and artistic expressivity is crucial if Catholic liturgy is to generate an adequate doxological ethos; the "glorious" in worship finds its dynamism in the eschatological. This thesis is a correlative of thesis four. If iconographic programming is crucial to widening and stabilizing the horizons of the worshiping assembly, the consequent effect will be to generate a strong doxological ethos in liturgical celebration. Numerous commentators have observed that Catholic liturgical practice today does not possess an adequate doxological style and character. Liturgical celebration is often pale, lifeless, and uninspiring.[26] The power of the ritual symbols seems to have declined, despite the emphasis placed upon their importance in recent liturgical renewal. An absence of depth and significance appears to characterize liturgical celebration at the pastoral level. A sense of cultural weightlessness has set in, and rites have taken on a commonplace, ordinary, insignificant, and nontranscendental state. The desire to replace the excessively solemn has too easily given rise to liturgical triviality.[27] The Latin liturgy since Vatican II, it is often said, lacks glory, beauty, awe, majesty, and splendor.[28]

This kind of complaint is not valid if what is lamented is the absence of the triumphalism that accompanied Catholic worship in certain post-Tridentine expressions; yet, I believe that the general diagnosis is fundamentally correct. The source of the problem is, I believe, in great part an impoverished eschatological consciousness in present-day Catholic worship and an inadequate liturgical sacramentalization of the vision of eternal life, of Christian hope in heavenly things, of the return of Christ in glory, and the lordship of Christ over history.[29] If, as already stated, the renewal of the iconographic will serve to widen and enrich Christian vision, this vision must have the eschatological at its heart. This will, in turn, serve to restore praise-filled energy, delight, awe, and fascination regarding the divine mystery that is at the heart of the liturgy.[30]

In my opinion, the engagement of the liturgy with the eschatological, that is, with Christ in glory and the vision of heaven, is the fundamental impulse which generates conceptions and expressions of praise, awe, and majesty in the liturgy. Visually powerful liturgical art and architecture have a crucial agency in sustaining and generating the doxological expressivity of the liturgy.[31] These multifaceted expressions impact profoundly all that occurs within a place of worship. Rites and ceremonies take on a glorious, majestic, awe-inspiring character. Altars, ambos, tabernacles, baptismal fonts, and other liturgical furnishings assume a noble and beautiful quality.[32] The ritual space is so configured as to invite, even require, noble and dignified rites and ceremonies. The language is not that of the everyday, but of the new Jerusalem. The music generated within and by such spaces is resonant, expansive, and soaring. The self understanding of the ordained and of those in lay liturgical ministry is characterized by a deep sense of reverence and self-effacement. For the future, then, Catholic churches must again become—even if in simple and modest ways—replicas and anticipations of the Holy City, the New Jerusalem, the Kingdom of Heaven, the heavenly wedding banquet, the Supper of the Lamb.[33] This development would accentuate the conception of the liturgy as a participation in the liturgy of heaven.[34] Ritual practice would, as a result, take on a more profound and expressive ethos and shed thereby the current tendency toward pragmatism and functionalism. Correlatively, a restoration of the doxological and the eschatological would allow the neglected element of beauty to find a new theological and practical importance in the liturgy of the West.[35] In this whole development, the church should, of course, rightly shy away from the triumphalism and the vainglorious that undoubtedly attended liturgical art, architecture, and rite especially in the Renaissance era and after. The exultation of the earthly church (which the baroque exemplified) must be carefully guarded against in seeking historical inspiration for the directions espoused here; but this danger is no excuse for not learning from history.

THESIS SIX: LITURGICAL ART AND ARCHITECTURE HAVE A PUBLIC CHARACTER

Liturgical art and architecture properly have a public rather than a domestic character; Catholic liturgy is ritually public, architecturally spacious, and socially inclusive. The church is, by its catholic and evangelical vocation, a "public church."[36] Catholic worship in every era since the time of Constantine has normally taken place in the public plaza, on the top of the hill, at the center of the city.[37] Except in times of crisis or persecution, authentic Catholic worship has never been closed to the public. The liturgy of the church belongs, by its very nature, at the center of the affairs of the city.[38] Christian worship assemblies are not, and never should be, regarded or enacted as private gatherings, spiritual-therapeutic communities, support groups, or common interest societies.

Church buildings are not, then, domestic spaces in the modern privatized sense of "domestic." Only in a theological rather than a sociological sense should a Catholic place of worship be spoken of as "the living room" or "household" of God's people.[39] A place of worship that is tame, plush, or comfortable in the manner of domestic spaces, clubs, or membership facilities is not able to sustain a strong theological or redemptive public presence and comprehensiveness. Liturgical architecture in the authentic Catholic tradition has more in common with the city hall, the public auditorium (even the concert hall) than with the living room, the small group facility, or the retreat space—all of which are characteristically private or at most partially accessible extensions of the phenomenon of privacy.[40]

In this matter, liturgical architecture and conceptions of Christian worship influence each other strongly. Church architecture that is not public in function and appearance generates liturgical practices and spiritualities that are not only non-public but that actively generate a withdrawal of Christian presence from public life. Non-public church buildings remove the liturgy from the public sphere. In turn, introverted liturgical ritualization fails to generate the kind of architecture that strategically positions the church to be public, socially concerned, and culturally influential. Most problematic of all, when liturgical worship and its architectural expression fail to be public, they tend to become sectarian and self-enclosed, so that patterns of social exclusion and cultural homogeneity easily become operative.[41]

These patterns derive in great part from what could be called "the cultural canonization of the intimate relationship." At least in the United States, we are losing a sense of the practical dignity of being neighbors, fellow citizens, even respectful strangers. When absorbed into the church, this outlook vitiates the recognition that there are many kinds and degrees of authentic human relationship, all of which may be civilized, baptized, and eucharistized.[42] The appropriate kind of intimacy to be sought in worship is not psychological intimacy in the accepted cultural sense: it is theological intimacy, that is, the bonding of persons of all degrees of relationship which occurs by their participation in the trinitarian life of God through sacramental initiation.[43]

The canonization of the intimate relationship goes hand in hand with the conviction that the public arena has become alien, fearsome, dangerous—an outlook which has been absorbed into North American Christianity to a notable degree. This generates an attitude in which public space is—often unconsciously—feared.[44] Accordingly, the very phenomenon of spaciousness is regarded today as a negative quality in church buildings, so that a bias now exists against large, ample churches. If they do not function well, large buildings are, of course, undesirable; but modern architectural technology has largely overcome this historic problem.[45] The proper desire for community and participation should not require an evasion of publicness.

In a culture in which public space and relationality are feared or rejected, the symbolic affirmation of publicness, spaciousness, and inclusiveness is a necessary feature of liturgical practice and its architectural expression.[46] Liturgical publicness is highly significant in that it symbolizes the redemption and sanctification of all human space and generates an affirmation of the potential redemption of all degrees of human relationship.[47]

Thesis Seven: Church Buildings Are Liturgical and Devotional

Church buildings serve both liturgical and devotional functions; the restoration of the devotional will render church architecture more genuinely popular; the devotional serves as a key conduit to the liturgical of the sacred and the "religious". While church buildings exist first and foremost for the celebration of the official liturgy of the church, they have also traditionally served as places for popular devotions (public and private), as well as for contemplation and meditation. The understanding that the function and character of a church building is not exhausted by the requirements of the official liturgy of the church is of long standing.[48] Places of worship have served as sites of complex religious transactions that include the intercession of particular saints, Marian devotion, the patronage of shrines, visits to the Blessed Sacrament, Stations of the Cross, and individual and corporate novenas.[49]

However, the mood in Catholicism (at least in the West) over the past thirty years has often been against the devotional and, in particular, against the devotional as it impinges upon or affects the formal elements of liturgy. The functionalist principles of modern architecture and their inability to handle the ambiguity and polyvalence of Catholic devotionalism have rendered church architecture since Vatican II exceedingly anti-devotional. Many have lamented the stripping from Catholic places of worship of popularly revered elements and artifacts: for instance the removal of kneelers, relics, and shrines, as well as the disappearance of conditions for the devotional life, such as silence before and after liturgical celebrations. It is no secret that what alienation exists on the part of the ordinary Catholic worshiper from modern church architecture derives in great part from the rejection by the newer architectural styles of traditional elements conducive to the devotional. This rejection was an outgrowth of an outlook which regarded popular religious practices and artifacts as superstitious and sentimental.

The results of this process are more serious than might be first apparent, for it is to a significant degree through the popular and the devotional that conceptions and expressions of the sacred find their way into the liturgy. In this matter, it is probable that Catholic liturgical theory around the time of Vatican II was too strongly influenced by the post-war Protestant espousal of a "religionless" Christianity, associated with figures like Dietrich Bonhoeffer and the proponents of secular theology, which sought a faith unencumbered by the cultural and emotional expressions of premodernity.[50]

Historically, Catholicism has attended with considerable intuition to the "religious" dimensions of faith, as well as to the manifestations of the sacred, the numinous, and the mystical that have accrued around central liturgical elements. The proper correlation of liturgical forms and natural religiosity is a critical matter and one requiring considerable vigilance. The extremes of excessive religiosity and rationalistic faith are well avoided.[51] What is required today is not so much new expressions of devotional life operating alongside liturgical forms, but an integration in which a profoundly religious ethos pervades the whole place of worship, entering into and flowing from, as well as being appropriately controlled by, the official liturgy itself.[52]

Liturgical buildings, then, may not be reduced without remainder to functional "eucharistic halls" narrowly defined. The roles that a church building serves are enormously complex and not easily limited. For this reason, the future of liturgical art and architecture requires, in my opinion, a renewed attention to the phenomenologies of devotional, the religious, and the sacred relevant to the conception, creation and use of Catholic places of worship in all their dimensions.[53]

Thesis Eight: The Modernist Movement Is Inadequate

The modernist movement in architecture is not adequate to the service of Catholic liturgy; modernism in liturgy and its art is undergirded by a mechanistic model of religion and culture. The modernist style of architecture has held sway for much of the twentieth century, finding its principal theoretical proponents in figures such as Le Corbusier and Walter Gropius.[54] In the area of liturgical architecture, modernism is well over a half-century old. While its functional achievements have been significant, the modernist movement is increasingly the object of criticism from a wide variety of sources and perspectives. Modernism is more readily today recognized as a "style" in the history of architecture. To name it as such is to say that it can and will be surpassed in new eras of creativity. The modernist movement is no longer regarded everywhere as the end point of architectural evolution.[55]

Why is the modernist style of architecture criticized? For the reason that it is characteristically driven by self-consciously rational conceptions of spatial operationality and performance. Modernist architecture is too readily divorced from nature, from the human environment, and from cultural context.[56] It is an architecture of separation, dualism, and opposition.[57] In its philosophical outlook, modernism is mechanistic, univocal, emotionally inhibited, and positivistic. The modernist outlook is obsessed by the grounding of form in function. Accordingly, it tends to reject forms that are not directly functional. From its inception, the modernist style has carried strong anti-historical and anti-traditional impulses. Architectural modernism embodies an explicit social agenda that is reconstructionist and revolutionary; thus it holds a general disdain for the past.[58] Because of its mechanist underpinnings, modernist aesthetics are generated largely in an abstract modality.

The philosophical origins of modernist architecture are in Protestantism and its secularization in the Enlightenment. The religious roots in Calvinism and Puritanism are particularly strong. Modernist architecture seems to have picked up those theological convictions of Protestantism which were neutral toward creation, fearful of human works, and cautious about religion as a human phenomenon.[59] It is hampered in its self-understanding and expressivity by the philosophical convictions of the "age of suspicion" and its "masters," Marx, Nietzsche, and Freud.[60]

The principles and practices of the modernist movement were readily assumed into the Catholic liturgical movement in the early part of the twentieth century. One reason for this development was the perceived congruence between modernist architectural ideals and the cultural simplicity of early Christianity.[61] The desire to establish the relevance of the church to contemporary culture provided an additional impulse.[62] A certain tendency toward behaviorism and mechanism also became a factor, generating in the later modern liturgical movement a radical review of the roles of art and architecture in Catholic worship.[63] By behaviorism and mechanism, I mean views derived from certain social-scientific schools which hold that liturgical rites operate by a limited and definite set of rational and predictable principles. Liturgical renewal in this model sought to control ambiguous expression and to curtail what seemed excessive or overwrought. The emphasis was simplicity, clarity, directness of expression, freedom from duplication, and a didactic model of ritual operationality.

To criticize the modernist movement in liturgical architecture is not to reject the genuine achievements of the functional and economic aims of twentieth-century architecture, or to seek a return to the past, following a revivalist agenda. Nor is it, by any means, to reject the principles of liturgical renewal, including those that arose in the areas of art and architecture before and since the Second Vatican Council. The achievements of modern liturgical architecture in helping restore the fundamental lines of liturgical action and freeing places of worship from inordinate expressive complexity were valuable and necessary. The desire (consistent with the democratic ideals of architectural modernism) to bring the liturgical action into the midst of the assembly and to rescue the latter from a certain obscurity was entirely commendable. Yet, the general spiritual results of modernist liturgical architecture have been disappointing. The new architecture is all too often cold, sparse, barren, and uninteresting.[64] In my opinion, the time has come to move past modernism into a new era of architectural creativity in the service of the liturgy which can assume the gains of modernism without being hampered by its deficits.[65]

THESIS NINE: THE POSTMODERN EMBRACE OF THE CLASSICAL

The emerging era in church art and architecture will be characterized by a postmodern embrace of the classical; postmodernity in art and architecture allows for a vital reappropriation of Catholic liturgical-architectural tradition. The postmodern is emerging at all levels of Western culture as (by definition) the successor to modernism. It finds diverse articulations in the various disciplines, including the architectural. In the latter, it assumes generally the criticisms of modernist architecture just outlined.[66] More specifically, for our purposes, postmodernism refers to an *architectural movement* which

- recognizes positive ideals and achievements in modern architecture;
- is critical of the functionalist, purist, and materialistic conceptions of architectural modernity; and
- advocates an architectural paradigm attentive to symbolism, idiomatic polyvalence, and transcendence.

The *different kinds* of architectural postmodernism—from new classicism to deconstructionism—are distinguished by their varying attitudes to architectural tradition and the authority of its principles and expressions for the future. See Thomas Gordon Smith, *Classical Architecture: Rule and Invention* (Layton, UT: Gibbs M. Smith, Inc., 1988); J. Mordaunt Crook, *The Dilemma of Style: Architectural Ideas from the Picturesque to the Post-Modern* (Chicago: The University of Chicago Press, 1987); Henrich Klotz, *The History of Postmodern Architecture* (Boston, MA: MIT Press, 1988); David Kolb, *Postmodern Sophistications: Philosophy, Architecture, and Tradition* (Chicago: The University of Chicago Press, 1990); Andreas Papadakis, ed., *Post-Modernism and Discontinuity* (London: Academy Group, 1987). Although criticized in more scholarly circles, the writings of Charles A. Jencks are instructive for popular readership. See *The Language of Post-Modern Architecture* (New York: Rizzoli International Publications, 1987); idem, *The Architecture of the Jumping Universe* (London: Academy Editions, 1995). The term *postmodernism* is not one with which all architectural theorists are comfortable, not least because it includes some deconstructionist strains or is simply synonymous with late modernism or mere eclecticism. I use the term here having in mind both "free-style" classicism and the more rigorously traditional "new classicism."[67] The postmodern alternative to architectural modernism operates according to an organic rather than a mechanistic model. This alternative recognizes that symbols, including art and architecture, communicate impressionistically, as an articulate whole, to a considerable degree subconsciously, and in a manner that is not always rationally accessible. It understands that artistic and architectural expressions generate a wide variety of reactions, perceptions, and emotions in participants. Architecture and art, in the postmodern view, speak polyphonically, in many voices, rather than, as in modernism, monophonically, or in one voice.

Postmodernism is attentive to symbolic richness, as well as more fully attuned to the spiritual and psychological dimensions of art. The postmodern perspective attends to popular idioms and is more exuberant and celebratory in its aesthetic. It recognizes the complexity of the architectural relation to nature, place, society, and culture. Postmodernism does not simply reject the modern, so much as move beyond it by contact with longer architectural history and tradition. Indeed, this notable attention to history and tradition is among the greatest strengths and most promising features of the movement.

Postmodern Catholic architecture will, in my opinion, be able to pick up and renew traditional idioms of church architecture, thereby restoring greater continuity with the Catholic past than is evident in liturgical-architectural modernism. This movement does not fear quotation from the received tradition of ecclesiastical architecture, nor does it share the bias against the medieval, Renaissance, and post-Tridentine eras that has been such a pervasive feature of Catholic thinking in recent decades.[68] The conceptual methodologies of this movement are able to "read" Catholic architectural history more adequately than are the narrower approaches currently operative. Postmodernism in Catholic art and architecture will be much more intuitive and creative than is modernism in dealing with the primordial religious qualities of material elements (water, stone, earth), as well as with atmospheric architectural qualities (darkness, emptiness, height, solidity, distance, profusion, and monumentality).[69] All in all, postmodern art and architecture will be able to serve well the rich polyvalent dimensions of liturgy and reconnect public worship with the complete history of church architecture.

Postmodern Catholic architecture is particularly well suited to incorporating two important sources of inspiration for a new Catholic architecture in the United States: that of Hispanic Catholicism with its rich expressive vocabulary, and that of Eastern Christianity with its strong iconographic theology and practice.[70] In this regard, it will serve as a receptive vehicle for the ideals of liturgical inculturation—so far almost completely without architectural expression in North American Catholicism today. Not least, postmodernism, especially in its "new classical" expressions, provides a more adequate paradigm than does modernism for the renovation of church buildings erected in previous eras. We cannot, of course, predict that postmodernism will be an outstanding success in reorienting Catholic liturgical architecture in more adequate directions than those presently operative. In my opinion, however, the promise of the movement is considerable.[71]

THESIS TEN: ORIENTATION OR DIRECTIONAL CONFIGURATION

Orientation or directional configuration within liturgical buildings is the fundamental programmatic factor regarding the placement and interrelationship of liturgical appointments. I promised at the outset that, due to my lack of competence, this essay would not spell out the practical implications of the theses I am proposing. This final thesis is as close as I will come to treating the specific issues of liturgical furnishings and appointments. The Constitution on the Sacred Liturgy of Vatican II had little to say on the details of liturgical design. The General Instruction of the Roman Missal published in 1969 provided more extensive foundational principles. These were later elaborated in detail in the American document *Environment and Art in Catholic Worship*—highly influential in the English-speaking Catholic world throughout the 1970s and 1980s.[72]

The norms established cumulatively and progressively by official postconciliar documents have provided a pattern of liturgical-architectural arrangements that has become standard in recent decades: a free-standing altar; an ambo to the side; a presidential chair behind or close to the altar; and a tabernacle in a side chapel or in a niche to the right or left of the altar. A good case can be made for this arrangement; it has in many respects worked well and should not be lightly abandoned. However, this now standard scheme may no longer be assumed today, as it was in the 1960s, to have entirely solid historical grounding and it may, in fact, require some refinement. In any case, the fundamental issue involved here, I suggest, is orientation or directional configuration.

Whatever the arrangement, the ordering of space and the orientation of elements within church buildings are highly significant.[73] The question of the orientation of the altar and the priest at Mass is the most controversial aspect of this issue.[74] While the so-called "traditionalist" desire to return simply to preconciliar arrangements must be rejected, there is something to be said for priest and people praying in the same direction, as long as the altar and the place of the people are closely coordinated. There are certainly strong historic precedents for such a scheme. This arrangement might rationalize the visual dynamics of worship, which are presently quite confused—with priest and people looking in different directions, especially during the Eucharistic Prayer. It could reverse neo-clericalist dominance of the assembly and reestablish a visual "register" of worship beyond that of the person of the priest.[75] This arrangement would symbolize more adequately the transcendent orientation of worship by reintroducing, through common focus on an iconographic program, the cosmic and heavenly dimensions of the liturgy.[76]

Again, the proper place of the tabernacle is fundamentally a question of orientation and spatial configuration. The position of the tabernacle in modern liturgical arrangements seems to remain unresolved at both theoretical and practical levels.[77] Popular sentiment in favor of its traditional prominence in churches has not been adequately analyzed or entertained by liturgical scholars. Something in the *sensus fidelium* on this matter remains impervious to current liturgical rationale. In my opinion, a more adequate theory of the tabernacle and of its significance and placement is necessary. Perhaps a new balance between altar and tabernacle along the lines of an incarnational-eschatological dialectic within the eucharistic liturgy would provide the key here.[78]

The question of the place and orientation of the priest's chair is another factor meriting reconsideration. The now standard location of the chair behind the altar may be based on a misunderstanding of the relationship between presiding and sitting in early Christian liturgy. The chair may not need to be at the center of the sanctuary facing the people, in which position neo-clericalist domination of the assembly easily occurs, but remain to the side facing the ambo, so that the priest may do when sitting what everyone else is doing: listen to the Word of God.[79]

Lest the proposals here seem to encourage a return to preconciliar arrangements, I would offer the renovation in the mid 1990s of St. James Cathedral in Seattle in the United States as a model in some respects (though not in others) of what I have in mind here. I would further insist that the traditional arrangements of Catholic churches—even of the baroque era, which was in general more inclusive of the congregation than many of its predecessors—are in many aspects not adequate to the needs of the revised liturgy. Yet the various historical models available are quite instructive in different ways and merit more examination than they have hitherto received in the post–Vatican II era. In any case, I would suggest that issues regarding the placement of liturgical elements for the future should be considered fundamentally within a framework of orientation and directional configuration.[80]

Conclusion

The new era of church art and architecture that the Catholic church is entering—or at least that I am proposing—does not signal in any way a "restorationism" which would seek to recover an imagined golden age; no such age ever existed. Nor do the new directions I am advocating simply reject the modern. Such an approach would be thoughtless and presumptuous. The genuine achievements of modern liturgical architecture deserve to be gratefully embraced, even as the church seeks to move beyond them, recognizing some severe limitations. The signs that a new era of church art and architecture is upon us are disparate and inconclusive. But they do exist and I believe we shall see these signs embodied in a new period of creativity as the church advances into the third millennium.

---

1. See the May–June 1997 issue of *Catholic Dossier* (3:3) devoted entirely to the issue of church architecture; also "Thomas Gordon Smith on the 'New Classicism,'" *Antiphon* (The Society for Catholic Liturgy) 2 (1997:1) 8–11.

2. The reciprocal dynamic here is elaborated in Piet Fransen in the essay entitled "Sacraments Signs of Faith," in *Intelligent Theology*, vol. 1 (Chicago: Franciscan Herald Press, 1969) esp. 140–43. See also the essay entitled "What Makes a Building a Church?" in Josef Pieper, *In Search of the Sacred: Contributions to an Answer*, trans. Lothar Krauth (San Francisco: Ignatius Press, 1991) 83–120.

3. The revised Roman rites for the dedication of places of worship display a notable dexterity in avoiding both simple functionalism and sacralism. See also the treatment of this matter in the *Catechism of the Catholic Church* (Rome: Libreria Editrice Vaticana, 1994, 1997) #1179–86; 1197–99; 1667–70.

4. Peter and Linda Murray state the distinction here pointedly: "The cardinal difference between a pagan temple and a Christian church is that the temple was believed to be the dwelling of the god or goddess, to whom priests or priestesses of the cult offered sacrifices. No matter how large it might be outside, it was not intended to be entered by devotees of the cult. In a Christian service the presence of the faithful is essential, and the buildings reflect the need to house a congregation" (*The Oxford Companion to Christian Art and Architecture* [New York: Oxford University Press, 1996] 105).

5. See the sermons entitled "The Gospel Palaces," "The Visible Temple," and "Offerings for the Sanctuary," in *Parochial and Plain Sermons* (San Francisco: Ignatius Press, 1987) 1344–49; 1350–58; 1359–69.

6. On the various aspects of this question, see John M. Lundquist, *The Temple: Meeting Place of Earth and Heaven* (New York: Thames and Hudson, 1993); Harold W. Turner, *From Temple to Meeting House* (The Hague: Mouton, 1979); Ben F. Meyer, *Christus Faber: The Master Builder and the House of God* (Allison Park, PA: Pickwick Press, 1992); Michael V. Fox, ed., *Temple in Society* (Winona Lake: Eisenbrauns, 1988); Yves M.-J. Congar, *The Mystery*

of the Temple, trans. Reginald F. Trevett (London: Burns and Oates, 1962); Joseph Keenan, "Temples and Churches," *Worship* 68 (1994) 222–31.

7. Among the more articulate advocates of architectural functionalism in the liturgy is Edward A. Sövik, who proposes a "non-church" or secular conception of liturgical architecture. See *Architecture for Worship* (Minneapolis: Augsburg Publishing House, 1973). See also Mark A. Torgerson, "An Architect's Response to Liturgical Reform: Edward A. Sövik and his 'Non-Church' Design," *Worship* 71 (1997) 19–41; Edward A. Sövik, "Notes on Mark Torgerson's Quire," *Worship* 71 (1997) 244–47. Though a Lutheran, Sövik's influence on Catholic liturgical architecture in the U.S. has been considerable.

8. Various aspects of this discussion are presented in Michael E. DeSanctis, *Renewing the City of God: The Reform of Catholic Architecture in the United States.* Meeting House Essays Number Five (Chicago: Liturgy Training Publications, 1993); Marchita Mauck, *Shaping a House for the Church* (Chicago: Liturgy Training Publications, 1990); Robin Gibbons, "Celebration and Sacrament: Holy Place and Holy People," *New Blackfriars* 77 (1996) 234–43; Tim Gorringe, "Sacred Space: Traditions and Conflict," *Church Building,* Autumn 1992 (Issue No. 23) 3–6. For an Anglican perspective, see Richard Giles, *Re-pitching the Tent: Re-ordering the Church Building for Worship and Mission in the New Millennium* (Norwich: The Canterbury Press, 1996).

9. See, for example, Caesarius of Arles, *Sermo* 229, 1–3, ed. G. Morin, CCL 104 (Turnhout: Brepols, 1953), 905–8.

10. Such a perspective is not only attentive to God's presence in the material world, but is cognizant of the proto-sacramentality of creation so well accounted for in Eastern Christian theology. For instance, see Alexander Schmemann, *The World as Sacrament* (London: Darton, Longman and Todd, 1966).

11. A refined approach to the issue in larger context is provided in Lawrence A. Hoffman, *Sacred Places and the Pilgrimage of Life.* Meeting House Essays Number One (Chicago: Liturgy Training Publications, 1991).

12. This process will be aided in no small degree by the insights of architectural anthropology. Valuable here are those resources of both philosophy and architectural theory which attend to the complex and mutually reciprocal relationships between people, place, and human dwelling. See Martin Heidegger, *Being and Time,* trans. John Macquarrie and Edward Robinson (New York: Harper and Row, 1962); idem, *Poetry, Language and Thought,* trans. Alfred Hofstader (New York: Harper Colophon, 1971); Christian Norberg-Schulz, *The Concept of Dwelling: On the Way to Figurative Architecture* (New York: Rizzoli, 1985); Anthony Vidler, *The Architectural Uncanny: Essays in the Modern Unhomely* (Cambridge, MA: The MIT Press, 1992); Stanley Tigerman, *The Architecture of Exile* (New York: Rizzoli International Publications, 1988); David Seamon and Robert Mugerauer, eds., *Dwelling, Place and Environment: Towards a Phenomenology of Person and World* (New York: Columbia University

Press, 1989); Gaston Bachelard, *The Poetics of Space,* trans. Maria Jolas (Boston, Beacon Press, 1969). Christian Norberg-Schulz argues that the "radical" interpretation which separates the Christian people from their buildings "is based on an insufficient understanding of the function of art and architecture in general. When Christ referred to the temple of his body (or the body of believers), he hardly implied that the community should isolate itself from the world of things to which it necessarily belongs." (*Architecture: Meaning and Place: Selected Essays* [New York: Electa/Rizzoli, 1988] 225). In other words, the incarnation did not suspend the natural laws of architectural anthropology!

13. Article 28 states: "Among the symbols with which liturgy deals, none is more important than this assembly of believers" (*Environment and Art in Catholic Worship,* National Conference of Catholic Bishops/Bishops' Committee on the Liturgy [Chicago: Liturgy Training Publications, 1986] 8).

14. For a qualified and nuanced interpretation of this principle, see John D. Laurance, "The Assembly as Liturgical Symbol," *Louvain Studies* 22 (Summer 1997) 127–52. See also R. Kevin Seasoltz, "The Liturgical Assembly: Light from Some Recent Scholarship," in Nathan Mitchell and John F. Baldovin, eds., Rule of Prayer, *Rule of Faith: Essays in Honor of Aidan Kavanagh,* OSB (Collegeville, MN: The Liturgical Press, 1996) 303–23; James Challancin, *The Assembly Celebrates: Gathering the Community for Worship* (New York: Paulist Press, 1989).

15. Anthropologist Clifford Geertz usefully points out that symbols are not only "of" but "for" a people: in a crucial sense, symbol systems stand over against the community within and in relation to which they operate. See the chapter entitled "Religion as a Cultural System," in Clifford Geertz, *The Interpretation of Cultures* (New York: Basic Books, 1973) esp. 91–94.

16. See the chapter entitled "Observations on Contemporary Issues," in John Dillenberger, *The Visual Arts and Christianity in America: From the Colonial Period to the Present* (New York: The Crossroad Publishing Company, 1989) 201–7.

17. It would be useful to study the relationship between the reticence about material symbolism and the modern resurgence of gnosticism. Illuminating here is Eric Owen Moss, *Gnostic Architecture* (New York, NY, 1999).

18. An engaging analysis is found in Margaret R. Miles, *Image as Insight: Visual Understanding in Western Christianity and Secular Culture* (Boston: Beacon Press, 1985) esp. 95–125. See also Eamon Duffy, *The Stripping of the Altars: Traditional Religion in England, 1400–1580* (New Haven, CT: Yale University Press, 1992); Carlos M. N. Eire, *War Against the Idols: The Reformation of Worship from Erasmus to Calvin* (Cambridge: Cambridge University Press, 1986); Sergiusz Michalski, *The Reformation and the Visual Arts: The Protestant Image Question in Western and Eastern Europe* (New York: Routledge, 1993); Lee Palmer Wandel, *Voracious Idols and Violent Hands:*

Iconoclasm in Reformation Zurich, Strasbourg, and Basel (Cambridge: Cambridge University Press, 1995); John Dillenberger, *A Theology of Artistic Sensibilities: The Visual Arts and the Church* (New York: Crossroad, 1986).

19. Numerous studies appearing on particular features of Western liturgical art are opening up a more coherent perspective in this area. See, for instance, Maurice B. McNamee, *Vested Angels: Eucharistic Symbolism in Early Dutch Painting* (Kampen: Kok Pharos Publishing House, 1997); Carol F. Lewine, *The Sistine Chapel Walls and the Roman Liturgy* (University Park, PA: The Pennsylvania State University Press, 1993); H. W. van Os, ed., *The Art of Devotion in the Late Middle Ages in Europe, 1300–1500* (Princeton, NJ: Princeton University Press, 1994); Marilyn Aronberg Lavin, *The Place of Narrative: Mural Decoration in Italian Churches, 431–1600* (Chicago: The University of Chicago Press, 1990); William Tronzo, ed., *Italian Church Decoration of the Middle Ages and Early Renaissance: Functions, Forms and Regional Traditions* (Bologna: Nuova Alfa Editoriale, 1989).

20. The notion of "architecture of subtraction" has been proposed as an ideal in some recent church renovations. See Marie Picard, "Renovating Past Renovations: St. Peter Church [Cleveland]," *Environment and Art Newsletter* 10 (1997) 28–30, 34–35.

21. The *Catechism of the Catholic Church* has this to say regarding the celebrants of the liturgy: " 'Recapitulated in Christ,' these are the ones who take part in the service of the praise of God and the fulfillment of his plan: the heavenly powers, all creation (the four living beings), the servants of the Old and New Covenants (the twenty-four elders), the new People of God (the one hundred and forty-four thousand), especially the martyrs 'slain for the word of God,' and the all-holy Mother of God (the Woman), the Bride of the Lamb, and finally 'a great multitude which no one could number from every nation, from all tribes, and peoples and tongues' " (#1138).

22. The kind of reserve about images and decoration found in figures like Saint Bernard in the twelfth century and the penchant for expressive abstraction in some strands of the period should not be mistaken for iconoclasm but understood as aversion to opulence and a disposition toward neo-Platonic conceptions of form and proportion. See, for instance, Bernard of Clairvaux, "An Apologia to Abbot William," in *The Works of Bernard of Clairvaux* (Shannon: Irish University Press, 1970) 1:63. The aniconic element of modern functionalism is also properly distinguished from the apophaticism of the Eastern Christian tradition. On the theological issues here, see Verna E. F. Harrison, "The Relationship Between Apophatic and Kataphatic Theology," *Pro Ecclesia* 4 (1995) 318–32.

23. The current Western liturgical fascination with the iconographic is, in my opinion, conceptually unstable. The highly subjectivist and expressive conceptions of art operative in Western Catholicism today (reflecting the wider culture) do not seem capable of incorporating—except at a superficial level—the

strongly sacramental understanding of the iconic. See, for instance, Michael Jones-Frank, *Iconography and Liturgy*. Meeting House Essays Number Six (Chicago: Liturgy Training Publications, 1994).

24. See Aidan Nichols, "On Baptising the Visual Arts: A Friar's Meditation on Art," *New Blackfriars* 74 (1993) 74–84. The literature on iconography is vast. A comprehensive bibliography is found in *Icons, Windows on Eternity: Theology and Spirituality in Color,* compiled by Gennadios Limouris (Geneva: World Council of Churches, 1990). Beyond the classic works by Weitzmann, Ouspensky, and Lossky, the following are recommended: Mahmoud Zibawi, The *Icon: Its Meaning and History,* trans. Patrick Madigan (Collegeville, MN: The Liturgical Press, 1993); Jaroslav Pelikan, Imago Dei: *The Byzantine Apologia for Icons* (Princeton, NJ: Princeton University Press, 1990).

25. The iconic tradition of the East, with its carefully prescribed liturgical programmatic, can also serve as a check on the recurring tendency of Western ecclesiastical art to become detached from the liturgical—a process operative to severely problematic degrees in the Renaissance and baroque eras.

26. See, for instance, Joseph Cardinal Ratzinger, *The Feast of Faith: Approaches to a Theology of the Liturgy,* trans. Graham Harrison (San Francisco: Ignatius Press, 1986); idem, *A New Song for the Lord: Faith in Christ and Liturgy Today,* trans. Martha M. Matesich (New York: The Crossroad Publishing Co., 1996); also the following essays by Hans Urs von Balthasar: "The Grandeur of the Liturgy," *Communio* 5 (1978) 344–51; "Liturgy and Awe," in *Explorations in Theology II: Spouse of the Word,* trans. A. V. Littledale with Alexander Dru (San Francisco: Ignatius Press, 1991) 461–72; "The Worthiness of the Liturgy," in *New Elucidations,* trans. Sister Mary Theresilde Skerry (San Francisco: Ignatius Press, 1986) 127–40. See also James Hitchcock, *Recovery of the Sacred: Reforming the Reformed Liturgy* (San Francisco: Ignatius Press, 1995).

27. On this, see M. Francis Mannion, "Worship in an Age of Subjectivism," *Liturgy 80* 20 (1989) 2–5.

28. That a similar process has been at work in North American Protestantism is pointed out by Amos Niven Wilder: "The church today has widely lost and all but forgotten the experience of glory which lies at the heart of Christianity" (*Theopoetic: Theology and the Religious Imagination* [Philadelphia: Fortress Press, 1976] 8).

29. This development is all the more striking in view of the powerful eschatological vision of the liturgy promoted in the Constitution on the Sacred Liturgy of Vatican II: "In the earthly liturgy we take part in a foretaste of that heavenly liturgy which is celebrated in the Holy City of Jerusalem toward which we journey as pilgrims, where Christ is sitting at the right hand of God, Minister of the holies and of the true tabernacle. With all the warriors of the heavenly army we sing a hymn of glory to the Lord; venerating the memory of the saints, we hope for some part and fellowship with them; we eagerly

await the Saviour, Our Lord Jesus Christ, until he our life shall appear and we too will appear with him in glory" (Text in *Vatican Council II: The Conciliar and Post Conciliar Documents,* Austin Flannery, gen. ed. [Collegeville, MN: The Liturgical Press, 1975] 5). See also the strong eschatological focus in the treatment of the liturgy in the Catechism of the Catholic Church (#1136–38).

30. Classic works relevant to these features of liturgical life include Josef Pieper, *In Tune with the World: A Theory of Festivity,* trans. Richard and Clara Winston (Chicago: Franciscan Herald Press, 1973); Romano Guardini, *The Spirit of the Liturgy,* trans. Ada Lane (London: Sheed and Ward, 1937) esp. 85–106; Hugo Rahner, *Man at Play or Did You Ever Practice Eutrapelia?,* trans. Brian Battershaw and Edward Quinn (London: Burns and Oates, 1965). See also Daniel W. Hardy and David F. Ford, *Jubilate: Theology in Praise* (London: Darton, Longman and Todd, 1984); Hughes Oliphant Old, *Themes and Variations for a Christian Doxology* (Grand Rapids, MI: William B. Eerdmans, 1992); Jurgen Moltmann, *Theology and Joy,* trans. Reinhard Ulrich (London: SCM Press, 1973); Piet Fransen, "Sacraments as Celebrations," *Irish Theological Quarterly* 43 (1975) 151–70.

31. That architecture has served as a particularly important vehicle for the eschatological in liturgical history is argued in the essay by C. Clifford Flanigan entitled "The Apocalypse in the Medieval Liturgy," in Richard K. Emmerson and Bernard McGinn, eds., *The Apocalypse in the Middle Ages* (Ithaca, NY: Cornell University Press, 1992) 333–51. Ironically, it was primarily by recovery of the verbal expression of early Christian eschatological consciousness that this feature was restored in the modern liturgical movement. See, for instance, Geoffrey Wainwright, *Eucharist and Eschatology* (New York: Oxford University Press, 1981).

32. A stronger eschatological-doxological framework would have strengthened the impressive proposals in Peter E. Smith, *Cherubim of Gold: Building Materials and Aesthetics.* Meeting House Essays Number Three (Chicago: Liturgy Training Publications, 1993).

33. For a brief historical overview of this theme, see the essay by P. Verdier entitled "Iconography of the Apocalypse," in *New Catholic Encyclopedia* (San Francisco: McGraw-Hill Book Co., 1967) vol. 1, 659–63.

34. Some recent writings on the eschatological character of worship include Robert Prestiano, "Pilgrimage and Parousia: Enduring Themes in Christian Tradition," *Ecclesia Orans* 10 (1993) 269–80; Mary M. Schaefer, "Heavenly and Earthly Liturgies: Patristic Prototypes, Medieval Perspectives and Contemporary Application," *Worship* 70 (1996) 482–505; Jean-Pierre Ruiz, "The Apocalypse of John and Contemporary Roman Catholic Liturgy," *Worship* 68 (1994) 482–504; Geoffrey Wainwright, "The Church as a Worshiping Community," *Pro Ecclesia* 4 (1993) 56–67; Laurence Hull Stookey, *Eucharist: Christ's Feast with the Church* (Nashville, TN: Abington Press, 1993);

Don E. Saliers, *Worship as Theology: Foretaste of Divine Glory* (Nashville, TN: Abington Press, 1994).

35. For an introduction to the vastly neglected area of liturgical aesthetics, see the special issue of *Liturgy Digest* 3 (1996) esp. 72ff.; also Don E. Saliers, "Liturgical Aesthetics," in *The New Dictionary of Sacramental Worship*, Peter E. Fink, ed. (Collegeville, MN: The Liturgical Press, 1990) 30–39; Nicholas Wolterstorff, *Art in Action: Toward a Christian Aesthetic* (Grant Rapids, MI: Eerdmans, 1980); Frank Burch Brown, *Religious Aesthetics: A Theological Study of Making and Meaning* (Princeton, NJ: Princeton University Press, 1989.

36. This theme has been developed in recent decades in Martin E. Marty, *The Public Church: Mainline-Evangelical-Catholic* (New York: Crossroad, 1981); David O'Brien, *Public Catholicism* (New York: Macmillan Publishing Co., 1989); Richard John Neuhaus, *The Naked Public Square: Religion and Democracy in America* (Grand Rapids, MI: William B. Eerdmans Publishing Co., 1984).

37. See Aidan Kavanagh, *On Liturgical Theology* (New York: Pueblo Publishing Company, 1984); John F. Baldovin, *Worship: City, Church and Renewal* (Washington, DC: The Pastoral Press, 1991) esp. 3–35.

38. See M. Francis Mannion, *The Cathedral as Sacrament of the Redeemed City*. The 1997 Anne Brand Stolberg Lecture (Covington, KY: The Cathedral Foundation, 1997).

39. While biblical and early Christian protocol can be invoked in favor of "domestic" language when speaking about the church, it would be inappropriate to impose modern experience on earlier epochs. The premodern household was characteristically a public entity. The household as a private space is very much a modern phenomenon. See Robert Banks, *Paul's Idea of Community: The Early House Churches in their Historical Setting* (Grand Rapids, MI: Eerdmans, 1980); Wayne A. Meeks, *The First Urban Christians: The Social World of the Apostle Paul* (New Haven, CT: Yale University Press, 1983) esp. 9–50; 74–110. See also David Herlihy, *Medieval Households* (Cambridge, MA: Harvard University Press, 1985; Kate Mertes, *The Noble English Household, 1250–1600* (New York: Basil Blackwell, 1988); Michael Mitterauer and Reinhard Sieder, *The European Family: Patriarchy to Partnership from the Middle Ages to the Present* (Oxford: Basil Blackwell, 1982).

40. In Eastern Christian thought, the church building is considered as a model of the whole universe. See, for instance, *The Church, the Liturgy and the Soul of Man: The Mystagogia of St. Maximus the Confessor*, trans. Dom Julian Stead (Still River, MA: St. Bede's Publications, 1982) esp. 68ff. See also William R. Lethaby, *Architecture, Mysticism and Myth* (New York: Braziller, 1975).

41. On the dynamics here, see Daniel V. A. Olsen, "Church Friendships: Boon or Barrier to Church Growth?" *Journal for the Scientific Study of Religion* 28 (1989) 432–47.

42. See M. Francis Mannion, "Worship and the Public Church," *Liturgy 80* 20 (1987) 11–14; also Patrick Kiefert, *Welcoming the Stranger: Worship and Evangelism* (Philadelphia: Augsburg/Fortress, 1989).

43. See Parker J. Palmer, *The Company of Strangers: Christians and the Renewal of American Public Life* (New York: Crossroad, 1983).

44. For a general analysis of this problem, see Richard Sennett, *The Fall of Public Man: On the Social Psychology of Capitalism* (New York: Alfred A. Knopf, 1977).

45. A defense of large public church buildings is to be distinguished from a promotion of the megachurch phenomenon in present-day American Protestantism. See David W. Fagerberg, "Was the Cathedral of Notre Dame a Megachurch?" *Pro Ecclesia* 6 (1997) 141–45.

46. On the need for a renewal of the "public" in architecture, see Nathan Glazer and Mark Lilla, eds., *The Public Face of Architecture: Civic Culture and Public Spaces* (New York: The Free Press, 1987).

47. On the wider theological features of this discussion, see William C. Placher, *The Domestication of Transcendence: How Modern Thinking About God Went Wrong* (Louisville, KY: Westminster John Knox Press, 1996).

48. See the essay entitled "Unmodern Prayer," in Hans Urs von Balthasar, *Elucidations,* trans. John Riches (London: SPCK, 1975) 113–18.

49. On the powerful "non-liturgical" effects of religious buildings, see John S. Dunne, *The House of Wisdom: A Pilgrimage* (San Francisco: Harper and Row, 1985).

50. This development is, in part, responsible for the "non-church" conception of places of worship currently operative (see note 7 above).

51. On this, see David N. Power, "Eucharistic Celebration: Action, Word, Sight," *Liturgical Ministry* 1 (1992) 77–84.

52. For a positive appreciation of the devotional in liturgical environments, see John Buscemi, *Places for Devotion.* Meeting House Essays Number Four (Chicago: Liturgy Training Publications, 1993). Some social and religious historians are beginning to pay more attention than previously to popular religion. See Colleen McDannell, *Material Christianity: Religion and Popular Culture in America* (New Haven, CT: Yale University Press, 1995); Robert A. Orsi, *Thank You, St. Jude: Women's Devotion to the Patron Saint of Hopeless Cases* (New Haven, CT: Yale University Press, 1996); idem, *The Madonna of 115th Street: Faith and Community in Italian Harlem* (New Haven, CT: Yale University Press, 1985).

53. Phenomenologies of the sacred which have been somewhat out of fashion in recent years deserve new consideration by students of liturgical art and

architecture. See Rudolf Otto, *The Idea of the Holy: An Inquiry into the Non-Rational Factor in the Idea of the Divine and Its Relation to the Rational*, trans. John W. Harvey (New York: Oxford University Press, 1923); Gerardus Van der Leeuw, Religion in Essence and Manifestation, trans. J. E. Turner (New York: Harper and Row, 1963). Mircea Eliade's extensive writings in this area are summarized in the chapter entitled "The Reality of the Sacred: Mircea Eliade," in Daniel L. Pals, Seven Theories of Religion (New York: Oxford University Press, 1996) 158–95. See also Mircea Eliade, Symbolism, the Sacred, and the Arts, Diane Apostolos-Cappodona, ed. (New York: Crossroad, 1986); Louis Bouyer, Rite and Man: Natural Sacredness and Christian Liturgy, trans. M. Joseph Costelloe (Notre Dame, IN: University of Notre Dame Press, 1963).

54. See generally, Le Corbusier, *Towards a New Architecture*, trans. F. Etchells (London: J. Rodker, 1931); idem, Apollo in the Democracy: The Cultural Obligation of the Architect (New York: McGraw Hill, 1968); *The New Architecture and the Bauhaus*, trans. P. Morton Shand (London: Faber and Faber, 1965); Henry-Russell Hitchcock and Philip Johnson, *The International Style* (New York: W.W. Norton and Company, 1996).

55. Various criticisms of architectural modernism are provided in: Roger Scruton, *The Classical Vernacular: Architectural Principles in an Age of Nihilism* (New York: St. Martin's Press, 1995); Patrick Nuttgens, *Understanding Modern Architecture* (London: Unwin Hyman, 1988); Alberto Pérez-Gómez, *Architecture and the Crisis of Modern Science* (Cambridge, MA: MIT Press, 1983). For popular, if somewhat exaggerated criticisms, see E. Michael Jones, *Living Machines: Bauhaus Architecture as Sexual Ideology* (San Francisco: Ignatius Press, 1995); Tom Wolfe, *From Bauhaus to Our House* (New York: Farrar Strauss Giroux, 1981).

56. See Vincent Scully, Architecture: The Natural and the Manmade (New York: St. Martin's Press, 1991); also Christopher Alexander, "The City as a Mechanism for Sustaining Human Contacts," in William Ewald, ed., *Environment for Man: The Next 50 Years* (Bloomington, IN: Indiana University Press, 1967) 60–109; *The Timeless Way of Building* (New York: Oxford University Press, 1979).

57. On these tendencies of modernist architecture, see the essay by Carroll William Westfall, "Thinking About Modernism and Classicism," *The Classicist*, No. 1 (1994–1995) 6–11.

58. For a general analysis of this matter, see James Holston, *The Modernist City: An Anthropological Critique of Brasilia* (Chicago: The University of Chicago Press, 1989).

59. See the chapter entitled "The Neutral City," in Richard Sennett, *The Conscience of the Eye: The Design and Social Life of Cities* (New York: W. W. Norton and Company, 1990) 48–68.

60. On the place of Marxian and Freudian analysis in architectural theory, see Roger Scruton, *The Aesthetics of Architecture* (Princeton, NJ: Princeton University Press, 1979) 137–57. See, more generally, William Lloyd Newell, *The Secular Magi: Marx, Freud and Nietzsche on Religion* (Lanham, MD: University Press of America, 1994).

61. See David H. Smart, "Gregory Dix and Architectural Modernism," *Antiphon* 4:1 (1999) 26–27.

62. See Norris K. Smith, "On Building Churches," *Communio* 3 (1979) 257–70. That the aims of the liturgical movement and of architectural modernism did not always sit well together is indicated in Martin Purdy, "Le Corbusier and the Theological Program," in Russell Walden, ed., *The Open Hand: Essays on Le Corbusier* (Cambridge, MA: MIT Press, 1982) 286–318. See also John Beaumont, "Bauhaus Architecture and the Catholic Church: Function at War with Form," *Culture Wars* 16 (1997:4), 26–39.

63. A useful introduction to criticisms of these aspects of liturgical reform by Catholic anthropologists Mary Douglas, Victor Turner, and Kieran Flanagan is provided in Aidan Nichols, *Looking at the Liturgy: A Critical View of Its Contemporary Form* (San Francisco: Ignatius Press, 1996) 49–86. See also Aidan Kavanagh, "Liturgy (*Sacrosanctum Concilium*)," in Adrian Hastings, ed., *Modern Catholicism: Vatican II and After* (New York: Oxford University Press, 1991) 68–73.

64. The comments of German liturgist Adolf Adam are relevant here: "The interiors of many modern churches do not earn good marks, because they seem so inhospitable and unattractive, so depressing, cold and empty. An unsuccessful arrangement of spaces, a bleak monotony in light and color, an artistic poverty in furnishings do not symbolize the dignity of the liturgical assembly nor do they invite the congregation into the mystery" (*Foundations of Liturgy: An Introduction to Its History and Practice* [Collegeville, MN: The Liturgical Press, 1992] 326–27).

65. For statements regarding the values of the modern movement in liturgical architecture, see Richard Hurley, "The Eucharist Room at Carlow Liturgy Center: The Search for Meaning," *Worship* 70 (1996) 238–50; Meredith L. Clausen, *Spiritual Space: The Religious Architecture of Pietro Belluschi* (Seattle: University of Washington Press, 1992). On a methodology for the study of modern liturgical architecture (from a sympathetic point of view), see Gerard Lukken and Mark Searle, *Semiotics and Church Architecture* (Kampen: Kok Pharos Publishing House, 1993); also the Fall issue of *Liturgy Digest* devoted to environment and art (2:1).

66. The term *postmodernism* continues to be controversial and to have diverging meanings in different fields. At its broadest, postmodernism refers to a general *cultural and religious movement* which a) consciously assumes the positive values and achievements of modernity; b) is critical of the individualistic,

rationalistic, and mechanistic features of the modern era; and c) advocates a worldview that is communal, spiritual, and organic. The *different kinds* of cultural and religious postmodernism—from neoconservatism to radicalism—are distinguished by their varying attitudes to history and the normativity of its conceptions and achievements for the future. See generally *Postmodernism: A Reader,* Thomas Docherty, ed. (New York: Columbia University Press, 1993); *The Post-Modern Reader,* Charles Jencks, ed. (New York: St. Martin's Press, 1992). On postmodernism in theology, see David Ray Griffin, William A. Beardslee and Joe Holland, *Varieties of Postmodern Theology* (Albany, NY: State University of New York Press, 1989, esp. 1–7); Terence W. Tilley, *Postmodern Theologies: The Challenge of Religious Diversity* (Maryknoll, NY: Orbis Press, 1995); Frederic B. Burnham, ed., Postmodern Theology: Christian Faith in a Pluralistic World (San Francisco: Harper and Row, 1989).

67. See David Watkin, *A History of Western Architecture* (London: Laurence King, second ed., 1996) 572–89.

68. See Giles Dimock, "Baroque Liturgy on Trial," *Sacred Music* 116 (1989:2) 19–24.

69. See Dennis McNally, *Sacred Space: An Aesthetic for the Liturgical Environment* (Bristol, IN: Wyndam Hall Press, 1985); also A.T. Mann, *Sacred Architecture* (Rockport, MA: Element, Inc., 1993; Gerhart B. Ladner, *God, Cosmos and Humankind: The World of Early Christian Symbolism,* trans. Thomas Dunlap (Berkeley, CA: University of California Press, 1995); Thomas Barrie, *Spiritual Path, Sacred Place: Myth, Ritual, and Meaning in Architecture* (Boston, MA: Shambala, 1996).

70. On the former, see the essay by Jaime Lara, "Passion and Power: Toward Understanding the Hispanic Aesthetic," *Faith and Form* 22 (1989) 14–15. See also Douglas Kent Hall, *Frontier Spirit: Early Churches of the Southwest* (New York: Abbeville Publishers, 1990); Peter Nabokov and Robert Easton, *Native American Architecture* (New York: Oxford University Press, 1989).

71. Leading centers of this movement already exhibiting concern for Catholic liturgical architecture are the School of Architecture at the University of Notre Dame and the Institute for the Study of Classical Architecture at New York University. The latter has, since 1994, published a yearly journal of considerable substance, *The Classicist,* which serves as a valuable guide to current discussions. See Randall S. Lindstrom, *Creativity and Contradiction: European Churches Since 1970* (Washington, DC: The American Institute of Architects, 1988).

72. *Editor's note:* Since the original publication of this essay, the United States Conference of Catholic Bishops has published *Built of Living Stones: Art Architecture and Worship* (Washington, DC: United States Catholic Conference, 2000). These guidelines are "presented to assist the faithful involved in the building and renovation of churches, chapels, and oratories of the Latin Church

in the United States. In addition, the document is intended for use by architects, liturgical consultants and artists, contractors and other professionals engaged in the design and/or places of worship. The text may also be helpful to those who wish to understand the Catholic Church's tradition regarding church buildings, the arts and architecture." (*Built of Living Stones*, no. 3).

73. On the significance of various floor plans, see Rudolf Schwarz, *The Church Incarnate: The Sacred Function of Christian Architecture*, trans. Cynthia Harris (Chicago: Henry Regnary Company, 1958); also DeSanctis, *Renewing the City of God*, esp. 13ff. In my opinion, church architecture should probably avoid exclusively circular or quasi-circular arrangements. These can easily lead to a radical domestication of the mystery of God and a positing of the dynamics of the church in the gathered assembly, generating congregationalism. Church architecture should probably also avoid exclusively linear or quasi-linear arrangements. These tend toward a spiritual exclusion of the people from the mystery of God and posit the foundational dynamics of the church in the clerical or the ritual order, generating clericalism and/or ritualism.

74. See Klaus Gamber, *The Reform of the Roman Liturgy: Its Problems and Background*, trans. Klaus D. Grimm (San Juan Capistrano, CA: Una Voce Press/Harrison, NY: The Foundation for Catholic Reform, 1993) esp. 77ff.; Jaime Lara, "*Versus Populum* Revisited," *Worship* 68 (1994) 310–221; Nichols, *Looking at the Liturgy*, 90ff.; Ratzinger, *The Feast of Faith*, 139–145. See the provocative comments on this matter in Matthew Fox, *The Coming of the Cosmic Christ*, (San Francisco: Harper, 1988) esp. 212–16.

75. *Editor's Note:* On September 25, 2000, Cardinal Jorge Medina Estevez, Prefect of the Congregation for Divine Worship and Discipline of the Sacraments responded to a letter from a European Cardinal's query regarding the position of the priest during the celebration of the Eucharistic liturgy (Prot. NO 2086/00/L). This letter "reaffirms that the position toward the assembly seems more convenient inasmuch as it makes communication easier (Cf. *Notitiae* 29 [1993] 245–49), without excluding the other possibility." The letter emphasizes that no matter what direction the priest faces as he celebrates the Eucharistic liturgy, "the physical position, especially with respect to the communication among the various members of the assembly, must be distinguished from the interior spiritual orientation of all. It would be a grave error to imagine that the principal orientation of the sacrificial action is [toward] the community. If the priest celebrates *versus populum*, which is legitimate [translation corrected] and often advisable, his spiritual attitude ought always to be *versus Deum per Jesum* [text corrected] *Christum* [toward God through Jesus Christ], as representative of the entire Church. The Church, as well, which takes concrete form in the assembly which participates, is entirely turned *versus Deum* [toward God] as its first spiritual movement." Finally, the letter reiterates that "whatever may be the position of the celebrating priest, it is clear that the Eucharistic Sacrifice is offered to the one and triune God, and that the principal, eternal, and high priest is Jesus Christ who acts

through the ministry of the priest who visibly presides as His instrument."
Note: The English translation is taken from http://www.adroemus.org/
12-0101cdw-adorient.html.

76. Studies in recent decades on the liturgical operationality of the retable or reredos in places of worship may suggest a way forward here. See Judith Berg Sobré, *Behind the Altar Table: The Development of the Painted Retable in Spain, 1350–1500* (Columbia: MO: The University of Missouri Press, 1989); Eve Borsook and Fiorella Superbi Gioffredi, eds., *Italian Altarpieces, 1250–1550: Function and Design* (New York: Oxford University Press, 1994); Peter Humfrey, *The Altarpiece in Renaissance Venice* (New Haven, CT: Yale University Press, 1993); Andrée Hayum, *The Isenheim Altarpiece: God's Medicine and the Painter's Vision* (Princeton, NJ: Princeton University Press, 1989); Barbara G. Lane, *The Altar and the Altarpiece* (New York: Harper and Row, 1984). See also Jacob Burckhardt, *The Altarpiece in Renaissance Italy,* ed. and trans. Peter Humfrey (Cambridge: Cambridge University Press, 1988).

77. See, for instance, the chapter entitled "The Location of the Tabernacle," in Peter J. Elliott, *Ceremonies of the Modern Roman Rite: The Eucharist and the Liturgy of the Hours* (San Francisco: Ignatius Press, 1995) 322–30; Timothy V. Vaverek, "The Place of the Eucharistic Tabernacle," *Antiphon* 4:2 (1999) 10–13. *Editor's Note:* Paragraph 315 from The *General Instruction of the Roman Missal* (2000), has clarified this matter by prescribing: "Consequently, it is preferable that the tabernacle be located, according to the judgment of the diocesan Bishop, a.) Either in the sanctuary, apart from the altar of celebration in a form and place more appropriate, not excluding on an old altar no longer used for celebration (cf. #303); b.) Or even in some chapel suitable for the faithful's private adoration and prayer and organically connected to the church and readily visible to the Christian faithful."

78. See M. Francis Mannion, "The Reserved Eucharist," *Antiphon* 3:2 (1998) 2–4.

79. See Bruce E. Harbert, "The Question of Liturgical 'Presidency,'" *Antiphon* 1:2/3 (1996) 6–8.

80. For additional consideration of these questions, see Giles Dimock, "The Beauty of God's House," *Catholic Dossier* 3:3 (1997) 11–16.

Chapter 8

The "Musification" of the Word: Cardinal Ratzinger's Theology of Liturgical Music

In the Catholic Church today, Cardinal Joseph Ratzinger continues to be a highly controversial figure. As prefect of the Vatican Congregation for the Doctrine of the Faith, the cardinal bears responsibility for the doctrinal integrity of Catholicism worldwide. Before he became prefect of the Congregation in 1981, Cardinal Ratzinger was Archbishop of Munich, a position to which he was appointed in 1977. Most of the cardinal's professional life hitherto was as professor of theology at the universities of Bonn, Münster, Tübingen, and Regensburg. His international reputation as a theologian had already been established by the time of the Second Vatican Council, at which he was a theological advisor to the German bishops.

Cardinal Ratzinger is not associated outside a limited audience with the field of liturgical music. The fact that he had lectured and written on the subject only became known widely in 1985 when an extended popular interview with the cardinal covering many aspects of ecclesial life was published in English under the title *The Ratzinger Report*.[1] Though the cardinal had no notable training as a musician, music ran in his family. For many years, his brother Monsignor Georg Ratzinger was choirmaster at Regensburg Cathedral. One of the cardinal's most recently published lectures on church music of which I am aware was prepared as a tribute to his retiring musician brother.[2]

Cardinal Ratzinger's corpus of writings on liturgical music is quite small: six longer essays and some short commentaries.[3] But read in the context of the cardinal's more extensive writings on liturgical, ecclesiological, and theological matters, the essays on music in the liturgy take on a strikingly impressive and substantive character.[4] Indeed, in my opinion, Cardinal Ratzinger's writings on liturgical music, because of their theological and philosophical comprehensiveness and profundity, represent the most significant corpus of writings on the subject produced in the Catholic Church in the twentieth century. An appropriate point at which to undertake analysis of Cardinal Ratzinger's thought on liturgical music is with the word with which the cardinal himself is often popularly associated: *orthodoxy*. Though the word has mostly a doctrinal reference, its literal meaning is highly significant in the present context: right or correct worship. Cardinal Ratzinger, more than most commentators, recognizes that issues of liturgical music are related not only to the proper ordering of liturgical worship itself, but to the right ordering of Christian conceptions and practice at all levels. Accordingly, he has written: The "controversy about Church music is becoming symptomatic for the deeper question about what the liturgy is."[5] Music has become "a question of the essence of liturgical action as such, of its anthropological and theological foundations."[6] Indeed, "the critical situation of church music today is part of the general crisis of the Church which has developed since Vatican 2."[7] He speaks of "the properly ecclesiastical and theological crisis of church music."[8] Problems of music, liturgy, and ecclesiology are, in the cardinal's outlook, deeply intertwined and mutually influential. These are further complicated by the general cultural crisis in the West which finds keen expression in the area of music.[9]

In this essay, I shall first set out the cardinal's analysis of what he perceives to be the postconciliar crisis of church music and its underlying characteristics. I shall then proceed to present the cardinal's theology of music in worship in its positive and constructive aspects. While I shall seek to follow the logic of the cardinal's various writings, some rearrangement of the material is necessary for the correlation of diverse insights—hopefully without distortion or misrepresentation.

Liturgical Music After Vatican II

Cardinal Ratzinger examines the crises in church music most concretely by reference to the ascendancy of what he calls "utility music" over art music in the recent life of the church. At the beginning of the essay on liturgical music in his book *The Feast of Faith*, he writes:

> It is astonishing to find that in the German edition of the documents of Vatican II, edited by Karl Rahner and Herbert Vorgrimler, the brief commentary which introduces the chapter on Sacred Music in the Constitution on the Liturgy begins with the observation that genuine art as found in church music, is "of its very nature—which is esoteric in the best sense—hardly to be reconciled with the nature of the liturgy and the basic principle of liturgical reform."[10]

The cardinal continues:

> Of course neither Rahner nor Vorgrimler want to banish all music from the worship of God; but what they do find alien to its nature is art music, i.e., the musical heritage of the Western Church. Consequently they feel that the Council, in recommending that "the treasury of sacred music is to be preserved and cultivated with great care" [CSL, 114], does not mean "that this is to be done within the framework of the liturgy."[11]

The cardinal states that the commentators, in a similar vein, stress the Council's recommendation that choirs should be cultivated especially in cathedral churches, but "the impression is given that the Council really wanted to limit them to cathedrals, and even then provided they did not obstruct the people's participation."[12] For Rahner and Vorgrimler, "the normal musical component of liturgy is hence not 'actual church music,' but 'so-called utility music.'"[13]

Such an interpretation of the intentions of Vatican II has given us, the cardinal observes, "the increasingly grim impoverishment which follows when beauty for its own sake is banished from the Church and all is subordinated to the principle of 'utility.'"[14] He continues: "One shudders at the lackluster face of the postconciliar liturgy as it has become, or one is bored with its banality and its lack of artistic standards."[15] In the cardinal's analysis, the problem of utilitarianism is far more significant than might first seem to be the case, for it expresses a utilitarian view not only of music, but of the liturgy, the church, and, indeed, all theological realities.

SPIRITUALIZATION, RATIONALISM, AND CHRISTIAN HERITAGE

The explanations offered by Cardinal Ratzinger for this general situation are of considerable complexity, not least because they are deeply interconnected and are in effect subtly different versions of each other.

The first is found in a phenomenon that goes back to the early church, to what the cardinal identifies as the ideal of spiritualization. This outlook emerged out of an early conviction of figures like Saint Jerome that Christians " 'should sing to God with their hearts, not with their voices.' "[16] This sort of admonition seems harmless enough, indeed almost virtuous. But it contains a deep prejudice—typical of early Christianity—against ritual and musical performance in divine worship in general. The conviction was strong in certain quarters that the church should not fall back into old legalistic or ritualistic Judaic ways, and rightly so. However, this belief spelled itself out, unfortunately, in an opposition to the material, the physical, and the sensual in favor of the spiritual. In the cardinal's words, the attitude was that "the 'spiritual' movement of the gospel must therefore be seen more or less as the renunciation of the sensual reality of musical sound in favor of the solely spiritual, i.e., the word alone."[17]

Cardinal Ratzinger indicates that the same pattern of thought repeated itself in Saint Augustine, Saint Gregory the Great, in many of the early fathers, and later in Saint Thomas Aquinas: "Church music is put at the level of what is pedagogically useful; in practice, therefore, it is subject to the criterion of 'utility' "[18] This early Christian outlook reappears severely today in a conviction which the cardinal summarizes as follows: "God can only really be praised in the heart means that no status can be accorded to music, to the audible form of this praise, within the act of praise itself in Christian worship."[19] Music, accordingly, "must be relegated to a secondary level."[20]

A second difficulty for sacred music and its current critical status originates, in Cardinal Ratzinger's view, in the perennial disposition toward rationalism. For the cardinal, this attitude is, in its essence, expressed in Aquinas's view that vocal worship is necessary not for God's sake, but for the sake of the worshiper.[21] Thomas reflects the conviction of Aristotle that piety finds its identity and meaning in self-cultivation, particularly the "cultivation of what is most pleasing to God, namely, reason."[22] Thomas's conviction finds fresh expression today in "a theory in which prayer is simply the activation of those of man's powers which are felt to be 'the best.' "[23] Hence, today, the cardinal says, "a shadow of rationalism is cast over the theory of liturgy" and over the conception and practice of music in the liturgy.[24]

A third problem attending sacred music today is the pervasive tendency to disown the venerable heritage of Christian culture. The cardinal speaks of an attitude in the postconciliar church "in which all church music, indeed all previous Western culture was not regarded as belonging to the present and hence could not be a part of contemporary practice."[25] As this outlook develops, "traditional culture is pushed aside into a more or less museum-like state of preservation in the concert hall."[26] In this way, "the link with history is broken, and history itself can only retain any value at all as a function, namely as an object in a museum. Thus history is completely relegated to the past, and loses all her vital power to shape life today."[27] This "disowning of Christian culture and search for new shores of cultural expression are, by way of protest, set over against the Christian world."[28] This process has its roots in a certain nihilism and a deconstruction of the traditional culture of Christianity and, indeed, ultimately emerges as a rejection of the inherited Western world at a very fundamental level.

Functionalism, Iconoclasm, Congregationalism

A fourth explanation of the modern liturgical-musical crisis is found in what Cardinal Ratzinger treats only very briefly: the phenomenon of functionalism. This outlook operates on the conviction that all of human reality is reducible to quantifiable dimensions and processes and that "this reducibility applies everywhere and in principle."[29] In the operative paradigm, the machine appears as the foundational symbol. "Here, there is no longer any place for artistic events which are unique, since all that is unique must be replaced by the merely calculable."[30] The consequence is that "art falls under the laws of the marketplace, and the marketplace abolishes it as art."[31] In the cardinal's view, the consequence is a view of creativity that is isolated and self-enclosed. However,

> the attempt to escape this consequence through a "creativity" which frees itself from anything established in advance and seeks a totally new reality, is futile. The intellectual underpinnings of the attempt to find in this way a new basis for art by dissolving the links to its religious origin have been most impressively elaborated by Ernst Bloch, for whom the artist is "the absolute breaker of boundaries," [and] "the pioneer at the frontier of an advancing world, indeed a most important component of the world which is only creating itself." Genius is "consciousness which has progressed the

farthest." Thus there disappears the qualitatively specific characteristic of art, which is mere anticipation of what is to come.[32]

Cardinal Ratzinger correlates this problem with the effects on liturgical music of the phenomenon of iconoclasm, which also has deep roots and finds recurring expression in church history. He writes:

> In the seventh and eighth centuries the Church of Byzantium was excited by this problem in a manner which touched the very nerves of her existence, and thus the Orthodox Church celebrates the Second Council of Nicaea as the "Feast of Orthodoxy," because this Council sealed the victory of images and thus in general the victory of art within the faith. In other words, the Orthodox Church sees in this question the salient point of the Church's existence in general, for on this point the basic decision about our understanding of God, the world and man is at stake.[33]

The cardinal points out that,

> though the Western Church was palpably convulsed by the question during the Carolingian age, it was really only the Reformation which ushered in the great iconoclastic drama, in which Luther sided with the ancient Church against Calvin and the leftists of the Reformation, the so-called Fanatics or Schwärmer.[34]

He concludes: "The earthquake that we are experiencing in the Church today belongs in this historical context: here is the real core of the theological question about the justification for images and music in the Church."[35]

Yet a further dynamic negatively operative in the area of church music today is the phenomenon of congregationalism. Cardinal Ratzinger's treatment of this matter is lengthier than those already outlined, because it is so fundamental to the problematic of his analysis. The cardinal spells out the troublesome starting point as follows:

> The liturgy takes its point of departure—we are told—from the gathering of two or three who have come together in the name of Christ. This reference to the Lord's words of promise in Matt. 18:20 sounds harmless and traditional at first hearing. But it receives a revolutionary turn when one isolates this one biblical text and contrasts it with the whole liturgical tradition. For the two or three are now placed in opposition to an institution with its institutional roles, and to every "codified" program. Thus this definition comes to mean: it is not the Church that precedes the group but the group that precedes the Church. It is not the Church as an integral

entity that carries the liturgy of the individual group or community; rather the group is itself the specific place of origin for the liturgy. Thus the liturgy does not grow out of a common given, a "rite" (which as a "codified program" now becomes a negative image of bondage); it arises on the spot from the creativity of those who are gathered.[36]

The cardinal continues: "The isolation of Matt. 18:20 from the entire biblical and ecclesiastical tradition of the common prayer of the Church has far-reaching consequences here. The Lord's promise to prayers of all places becomes the dogmatization of the autonomous group."[37] In such a perspective, "every given coming from the whole is a fetter one must resist for the sake of the freshness and freedom of the liturgical celebration. It is not obedience to the whole but the creativity of the moment that becomes the determining form."[38]

The attitude to the liturgical and musical traditions of the church in an emerging congregationalism is one of hostility and suspicion: "Traditional (and also conciliar!) concepts such as 'the treasury of *musica sacra*,' the 'organ as queen of the instruments,' and the 'universality of Gregorian chant' now appear as 'mystifications' for the purpose of 'preserving a certain form of power.'"[39] In this view, "Gregorian chant and Palestrina are tutelary gods of a mythicized, ancient repertoire, elements of a Catholic counterculture that is based on remythicized and supersacralized archetypes, just as in the historical liturgy of the Church it has been more a question of a cultic bureaucracy than of the singing activity of the people."[40] Cardinal Ratzinger here is basing his observations on a respected modern Italian encyclopedia on liturgy; thus he cannot fairly be accused of exaggerating.[41]

Worship as Feast

Beyond this, there exists the problem for sacred music created by debates over the nature of the liturgy itself. It is often said today, Cardinal Ratzinger points out, that the liturgy "should be made non-cultic and reduced to its very simple point of origin, a community meal."[42] But as this conviction plays itself out, the traditional understanding of the liturgy as feast falls away. When conceived as a feast, "the liturgy thrives on splendour and thus calls for the transfiguring power of art."[43] In the cardinal's words, "When exaggerated meal-theories fail to take this fundamental [feast] character of the liturgy into account, they no longer explain the essence of the liturgy but rather conceal it."[44] The result is that "where a genuine feast no longer exists, art becomes a mere museum piece, and this precisely in its most splendid manifestations."[45] The consequences are that "church music can continue to exist only in the form of congregational singing, which in turn is not to be judged in terms of its artistic value but only on the basis of its functionality, i.e., its 'community-building' and activating function."[46] This has led, as the cardinal sees it, to the view after Vatican II that "none of the traditional church music could satisfy the liturgical norms now in force: everything would have to be created anew."[47] Plainly, in this view, "liturgical music is not regarded as art, but as a 'mere commodity.'"[48] The music of the splendid feast is replaced by the music of the utilitarian meal.[49]

We may conclude from Cardinal Ratzinger's analysis, as I have briefly summarized it, that deep theological, ecclesiastical, and cultural problems are today imbedded in the conceptual and practical structures of Catholic liturgy and its musical expression. The dynamics of spiritualization of a particular kind continue to create a deep prejudice against music itself. The outlook of rationalism generates an intolerance of the emotional and expressive ambiguities of musical praise. The suspicion of Christian culture means a rejection and abandonment of the traditional heritage of music. Functionalism is intolerant of liturgical music's aspirations to artistic significance. Iconoclasm, fearful of imagery in worship, is theologically inhospitable to the aural imagery of musical art. Congregationalism rejects complexity and received forms in favor of institutional immediacy and the preeminence of local creativity. The collapse of the festive and the splendid in the liturgy and its replacement by the functional clearly takes with it the great tradition of sacred music, replacing it with the "utility music" that Cardinal Ratzinger criticizes at the outset.

LITURGY AS OPUS DEI

Cardinal Ratzinger's analysis of the state of liturgical music is not, as I said at the beginning, merely negative; far from it. The identification of problems and analysis of their particular character are, he himself states, a necessary prerequisite to constructing a positive theology of Christian liturgy and its musical forms. The positive and constructive aspects of Cardinal Ratzinger's theology of liturgical music, which may be regarded as the necessary reversal of the analysis already portrayed, are embedded within the theological circles of liturgy, ecclesial life, human history, and divine revelation.

For Cardinal Ratzinger, the liturgy is the *opus Dei*, enacted in and through the church's *communio sanctorum* of all places and times, an act of being and participation, bearing three ontological dimensions: history, mystery, and cosmos. This framework provides rich and detailed attention to liturgical music in its most profound, synthetic, and comprehensive dimensions.

That the liturgy is *opus Dei*, the work of God, is, for Cardinal Ratzinger, a starting point of the greatest importance. The affirmation of the liturgy as *opus Dei* stands in opposition to the notion that formal acts of worship are the work of any particular group or congregation. It is not unusual in liturgical discourse in the United States today to hear that the worshiping assembly is the primary symbol or subject of the liturgy.[50] When proposed in a precise theological sense, the assertion has truth, albeit somewhat tautologously. Yet, when understood in an undifferentiated and unqualified manner, a serious distortion easily and quickly develops. In Cardinal Ratzinger's words: "Where all act so that they themselves may become the subject, the One who truly acts in the liturgy also disappears with the collective subject 'Church.'"[51] As a result, "the group celebrates itself and in doing so celebrates nothing at all. For it is no cause for celebration. That is why the general activity becomes boredom. Nothing happens when he whom the whole world awaits is absent."[52] The liturgy loses its fundamental subjectivity in God and is conceptually situated instead in self-referential human activity. The cardinal thinks that a recovery is critically necessary today of the conception that "the liturgy is to be the opus Dei in which God himself acts first and we are redeemed precisely through the fact that he acts."[53] The conception of the liturgy as a participation in the triune dialogue between Father, Son, and Holy Spirit is foundational for the development of a constructive theology of worship.[54] The liturgy is not primarily a human doing, but is God's action in, with, and through the church and all its particular manifestations.

This act of God, the *opus Dei*, is enacted within the mediacy of the *communio sanctorum*, the whole church of heaven and earth, the church of all times and all ages. Once again, Cardinal Ratzinger opposes the notion that the liturgy is fundamentally the act of this or that group. It is, he says, fundamental that the conception of the whole church of heaven and earth as active and present in the liturgy be rediscovered, the church understood not as an "institution inimical to man, but one in which there is the new We in which the I can first win its foundation and its dwelling."[55]

It follows that if in the liturgy God himself is the principal actor and the whole church is its performative arena, the liturgy may not be conceived of primarily as an *activity*, but as a mode of *being* in the life of God. The cardinal here invokes Romano Guardini, who "stressed emphatically that in the liturgy it is not a question of *doing* something but of *being* something."[56] Put simply, the liturgy is not primarily something the church or a group makes, something actively instituted. It is something *received*, and in which believers participate receptively.

Inspired by Guardini, Cardinal Ratzinger sums up the basic understanding of liturgy he espouses:

> The realization that the genuine subject of the liturgy is the Church, that is the *communio sanctorum* of all places and all times, is, from this point of view, really of great importance. For as Guardini showed in detail in his early writing, *Liturgische Bildung*, there follows from this realization a removal of the liturgy from the caprice of the group and individual (including clerics and specialists).[57]

Ontological Dimensions

Cardinal Ratzinger goes on to speak of the liturgy in terms of three ontological dimensions: the cosmological, historical, and mysteriological—all of which are profoundly interconnected and mutually generative.

The Historical Dimension

The historical dimension refers to the evident truth that the church's worship possesses an actual history. The liturgy is a living reality that "has a beginning, continues in effect, remains present but is not yet finished, and lives only insofar as it is further developed."[58] In the historical process, "many things die out, many things are forgotten and return later in a new way, but development always means participation in a beginning opened to what lies ahead."[59] A most important implication of this attention to the historical dimension of the liturgy is that, "No one is its one and only creator, for each one is a participant in something greater, but each one is also an agent precisely because he is a recipient."[60]

To say that liturgy has a historical dimension is to recognize that it has a pre-existence, thus a stability, a power, and an authority beyond the creativity of the immediate or specific group. When liturgical history is denied, there appears as a consequence a creativity which inappropriately asserts individual and group autonomy. Such a view encourages "unrepeatability" in liturgical events, giving rise to the direct antithesis to the "objectivity and positivity that belong to the essence of the Church's liturgy. The group always has to fabricate itself anew, only then is it free."[61]

If the liturgy and its music are not constitutively from the individual or group—that is, do not originate in them—from where do they come? Cardinal Ratzinger's answer is that the liturgy is "Spirit-guided;" it is a medium "molded by the Word."[62] The liturgy has an objectivity founded in and sustained historically by God's revealing and saving activity. It grows out of the historical reality of the Word becoming flesh and dwelling among humankind in glory. The continuing reality of the Word incarnate, generating and sustaining the liturgical life of the church, is solidified in the declaration of Christ: "I am going now, but I shall return to you. It is by going that I return. It is good that I go, for only in this way can you receive the Holy Spirit" (John 14:2; 14:18; 16:5).[63] Christ's ongoing presence in and with the church is the very source of the liturgy itself. In the events of the Word made flesh and the action of the Spirit ever renewed, Christ "carries the flesh, i.e., man and the whole created world, into the eternity of God."[64] The word *carry* is most expressive here in that it suggests in one more way the pre-existence and properly autonomous agency and dynamism of the liturgy.

Some would criticize Cardinal Ratzinger for downplaying the manner in which human creativity acts to shape and mold the liturgy. Yet the cardinal's principal objective is not to discourage genuine creativity but to offer an important corrective to the manner in which the liturgy is often conceived today as a human or congregational fabrication. In view of the extent of postconciliar misunderstanding, the cardinal understandably goes to great lengths to underscore that the liturgy possesses a divinely constituted autonomy, a pre-given character, and an objectivity that may not be compromised. Liturgy and its music are in great part, the cardinal holds, *given* to us, and their constitutive inspiration and effective power are beyond that to which an individual or particular group may lay claim. As Cardinal Ratzinger puts it: "At bottom, great works of Church music can only be bestowed because the transcendence of self, which is not achievable by man alone, is involved."[65] This means, in turn, a willingness to submit to what we have not created, but what is offered to us by the genius of a greater tradition. The composer must have a similar receptivity to tradition; he or she is not primarily fabricator but inspired recipient. "To this extent, reverence, receptivity, and the humility that is ready to serve by participating in the great works that have already issued forth necessarily stand at the beginning of great sacred music."[66]

The Mysteriological Dimension

The second of the ontological dimensions of liturgy elaborated in Cardinal Ratzinger's scheme is that of mystery. The dimension of mystery cannot, of course, be separated fundamentally from the historical and the cosmic, and all that is said of each dimension implies the existence of the other two. To say that liturgy has a dimension of mystery is to say that in its various forms and specifically in its music, God discloses himself. The Word of God takes flesh in music, so that liturgical music may be said to have a sacramental, revelatory, holy character. God is the model of human creativity, and human artistic creativity is the discovery of "the beauty that is already waiting and concealed in creation."[67] To spell this out, the cardinal refers to Old Testament psalmody, specifically to Psalm 47, which contains the line "sing artistically for God," on which he sets out a musical theology of the psalms.[68] In contrast to those Christian theologies suspicious of music, "the psalms manifest an utterly unpuritanical delight in music."[69] This delight in the Lord was felt to be meaningful and beautiful in itself and to be a powerful expression of the presence and the glory of God. "The Creator's glory cannot be manifested in word only: it needs to be expressed in the music of creation, too."[70] Music is a means by which God relates to humanity and through which the human person ascends to God: "Praise itself is a movement, a path; it is more than understanding, knowing and doing—it is an 'ascent,' a way of reaching him who dwells amid the praises of the angels."[71] Liturgy and its musical expression constitute a response to the call and presence of the self-disclosing God. They demand from the worshiper a "yes," an obedience.[72]

Consistent with this conviction, the cardinal emphasizes the strongly contemplative and receptive element of liturgical music. While the Second Vatican Council emphasized active participation, it did not intend to do so in such a way as to suggest that congregational singing is the only proper mode of musical participation. If music embodies the mystery of God in the liturgy, this requires of the worshiper a correspondingly deep and attentive musical receptivity. Cardinal Ratzinger spells out the practical implications of this for actual musical performance in the liturgy:

> There are a good number of people who can sing better "with the heart" than "with the mouth"; but their hearts are really stimulated to sing through the singing of those who *have* the gift of singing "with their mouths." It is as if they themselves actually sing in the others; their thankful listening is united with the voices of the singers in the one worship of God."[73]

Accordingly, the cardinal does not accept the notion that church music can continue to exist only in the form of congregational singing. The choir also is most important and it has a representative character, a role of deputyship which provides a powerful form of general participation in the liturgy.[74] That liturgy is mystery, then, invites the recognition that music is not primarily human activity directed toward God, but God's activity toward humanity—to which the latter responds not by self-centered initiatives but by an active receptivity and the profound contemplation, obedience, and appropriation that true hearing implies.

The Cosmic Dimension

The third of the three intertwined dimensions of the liturgy for Cardinal Ratzinger is the cosmic. By this, the cardinal means that the liturgy is in its ontological structure an event of heaven and earth, an action of all creation founded in the divine. The liturgy, he says, must "orchestrate the mystery of Christ with all the voices of creation."[75] This is what the process of glorification means. The church, then, "must not settle down with what is merely comfortable and serviceable at the parish level; she must arouse the voice of the cosmos and, by glorifying the Creator, elicit the glory of the cosmos itself, making it also glorious, beautiful, habitable and beloved."[76] The liturgy is a participation in the cosmic heavenly liturgy, indeed is "anticipated parousia."[77]

That the liturgy has a cosmic dimension means that it must have more than a grim predictability or utility founded in the needs of the isolated group. The liturgy is properly an event of all creation, an act of the whole temple of God. Since the temple of the New Covenant dwells where Jesus Christ dwells, namely in heaven and in the church wherein God's people are gathered, "the Church's liturgy, which now regards the whole cosmos as its temple, must have a cosmic character, must make the whole cosmos resound."[78] On this, Cardinal Ratzinger quotes Erik Peterson:

> It is not pure coincidence that the medieval music theorists begin their treatises by referring to the harmony of the spheres. Since the Church's hymn of praise tunes in to the praises of the cosmos, any consideration of the musical element in the Church's cult must also take into account the sort of praise offered by sun, moon, and stars.[79]

The cardinal comments:

> What this means *in concreto* becomes clearer when we recall the prayer in Ps. Cyprian which speaks of God as the One Who is praised by angels, archangels, martyrs, apostles and prophets, "to whom all the birds sing praises, whom the tongues of those in heaven, upon the earth and under the earth glorify: all the waters in heaven and under the heavens confess Thee."[80]

Cardinal Ratzinger asserts that in this context

> church music with artistic pretensions is not opposed to the essence of Christian liturgy, but is rather a necessary way of expressing belief in the world-filling glory of Jesus Christ. The Church's liturgy has a compelling mandate to reveal in resonant sound the glorification of God which lies hidden in the cosmos. This, then, is the liturgy's essence: to transpose the cosmos, to spiritualize it into the gesture of praise through song and thus to redeem it; to "humanize" the world.[81]

The cardinal summarizes his conception of the cosmic dimension of the liturgy very expressively by referring to something Mahatma Gandhi wrote:

> Gandhi refers to the three living spaces of the cosmos and to the way in which each of these living spaces has its own mode of being. Fish live in the sea, and they are silent. Animals on the earth cry. But the birds, whose living space is the heavens, sing. Silence is proper to the sea, crying to the earth and singing to the heavens. Man, however, has a share in all three.

> He bears within himself the depths of the sea, the burden of the earth, and the heights of heaven, and for that reason all three properties belong to him: silence, crying and singing.⁸²

The cardinal adds:

> We see how the cry is all that remains for the man without transcendence because he wills to be only earth and also attempts to make heaven and the depths of the sea into his earth. The right liturgy, the liturgy of the communion of saints, restores his totality to him. It teaches him silence and singing again by opening up the depths of the sea to him and by teaching him to fly like the angels. By lifting up his heart, it brings the song buried in him to sound again. Indeed, we can even say the reverse: one recognizes right liturgy in that it frees us from general activity and restores to us again the depths and the heights, quiet and song. One recognizes right liturgy in that it has a cosmic not a group character. It sings with the angels. It is silent with the waiting depths of the universe. And thus it redeems the earth.⁸³

MUSIC, INCARNATION, AND CULTURE

Building on what has already been set forth, Cardinal Ratzinger's writings offer further specific considerations on the incarnational character of music, the anthropological and sociological structures of music as a human phenomenon, and the question of musical styles in the liturgy. These reflections find their starting point once again in the reality of the Incarnation.⁸⁴ The Word of God entering history takes shape in the whole cosmos, assuming its definitive incarnate form in Christ and then in the church. The Word in the church is not merely verbal, of course; it is effected in the sacraments, which are the central modalities in which the Incarnation is elongated historically. The whole sacramental and liturgical system forms an expansion of the Word into the realms of the bodily and that of all the human senses. The Word of God finds expression in a process the cardinal calls the "musification" of the Word, itself a feature of the incarnational process by which "the flesh itself is 'logicized.'"⁸⁵

As the Word takes flesh, it draws into itself and reshapes the diversity of created things and the multifaceted dynamics of the human world. As all the features of creation are shaped and conformed to the cross of Christ, so, too, is music. This means a process of the attraction and reshaping of "pre-rational and trans-rational forces, attraction of the hidden sounds of creation, discovery of the song that lies at the bottom of things."[86]

As the " 'spiritualization' of the flesh" occurs, "wood and metal become tone, the unconscious and the unreleased become ordered and meaningful sound. A corporealization takes place which is a spiritualization, and a spiritualization which is a corporealization."[87] The Word takes form in music; music is assumed into the Word.

In Christian liturgy, then, there is a profound and magnificent interplay between word, music, and rite. Word and rite, founded in the incarnation, reach out and draw the world of music into the shape of the mystery enacted and celebrated in the liturgy. Accordingly, authentic liturgical music may be said to result "from the claim and the dynamics of the Incarnation of the Word."[88] Sacred music serves the process by which humanity is assumed into the life-giving glory of God— a facility of music that gives it its powerfully transformative and transcending agency.

Intrinsic to this whole process is the transformation that necessarily occurs to music so that it is adequate to its liturgical role. Not all musical forms and styles, according to the cardinal, fit the liturgy. Here Cardinal Ratzinger invokes the familiar platonic distinction between the Apollonian and Dionysian in music. He writes:

> Let us think first of all, for example, of the Dionysian type of religion and music with which Plato grappled from the standpoint of his religious and philosophical view. In not a few forms of religion, music is ordered to intoxication and ecstasy. The freedom from the limitations of being human towards which the hunger for the infinite proper to man is directed is to be attained through holy madness, through the frenzy of the rhythm and of the instruments. Such music lowers the barriers of individuality and of personality. Man frees himself in it from the burden of consciousness. Music becomes ecstasy, liberation from the ego, and unification with the universe. We experience the profane return of this type today in rock and pop music, the festivals of which are an anti-culture of the same orientation— the pleasure of destruction, the abolition of everyday barriers, and the illusion of liberation from the ego in the wild ecstasy of noise and masses.[89]

This kind of redemption, the cardinal says, is thoroughly opposed to that offered by the Christian faith:

> Because rock music seeks redemption by way of liberation from the personality and its responsibility, it takes, in one respect, a very precise

position in the anarchical ideas of freedom which predominate today in a more unconcealed way in the West than in the East. But precisely for that reason, it is thoroughly opposed to the Christian notion of redemption and of freedom as its exact contradiction. Not for aesthetic reasons, not from reactionary obstinacy, not from historical immobility, but because of its very nature music this type must be excluded from the Church.[90]

The cardinal goes on analyze the anthropological grounding of different types of music:

> There is agitation music which animates man for different collective purposes. There is sensual music which leads man into the erotic or essentially aims in other ways at sensual feelings of pleasure. There is light music which does not wish to say anything but only to break up the burden of silence. There is rationalistic music in which the tones serve only rational constructions but in which no real penetration of spirit and sensibility results.[91]

However, "The music that corresponds to the liturgy of the incarnate Christ raised up on the cross lives from another, greater and broader synthesis of spirit, intuition, and sensuous sound."[92] To be authentic, liturgical music must be christologically transformed.[93]

In this context, Cardinal Ratzinger offers an evaluation of the church's tradition of music:

> One can say that Western music, from Gregorian chant through the cathedral music and the great polyphony, through the renaissance and baroque music up until Bruckner and beyond, has come from the inner wealth of this synthesis and developed it in the fullness of its possibilities. This greatness exists only here because it alone was able to grow out of this anthropological ground that joined the spiritual and the profane in an ultimate human unity. This unity is dissolved in the measure that this anthropological order disappears.[94]

This is why "the liturgical music of the Church must be ordered to that integration of human being that appears before us in faith in the Incarnation. Such a redemption is more laborious than that of intoxication. But this labor is the exertion of truth itself. In one respect, it must integrate the senses into the spirit; it must correspond to the impulse of the *sursum corda*."[95] The music of Christian faith "seeks the integration of man in the *sursum corda;* man does not find this integration in himself, but only in self-transcendence towards the Incarnate Word."[96] Accordingly, "sacred music, which stands in the structure of this movement, thus becomes the purification and the ascent of man."[97] Liturgical music, to be authentic, must be christologically transformed.[98]

The cardinal does not deny that a similar process of the "musification" of Catholic faith can occur in the non-Western cultures of the world. He is not by any means canonizing Western classical music, although he does not hesitate to assert that the processes of "musification" have been exceptionally well achieved in Western music. "The work of a Palestrina or a Mozart would be unthinkable apart from this dramatic interplay in which creation becomes the instrument of the spirit, and the spirit, too, becomes organized sound in the material creation."[99] He does insist, however, that a certain caution is required in the whole matter of cultural adaptation of the liturgy, particularly in its musical aspect. "The taking up of music into the liturgy must be its taking up into the Spirit, a transformation which implies both death and resurrection. That is why the Church has had to be critical of all ethnic music; it could not be allowed untransformed into the sanctuary."[100] If music is to be the medium of the Spirit in the variety of cultural situations, it needs purifying; "only then can it in turn have a purifying and 'elevating' effect."[101]

For the cardinal, it is in the dynamics of an exceptional interplay of Word, Spirit, and music in history that are found the theological and practical criteria and protocols for music in the liturgy. The degree to which music discovers and embodies the excellence of the Logos in history is the degree of its liturgical and, therefore, artistic excellence. The products of the success of this historical process constitute what Vatican II calls the "treasury of sacred music"—which, the cardinal points out, is offered as the norm and point of departure for all new compositions and developments. For the cardinal, then, music is sacred or profane not in itself but in accordance with its ability to be assumed into and serve the liturgy. Musical styles which resist such an assumption and fail such service are what constitute the profane in the liturgical arena. The cardinal here points to two criteria for liturgical appropriateness of music. First, particular forms "must correspond to the demands of the great liturgical texts—the *Kyrie, Gloria, Credo, Sanctus, Agnus Dei.*"[102] The second criterion is reference to Gregorian chant and to Palestrina, which provide a fundamental basis for ongoing development.[103] Cardinal Ratzinger is not espousing here a restrictive assessment of liturgical appropriateness but is offering norms for orientation and direction: "What may arise through the creative appropriation of such an orientation is not to be established in advance."[104] Indeed, the cardinal points favorably to the possibilities inherent in "a new blossoming of faith in Africa, Asia, and Latin America from which new cultural forms may sprout forth."[105]

Conclusion

Cardinal Ratzinger's theology of music provides, as I stated at the outset, remarkable insight into the modern crisis of the liturgy and its music. The crisis, he is convinced, has deep ecclesiological, theological, and anthropological roots. His analysis of the problems that the church experiences today in its liturgy and music goes a long way in helping to articulate the present intuitions that bother many but seem to elude adequate statement. The cardinal's theology of liturgy and its music as *opus Dei* in the midst of the *communio sanctorum,* unifying history and cosmos in an eternal festival of divine worship, is as rich as any I know.

---

1. Joseph Cardinal Ratzinger with Vittorio Messori, *The Ratzinger Report: An Exclusive Interview on the State of the Church* (San Francisco: Ignatius Press, 1985) esp. 119–34. All sources cited in this essay are by Joseph Ratzinger unless noted otherwise.

2. "Church Music in the Cathedral of Regensburg, 1964–1994: Betwixt and Between the Regensburg Tradition and Postconciliar Reform," *Sacred Music* 122:2 (Summer 1995) 5–17. A later version of this essay appears under the title " 'In the Presence of Angels I will Sing Your Praise:' The Regensburg Tradition and the Reform of the Liturgy," in *A New Song for the Lord: Faith in Christ and Liturgy Today* (New York: Crossroad Publishing, 1996) 128–46; hereafter cited as "The Regensburg Tradition." For the German original, see "In der Spannung zwischen Regensburger Tradition und nachkonziliarer Reform," *Musica Sacra* 114 (1994) 379–89. I am indebted to Robert F. Skeris and Anthony Ruff, OSB, for information on the German originals of the principal essays quoted in this article.

3. This essay was written before the publication of Cardinal Ratzinger's work, *The Spirit of the Liturgy,* trans. John Saward (San Francisco: Ignatius Press, 2000), which contains one chapter entitled, "Music and Liturgy." No attempt has been made or thought necessary to adapt this essay in light of the more recent material.

4. See the various essays in *The Feast of Faith: Approaches to a Theology of the Liturgy* (San Francisco: Ignatius Press, 1986); also in *A New Song for the Lord.* For a useful introduction to the cardinal's thought, with a bibliography spanning the years 1954–1986, see Aidan Nichols, OP, *The Theology of Joseph Ratzinger: An Introductory Study* (Edinburgh: T. and T. Clark, 1988) esp. 207–24.

5. "Liturgy and Sacred Music," *Communio* 13:4 (Winter 1986) 377–78; hereafter cited as "Sacred Music." A version of this essay appears in a documented supplement as "Liturgy and Church Music," in Robert A. Skeris, *Divini Cultus Studium: Studies in the Theology of Worship and of Its Music* (Altötting: Alfred Coppenrath, 1990) 185–97. See also the chapter entitled, "The Image of the World and of Human Beings in the Liturgy and Its Expression in Church Music," in *A New Song for the Lord,* 111–27. For the original, see "Liturgie und Kirchenmusik," *Musices Aptatio Yearbook 1986* (Rome: Consociatio Internationalis Musicae Sacrae, 1986) 60–74.

6. "Sacred Music," 377.

7. "Theological Problems of Church Music," in Robert Skeris, ed., *Crux et Cithara: Selected Essays on Liturgy and Sacred Music* (Altötting: Alfred Coppenrath, 1983) 214; hereafter cited as "Theological Problems." For the original, see "Theologische Probleme der Kirchenmusik," *Communio: Internationale Katholische Zeitschrift* 9 (1980) 148–57.

8. "Theological Problems," 214.

9. "'Sing Artistically for God': Biblical Directives for Church Music," *A New Song for the Lord,* 104–105; hereafter cited as "Biblical Directives." For the original, see "Biblische Vorgaben für die Kirchenmusik," in *Brixner Initiative Musik U. Kirche: 3. Symposium "Choral und Mehrstimmigkeit"* (Brixen: Verlag A. Weger, 1990) 9–21.

10. "On the Theological Basis of Church Music," in *The Feast of Faith,* 97; hereafter cited as "Theological Basis." The original appears as "Zur theologischen Grundlegung der Kirchenmusk," in Franz Fleckenstein, ed., *Gloria Deo-Pax Hominibus,* Festschrift zum 100 jährigen Bestehen der Kirchenmusikschule Regensburg (Bonn: Allgemeiner Caecilianverband, Sekretariat, 1974) 39–62.

11. "Theological Basis," 97–98. See Karl Rahner and Herbert Vorgrimler, *Kleines Konzilskompendium,* 2nd ed. (Freiburg: Herder, 1967) 48.

12. "Theological Basis," 98. A specific program for the continued use of Masses from the church's "treasury" is set out in "The Regensburg Tradition," 141–46. See also Anthony Ruff, OSB, "The Choral Sanctus After Vatican II?" *Antiphon* 2:3 (1997) 18–23.

13. "Theological Basis," 198.

14. ___, 100.

15. ___.

16. ___, 103; See Jerome, *Comm in ep ad Eph* III 5, PL 26: 258, C–D. See also "Biblical Directives," 104–105.

17. "Theological Basis," 106.

18. ___, 111.

19. ___, 110.

20. ___.

21. ___, 112.

22. ___, 113.

23. ___.

24. This problem finds possibly its strongest expression in what may be described as the ritual-functional paradigm of church music associated in Europe with Universa Laus and in the United States with the document, *The Milwaukee Symposia for Church Composers: A Ten-Year Report* (Washington, DC: The National Association of Pastoral Musicians, 1992).

25. "Theological Problems," 214.

26. ___.

27. ___; also "The Regensburg Tradition," 130–32.

28. "Theological Problems," 216.

29. ___, 217.

30. ___.

31. ___.

32. ___, note 7.

33. ___, 216.

34. ___.

35. ___; also "The Regensburg Tradition," 128–30.

36. "Sacred Music," 378.

37. ___, 379.

38. ___; also "The Regensburg Tradition," 132–35.

39. "Sacred Music," 379.

40. ___.

41. See Felice Rainoldi and Eugenio Costa, "Canto e musica," in *Nuovo dizionario di Liturgia,* ed. Domenico Sartore and Achille M. Triacca (Rome: Ed. Paoline, 1984) 199ff.

42. "Theological Problems, 214.

43. ___, 215.

44. ___.

45. ___.

46. ___, 214.

47. ___.

48. ___.

49. The necessity of the renewal of the eschatological features of liturgical music is set forth in The Snowbird Statement on Catholic Liturgical Music (Salt Lake City: The Madeleine Institute, 1995), especially in the following: "The choir bears witness to the eschatological fulfillment of the church, the song of which prefigures that of the saints and angelic choirs in the New Jerusalem; the choir is a joyful attendant of the pilgrim people of God and a festive sign of their heavenly home" (no. 20). What is said of the choir applies equally to all forms and expressions of liturgical music.

50. The apparent origin of this principle is no. 28 of *Environment and Art in Catholic Worship*, National Conference of Catholic Bishops/Bishops' Committee on the Liturgy (Chicago: Liturgy Training Publications, 1986), which states: "Among the symbols with which liturgy deals, none is more important than this assembly of believers" (8).

51. "Sacred Music," 382.

52. ___.

53. ___.

54. ___, 383.

55. ___, 382. For a useful elaboration of this dimension of the liturgy, see Catherine Pickstock, *After Writing: On the Liturgical Consummation of Philosophy* (Oxford: Blackwell Publishers, 1998) esp. 180ff.

56. "Sacred Music," 383.

57. See Romano Guardini, *Liturgische Bildung. I: Versuche* (Rothenfels: Deutsche Quickbornhaus, 1923); with a revised edition under the title *Liturgie und liturgische Bildung* (Wüzburg: Werkbund–Verlag, 1966). See also the essay entitled "Von der Liturgie zur Christologie," in Josef Ratzinger, ed., *Wege zur Wahreit: Die bleibende Bedeutung von Romano Guardini* (Dusseldorf: Patmos Verlag, 1985) 121–44.

58. "Sacred Music," 383–84.

59. ___, 384.

60. ___.

61. ___.

62. ___, 385.

63. ___, 386.

64. ___.

65. ___, 389.

66. ___.

67. "Biblical Directives," 102–103.

68. ___, esp. 96–103; 109–110.

69. "Theological Basis," 114.

70. ___, 115.

71. ___, 116.

72. "Sacred Music," 384.

73. "Theological Basis," 124.

74. See "The Regensburg Tradition," 139–41; also Karl-Heinz Menke, *Stellvertretung: Schlüsselbegriff christlichen Lebens und theologische Grundkategorie* (Einsiedeln-Freiburg: Johannes Verlag, 1991).

75. "Theological Basis," 115.

76. ___ 24.

77. "The Regensburg Tradition," 129.

78. "Theological Problems," 220.

79. ___. The reference is from Erik Peterson, *The Angels and the Liturgy* (New York: Herder and Herder, 1964), 29.

80. "Theological Problems," 220; see Erickson, *The Angels and the Liturgy*, 22–23. The cardinal comments in this context on the cosmology attending the liturgical use of the organ: "The organ is a theological instrument whose original home was the cult of the emperor. When the Emperor of Byzantium spoke, an organ played. On the other hand the organ was supposed to be the combination of all the voices of the cosmos. Accordingly, the organ music at imperial utterances meant that when the divine emperor spoke, the entire universe resounded. As a divine utterance, his statement is the resounding of all the voices in the cosmos. The 'organon' is the cosmic instrument and as such the voice of the world's ruler, the *imperator*" ("Theological Problems," 220).

81. "Theological Problems," 221. The reader will note the striking resemblance of the cardinal's expressions here with the rich cosmological vision of the liturgy set out in the *Catechism of the Catholic Church*, esp. in nos. 1136–39.

82. "Sacred Music," 390.

83. ___, 390–91.

84. ___, esp. 385ff.

85. ___, 386. The cardinal also speaks of "the musification of faith" and the process by which "the flesh itself is 'logicized'."

86. "Sacred Music," 386.

87. ___.

88. ___.

89. ___, 387.

90. ___, 387–88. The further refinement of the cardinal's thought that has occurred since these words were written offers a more subtle distinction between the rhythmic music of genuine folk genres and commercialized Western rock or "pop" music. Thus the cardinal would not reject genuine folk elements in the church's liturgical music repertoire. See "Biblical Directives," 95–96; 107–109.

91. "Sacred Music," 388.

92. ___.

93. "Biblical Directives," 103–105.

94. "Sacred Music," 388.

95. ___.

96. ___, 388–89.

97. ___, 389.

98. "Biblical Directives," 103–105.

99. "Theological Basis," 119.

100. ___, 118.

101. ___, 119.

102. "Sacred Music," 389.

103. "Biblical Directives," 105; "The Regensburg Tradition," 136.

104. "Sacred Music," 389.

105. ___. In this matter, I do not find compelling the arguments that Cardinal Ratzinger espouses a restrictive or closed classicism regarding future developments in liturgical music. See, for instance, Jan Michael Joncas, "Whose Culture? Whose Tradition? Educational Challenges," *Pastoral Music* 14 (1990) 32, note 9.

Part IV

The Liturgical Future

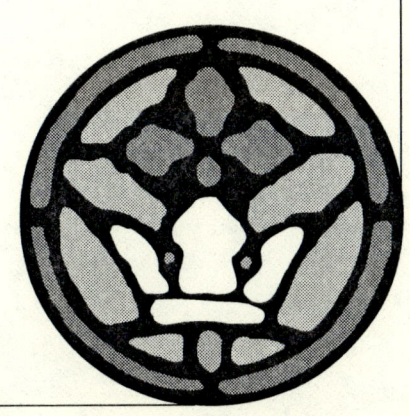

Chapter 9

The Catholicity of the Liturgy: Shaping a New Agenda

On a regular basis over the past two decades, the need for a new liturgical movement in Catholicism has been proposed in various quarters. No new movement of the high profile envisaged as desirable by many presently exists and certainly none of those now operational seems entirely capable of unifying the disparate directions proposed for Catholic liturgy as it moves into the third millennium. What liturgical movement does exist today seems highly diffuse and appears to fan out in a variety of directions. In this essay, I will suggest that, in fact, there exist at present not one but five identifiable liturgical movements in the English-speaking world, particularly in that part with which I am most familiar: the United States. These take the form of five distinct agendas of liturgical reform, which I propose to treat under the following headings: advancing official reform; restoring the preconciliar; reforming the reform; inculturating the reform; and recatholicizing the reform. An understanding of the character and ideals of the various agendas is a necessary prelude to discussion about the future shape of Catholic liturgical renewal, which, I shall suggest, will be most adequately served by the agenda of *recatholicizing the reform*.[1]

It is necessary to preface this analysis with the appropriate cautions about the dangers of a methodology of agenda differentiation. I learned the fundamental elements of this methodology from my teacher Avery Dulles who has used such an approach in many of his writings to bring at least tentative clarity to complicated theological data.[2] Following Dulles, I would protest that my aim is neither to suggest clearer lines of distinction between the various agendas than exist in reality nor to box individuals and groups in, as though ecclesial life is free of overlap, complexity, or ambiguity. My approach will, I hope, have the general strengths of the methodology employed, principally clarity; but it will also have the weaknesses, mainly simplicity tending toward excessive simplification. I am aware that the various existing liturgical agendas are not entirely separate, free of overlap, or mutually exclusive. While there exists a considerable variety of opinions and commitments within the perspectives I shall identify, it can readily be admitted that some elements of difference are more a matter of emphasis or of priority than of fundamental principle. At the same time, the differences between the various agendas should not be underestimated. As will become clear, each of these agendas stands in a particular relationship to the Constitution on the Sacred Liturgy of the Second Vatican Council, and each may be seen as based on a particular reading of the Constitution.

The Official Agenda

The first of the agendas presently operative I propose to call "advancing official reform." This agenda, which has its roots in the more theologically and historically conscious features of the modern liturgical movement, was formulated immediately after the Second Vatican Council and institutionalized in the Consilium for the Implementation of the Constitution on the Sacred Liturgy established in 1964, in the Congregation for Divine Worship in 1969 (into which the Consilium was subsumed), and in the subsequent evolution of that congregation. Because of its official character, this agenda regards itself with considerable justification as the legitimate executor of the program for liturgical reform set forth in the Constitution on the Sacred Liturgy. The principal fruits of the official agenda are the actual revised liturgical books of the Catholic Church as we now know and celebrate them.

The agenda of advancing official reform is concretized in the work of the Bishops' Committee on the Liturgy in the United States and in the various liturgy secretariats of the English-speaking episcopal conferences.[3] Today this agenda finds notable focus in the deliberations and activities of the International Commission on English in the Liturgy (ICEL), founded during the Council to provide a cooperative agency in translation matters for the episcopates of the English-speaking world.

This agenda operates in liturgical faculties of the more conservative kind, most notable among which is Sant' Anselmo in Rome. Its principal organs include *Ecclesia Orans, Notitiae,* the various progress reports and communications from ICEL, and the official newsletters and publications of the liturgy secretariats of the various episcopal conferences. Organizations in the United States such as the Federation of Diocesan Liturgical Commissions and We Believe! are strongly supportive and even occasionally defensive of the official agenda. If the organizations just mentioned belong on the more progressive end of this agenda, it seems fair to say that the present Congregation for Divine Worship and the Discipline of the Sacraments stand on the more conservative end.[4]

The most comprehensive narrative account of the agenda of advancing official reform based on the trajectory established by the postconciliar Consilium is found in Archbishop Annibale Bugnini's work, published in 1990, entitled *The Reform of the Liturgy 1948–1975*.[5] Indeed, Bugnini himself may be regarded as among the principal authors and advocates of this agenda. His book is probably the most insightful guide to the history of liturgical reform from the Constitution on the Sacred Liturgy through the massive revision of the liturgical books, to its present focal point, as far as the English-speaking world is concerned, in the work of ICEL.

The agenda I am describing here is, by its official character, the norm and standard around which the various other agendas I will identify are organized. For this reason, the other agendas may be seen in one way or another as centering on points of criticism or some form of questioning or probing of the official agenda.

In a certain sense, the official agenda is the most challenging to define, because it is so monumental and all-embracing. This agenda operated after the Council, as the Constitution on the Sacred Liturgy indicated it must, with a high and unified theological consciousness in which the liturgical life of the church was connected more adequately to trinitarian doctrine, christology, ecclesiology, and eschatology. It followed a path conceived within a set of dialectics: tradition and progress; unity and diversity; simplicity and complexity. An overriding concern was the renewal of the active participation of the Christian people and the need to reestablish diverse ministerial roles within the worshiping assembly. The operational principles of this agenda included arriving at lucidity of liturgical understanding; recovery of the instructive facility of the liturgy; achieving "noble simplicity," clarity and brevity; and facilitating freedom from useless repetition and the necessity of much explanation.[6] The inspiration and ideal of the official agenda was the early Roman liturgy, the general features of which it sought to uncover and reappropriate in a methodologically scientific and historically critical manner. The scholarship of this agenda was from the beginning highly ecumenical, drawing upon Orthodox, Anglican, and Reformed sources.

Among the more notable features of this agenda since the Council has been its internally evolutionary character. The Consilium in charge of the specific reforms of the various liturgical books regarded its work as both an elaboration and development of the conciliar Constitution on the Sacred Liturgy.[7] The process of evolution found particular expression in the area of language. The conciliar Constitution allowed a very restricted use of the vernacular in the Mass, but it left open the way for appeals to the Holy See by episcopal conferences for more substantive concessions. Accordingly, restrictions on the use of the vernacular were progressively lifted in the face of requests from hierarchies throughout, until by 1971 the use of the vernacular in public Masses was left entirely to the judgment of particular conferences.[8]

The present projects of ICEL highlight a second notable feature of the official agenda: This is the two-phase understanding of the program of reform that has been operative for nearly two decades. In 1981, ICEL began a process of looking toward the systematic revision of the nearly thirty liturgical books issued since the Second Vatican Council. The current work of ICEL in proposing a new wave of changes is seen by its sponsors as a further legitimate development of the official conciliar and postconciliar programs. A key protocol for this aspect of the postconciliar agenda is found in the opening paragraph of the now controversial 1969 Instruction on the Translation of Liturgical Texts (*Comme le prévoit*) which states that, "after sufficient experiment and passage of time, all translations will need review."[9] This review process, now well advanced in the English-speaking world, envisages not only new translations but also original texts and some degree of ritual revision.[10]

Ongoing developments within the official agenda are not, of course, limited to ICEL, or to the English-speaking world. The various initiatives undertaken by the Congregation for Divine Worship and the Discipline of the Sacraments and by other Roman dicasteries, as well as by the Pope himself, are of primary importance. Chief among such developments is the third edition of the Roman Missal presently in vernacular translation. Proposals from a wide variety of scholarly and pastoral sources for additional liturgical reform within the trajectory of the official agenda established after the Second Vatican Council continue to be espoused in conferences and publications.[11]

We turn now to the two agenda groups that exist on the conservative or traditionalist end of the spectrum of present-day liturgical movements. The first of these is committed to what I shall call "restoring the preconciliar."

TRADITIONALISM AND RESTORATION

Among the restorationist agenda group, there exists a fundamental suspicion of the Second Vatican Council, of the Constitution on the Sacred Liturgy, and therefore of all liturgical developments, both theoretical and practical, subsequent to 1963. To more or lesser degrees, a conviction operates among adherents of this agenda group that the authentic liturgy of Catholicism has been compromised since the Second Vatican Council and that the Mass of 1969 is fundamentally objectionable because it is neither in continuity with the preconciliar liturgical order nor an adequate expression of the fullness of the mystery of faith.[12]

The followers of Archbishop Marcel Lefebvre and the clerical Society of St. Pius X, which include a diverse following in the English-speaking world, represent the more extreme exponents of the restorationist agenda. These are unambiguously and unalterably committed to the return of the so-called Tridentine Mass; no other avenue of liturgical development is acceptable.[13] This wing of the restorationist agenda fundamentally rejects the ability of any Pope to reform the Tridentine Mass and, for that reason, it objects in principle to the Missal of Paul VI.[14] Apologists of this school have argued variously that the Mass of Paul VI must be rejected due to its Protestant inspiration, its formal invalidity and the defective priestly intention it enshrines. The new Mass is said to be a symbol of resurgent modernism and an instrument of revolutionary errors in the church.[15]

Not all who espouse the restoration of the preconciliar have been so radical in their objections to liturgical reform.[16] Many Catholics whose loyalty to the Holy See remained strong sought forthrightly the restoration of the Tridentine Mass after 1970 without rejecting out of hand the Missal of Paul VI. All in all, however, Catholics of this persuasion remain most suspicious of the Second Vatican Council and they are deeply disappointed in what the postconciliar liturgical reforms have produced. The leadership of the Latin Liturgy Association in the United States expressed this outlook pointedly in writing recently that the Constitution on the Sacred Liturgy belongs to a set of "fallible human documents written by fallible human bishops as a result of a process which was not devoid of politicking."[17] In the writer's opinion, "much harm has been done to the Church by regarding the conciliar documents as the Revealed Word of God."[18] The commentary continued: "There is clearly no consensus within the Church on the important question of the Council's liturgical reforms"[19] and it concluded: "The ranks of those who regard the conciliar program on liturgy as being quite ill conceived are not limited to the ignorant and the embittered."[20]

The 1984 Vatican indult allowing the use of the old Mass under strictly controlled conditions and the more generous 1988 document *Ecclesia Dei* were proposed largely in response to increasing expressions of disaffection and even defection on the part of traditionalist Catholics.[21] The official provisions for the Tridentine Mass since 1984 seem to have provided some relief from the tense situation that was developing in Catholic traditionalist circles. A result was the reconciliation with the Holy See of some followers of Archbishop Lefebvre, creating in 1988 the Priestly Fraternity of St. Peter, now found in a number of dioceses in the United States and Europe. The traditionalist Benedictine monastery of St. Madeleine in Le Barroux in France seems to have become a center for those following and promoting the preconciliar rite.[22] Groups in the United States such as the Coalition in Support of *Ecclesia Dei* and the Traditional Mass Society have proposed initiatives, as yet unsuccessful, to advance a separate vicariate system for Catholics who seek a complete restoration of all features of the liturgical life of the church before the Second Vatican Council.[23]

The activities and perspectives of this agenda group may be gleaned from papers and newsletters such as *The Wanderer, The Remnant, Precious Blood Banner,* and *The Latin Mass.* Very little scholarly material has up to now been available in support of liturgical restorationism. The outlook of this agenda group calls to mind what scripture scholar Raymond Brown has described in other circumstances as "non-scholarly conservatism."[24] This does not mean that this agenda is, for this reason, to be dismissed; it is simply to recognize that it has a popular rather than an academic base. However, a movement to provide a scholarly foundation for this agenda seems to be underway more recently. While the center of such activities is Europe, notably France and Germany, developments are followed with a lively interest in traditionalist Mass circles in the United States. The movement "Renaissance Catholique" in France has taken the initiative of organizing in Paris, with the support of Cardinals Alfons Stickler and Silvio Oddi, the International Center for Liturgical Studies (CIEL), which seeks to provide a theological defense of the Tridentine Mass.[25]

William D. Dinges estimates that there are over 375 Tridentine Mass centers in the United States and that these are attended by between 15,000 and 20,000 Catholics. Nearly half of these centers are unauthorized, while the rest operate with official ecclesiastical approval. About half of American dioceses now sponsor regularly celebrated Tridentine Masses.[26]

Probably the mildest form of the restorationist agenda is that espoused by an indeterminate body of Catholics who have learned to live with the Mass of 1969, but whose preference would be for the Tridentine Mass.[27] Those who espouse the restoration of the preconciliar liturgy do not always argue for the discontinuation of the Mass of Paul VI; for some the coexistence of the various orders of the Mass is both acceptable and desirable.[28]

Reforming a Reform

Not all on the conservative or traditionalist end of the spectrum of liturgical positions are restorationists. A much more moderate grouping is committed to what has been described as "reforming the reform." This expression was popularized with the appearance of the book, *The Reform of the Roman Liturgy* by Klaus Gamber, published in English in 1993.[29]

The reform of the reform does not seek to restore the Tridentine Mass, but rather to return to what it regards as the true intentions of the Constitution on the Sacred Liturgy and to review in depth the processes and actual achievements of the liturgical reform. The proponents of this agenda have in common with Tridentine restorationism a strong, if less radical, dislike of much of what came after the Second Vatican Council, but, unlike the restorationists, they insist that they embrace fundamentally the vision of the Council and the

Constitution on the Sacred Liturgy. The critical concerns of this group are the programmatic decisions and initiatives of the postconciliar Consilium and the character of the reformed liturgical books themselves. The central program espoused in this agenda appears to be a revisitation of the 1962 Missal (and its 1965 and 1967 amendments) and a revision of the order of Mass in a less severe direction than actually occurred, in light of what proponents perceive to be the true intentions of the preconciliar liturgical movement and of the Second Vatican Council.

The broad lines of this agenda are set out as follows by Gamber: "It is generally accepted that, in one way or another, a liturgical reform, particularly an enrichment of the Roman rite, had become necessary because, since the Council of Trent, it had become ossified into a form of rubricism. There is also a consensus that the Constitution on the Sacred Liturgy of the Second Vatican Council corresponded in many respects to the legitimate pastoral requirements of our time. But no such consensus exists when we look at the reforms that were actually introduced, particularly the new liturgical books composed by a group of experts after the conclusion of the Council."[30] Gamber's book contains a testimonial by Wilhelm Nyssen that sharply identifies the focus of Gamber's discontent. "[Gamber] deplored the postconciliar *Instructions for the Implementation of the Constitution* because he felt that they had been published with undue haste, that their content was shallow, and that much of it was manifestly incompetent."[31]

The agenda to reform the reform has been taken up in the United States by Father Joseph Fessio and the leaders of the organization Adoremus: Society for the Renewal of the Sacred Liturgy. Adoremus is, in its own words, committed to "a complete rethinking and *authentic renewal* of the reform of the liturgy, using both *Sacrosanctum Concilium* and an evaluation of the experience of the postconciliar years to arrive at a renewed liturgy in keeping with the principles of the Second Vatican Council."[32] The guiding prescription invoked is article 23 of the Constitution on the Sacred Liturgy which states: "There must be no innovations unless the good of the Church genuinely and certainly requires them, and care must be taken that any new forms adopted should in some way grow organically from forms already existing."[33] This principle is clearly thought to have been offended against in the agenda of official reform.

As with the other agendas, a spectrum of positions exist within this one and a variety of perspectives are espoused. The actual project of reforming the reform has not by any means achieved complete clarity or unanimity. However, the leaders of this movement appear to share a common conviction that liturgical renewal has gone beyond anything legitimately envisaged by the Second Vatican Council; that the episcopate has in liturgical matters abdicated its authority to specialists and scholars; that ICEL bears much responsibility for the current state of affairs; and that an order of the Mass more closely related to the 1962 Missal than to the Mass of 1969 is desirable.

A more detailed account of how, in regard to the Mass, the reform of the reform might be carried out is found in the first issues of *Adoremus Bulletin*, which featured a three-part essay by Brian W. Harrison in late 1995 and early 1996. Harrison espouses the position of Gamber that the Roman rite has been destroyed in the postconciliar reforms and that a new rite of the Mass should now be created and instituted, "having *equal status and recognition* with the rite introduced by Paul VI."[34] Long-Term Solution," *Adoremus Bulletin*, January 1996, 1; emphasis in original. The other parts of this essay are "The Crisis in Eucharistic Faith: Implications for Post–Vatican II Reform," Adoremus Bulletin, November 1995, 1, 8; "Planning a 'Reform of the Reform:' Part II: Some Inadequate Solutions to the Eucharistic Liturgy Crisis," *Adoremus Bulletin*, December 1995, 1, 8. Significantly, the "Reform of the Reform" for which Harrison calls involves an explicit rejection of "the Traditionalist Proposal," that is, the view that the solution to the present crisis in Catholic worship is simply the restoration of the Mass as it was before the Council ("Planning a 'Reform of the Reform'," 8). This new rite would not displace the Mass of 1969, but would be regarded as "an alternative implementation of Vatican Council II."[35] Toward this end, Harrison calls for a modification of the Missal of 1962 in light of the principles of the Constitution on the Sacred Liturgy. Among his proposals are the following: the restoration of the recitation of the Canon in Latin; exclusive use of the Roman Canon; the restriction of communion to one species; priest and the people facing in the same direction during the eucharistic liturgy; the use of two scripture readings instead of three; and the exclusive use of men in liturgical ministries.[36]

How widely shared these proposals are in this agenda group, I am uncertain. Overall, my impression is that the directions outlined by Gamber and Harrison are received with considerable sympathy by many who speak generally of "reforming the reform." Cardinal Joseph Ratzinger wrote a preface to the French, but not the English, edition of Gamber's book and he has spoken positively of Harrison's proposals. Dominican theologian Aidan Nichols has suggested a direction similar to Harrison's in his recent book, *Looking at the Liturgy,* written to advance the proposal to reform the reform.[37] Fessio, who is probably the leader in the United States of this agenda, focuses the reform of the reform on three central measures: priest and people facing in the same direction; the use of the Roman Canon with a minimum of options; and the reinstitution of the sung Gregorian chant Ordinary of the Mass.[38] However, unlike Gamber and Harrison, Fessio and the leadership of *Adoremus* seem less intent on a return to the 1962 Missal as the point of departure than on seeking a normative reordering of the Mass of 1969 along lines inspired by the 1962 Missal and its 1965 and 1967 revisions. This would inevitably involve some structural changes in the present order of liturgy.[39]

I want to turn now to the two agenda groups that represent respectively progressive and corrective programs for ongoing liturgical reform. The first of these may be described as committed to "inculturating the reform" and the second to what I propose to call "recatholicizing the reform." What both of these agenda groups have in common is a fundamental affirmation of the Second Vatican Council and the Constitution on the Sacred Liturgy, as well as an *acceptance of the reformed rites as they now exist as the basis for any further development.* Unlike the two conservative groups—which wish more or less to go back to or behind the Council—the two groups which I am now introducing seek to go beyond the reform as it has been carried through in recent decades, but in rather different ways.

Worship, Culture, and Creativity

The fundamental conviction operative in the agenda of "inculturating the reform" is that while the revisions of the past thirty years have more or less successfully given the church a new set of liturgical books, these achievements are but a prelude to a much more profound and far-reaching reform of the liturgy. An entirely new phase of creativity must be initiated by which the officially revised liturgical rites will be adapted to the various cultures of the world, including those of the modern West. This position proposes a new pluralization, diversification and decentralization of Catholic liturgical life.

I stated at the outset that a certain overlap may be identified in the relationship between the various agendas described in this essay. This is evident in the connection between the official agenda and the inculturation agenda. The latter does not simply take up where the former leaves off. If the roots of the inculturation agenda are in the official reform, it is clear that the official agenda—notably in regard to the translation processes that have engaged ICEL and the English-speaking bishops' conferences—embraces at least in principle the beginnings of liturgical inculturation.[40] Yet it may be argued that the thoroughgoing inculturation ideals as they are now developing in academic circles go considerably beyond the present scope of the official agenda.

The positions espoused within the agenda of inculturation are as diverse as in the other groups. Some envisage the need to adjust the Roman liturgy to modern Western European and North American needs and conceptions. This concern was central to the meeting in Scottsdale, Arizona, in December 1974 that gave rise to the North American Academy of Liturgy.[41] Others focus on the necessity of liturgical adaptation to the religious ethos of particular cultural communities within the United States, for instance, African American, Hispanic, and Native American.[42] Dialogue between feminist theology and spirituality and Catholic liturgical tradition represents a particularly strong movement within the inculturation agenda. The need for "inclusive" gender language both in relation to God and the human person generally provides the focal point in this area.[43] Likewise, those influenced by liberation and political theologies bring their own set of concerns to the liturgical inculturation agenda.[44]

The spirit of experimentation and adaptation that has characterized liturgical celebration at the parish level in the United States since the Second Vatican Council may be understood as inculturation, even if it is not consciously adverted to as such. Popular styles of priestly presidency, preaching, music, and art, as well as the advent of small group dynamics in the liturgy, represent an absorption into Catholic worship of celebrative idioms native to popular American culture. As the Roman liturgy is adapted to the mainstream culture of the United States, it becomes notably "informal" and personalized and a high value is placed on stylistic creativity and variety.

The inculturation agenda claims theoretical legitimacy by reference to articles 37 to 40 of the Constitution on the Sacred Liturgy, which talk about the need for renewal to proceed beyond a reform of the liturgical books to an adaptation of those books to new cultural circumstances. The intention of the Second Vatican Council, it is argued, was not only to recover the historic core of the Roman rite but also to adapt the liturgy to new and diverse cultural environments. Article 37 of the Constitution states: "The Church does not wish to impose a rigid uniformity in matters which do not involve the faith or the good of the whole community. Rather does she respect and foster the qualities and talents of the various races and nations."[45] Accordingly, "anything in these peoples' way of life which is not indissolubly bound up with superstition and error she studies with sympathy, and, if possible, preserves intact. She sometimes even admits such things into the liturgy itself, providing they harmonize with its true and authentic spirit."[46]

Once the substantial unity of the Roman liturgy is safeguarded, the Constitution declares, "provision shall be made, when revising the liturgical books, for legitimate variations and adaptations to different groups, regions and peoples, especially in mission countries."[47] Article 40 allows for even more radical adaptation of the rites and prescribes that local ecclesiastical authority must "carefully and prudently consider which elements from the traditions and cultures of individual peoples might appropriately be admitted into divine worship."[48] The same article indicates that this process should be carried out through a program of approved experimentation and involve the input of experts in cultural adaptation.

At the international level, Father Anscar Chupungco remains the most notable and respected theoretical proponent of the inculturation agenda.[49] This agenda is widely embraced in the better known graduate programs in liturgy in the United States, and it finds strong advocacy in the nation's Catholic Black, Hispanic, and Native American organizations, as well as in various research projects and conferences, both academic and pastoral.[50]

Catholicity and the Liturgy

This brings me to the fifth and final agenda which I describe as "recatholicizing the reform." At this point, I move from a descriptive to a prescriptive mode. As I stated at the outset, I believe that ongoing liturgical reform will be most adequately advanced by the agenda I am now introducing. As will become clear, the recatholicizing agenda draws on elements of the agendas already described, indicating again that the agendas are not necessarily mutually exclusive. In the final section of this essay, in which an evaluation of the various agendas will be offered, I shall argue that among the strengths of the recatholicizing agenda is that it unifies with a considerable degree of adequacy the perceived values of the other agendas.

The words *recatholicizing* and *recatholicization* invoke the understanding of "catholicity" found in such theologians as Avery Dulles and Henri de Lubac, for whom the catholicity of the church is found not primarily in its geographic extensiveness, but in the spiritual depths, sacramental richness, religious exuberance and creativity of ecclesial institutions.[51] Avery Dulles's magisterial work, *The Catholicity of the Church*, published in 1985, provides the immediate inspiration, as far as nomenclature is concerned, for the agenda I am describing here.[52] In this book, Dulles presents a rich and compelling vision of the catholicity of the church. When the church is truly catholic, it is characterized by a high trinitarian consciousness; it reaches into the very depths of the human soul; it engages profoundly the spiritual heritage of historic Christianity; and its vision is centered on the glory of God and the coming of the kingdom. It is this kind of comprehensive framework that constitutes the agenda for recatholicizing the reformed liturgy.[53]

Dulles introduces his analysis of ecclesial catholicity as follows: "As we read in the Letter to the Ephesians, Paul prays that his readers may be enabled to comprehend 'the breadth and length and height and depth' of the love of Christ, even thought this 'surpasses knowledge' (Ephesians 3:18–19). Like the love of Christ, the Church may be viewed as a mystery with four dimensions: height, depth, breadth, and length" (30).[54] First there is "catholicity from above" or "the 'height' of catholicity." By "catholicity from above," Dulles means that "The triune God, who communicates himself in the incarnate Word and in the Holy Spirit, is the source and ground of catholicity" (47). The catholicity of the church is constituted in this dimension by the glory of God flowing in its trinitarian dynamism into the whole earth. Out of the fullness of love, God bounteously and splendidly shares his life with created beings, so that in him "we live and move and have our being" (Acts 17:78). In this marvelous and all-encompassing trinitarian movement, Dulles says, the Word of God "entered into a kind of union with the cosmos" (34). Christ becomes the "head of creation" (34) and "the Church is the fullness or completion of Christ" (41). The church then is understood as "a participation in Christ's dynamic power to recapitulate both humanity and the cosmos under his universal leadership" (43).

Turning next to the depth dimension of the church, Dulles introduces "catholicity from below" in the following manner: "According to the Catholic understanding, the Spirit of God does not merely hover above the world, nor does it simply touch the world as a tangent touches a circle, but it reaches into the depths. Divine life, when it enters the human realm, penetrates not only the spiritual faculties of the intellect and will, but the person's whole being, including the sensory and bodily aspects" (48). Catholicity from below is constituted by the truth that "justification stands in a cosmic setting" (51). In this regard, Dulles identifies in Catholicism a profound "reverence for human nature" (53), for the bodily, the sensory, and the beautiful. Human nature and the created order have an internally transcendental orientation and are "intrinsically ordered toward the goal of eternal blesssedness in God through Christ" (57; cf. 55ff.). Dulles here attends to what might be described as ecclesial anthropology, "the human material that goes into the Church" (48).

The quantitative or horizontal aspect of catholicity, what Dulles calls "catholicity in breadth," is treated next. This dimension refers to the expansive and inclusive features of the church, to the intrinsic ability of the church "to communicate itself without limit to persons of every kind and condition" (68). Dulles points out, quoting de Lubac, that, in this sense, the church was catholic on the day of Pentecost as it was ever to become in the course of its history (68). For Dulles, "The catholicity of the Church became manifest when the Gentiles turned to the gospel as giving the answers to their own questions about the meaning of life and death. Subsequent history has confirmed the capacity of men and women of every kind and condition to find faith and hope in the Christian proclamation" (73). Furthermore, "As the Church spreads her faith, she shows forth the transcendence of the gospel and the universal working of the grace of the Holy Spirit. At the same time, the Church actualizes her own catholicity. Constituted in the world as a sacrament, or efficacious sign, of God's universal redemptive will in Christ, the Church is driven by an inner dynamism to represent the whole of humanity as the recipient of redemption" (74). There is thus "in the Church a universality in her capacity as sign" (74).

Dulles turns finally to what he calls "catholicity in length" or "catholicity in time" (87). He points to Saint Thomas Aquinas's assertion that the church, on the one had, has existed since the time of Abel and, on the other, that it stretches forward into eternity, into eschatological fulfillment (cf. 87–89). In the New Testament, the dynamic eschatological vision was symbolized in the language of the marriage of the Lamb, the heavenly banquet, the Sabbath rest, the New Jerusalem, the completed Temple (90). Dulles recognizes that "Catholic theology has not always found it easy to come to terms with the realities of history" (99). The dangers of an exaltation of the past at the expense of the present and of the present over the past are perennial in Christian history (94ff.). In its Constitution on Divine Revelation, the church at the Second Vatican Council opted for "a dynamic, progressive view of tradition," avoiding both of the dangers just mentioned (100; cf. 101–103). The church, accordingly, is called to "show forth in the world the mystery of the Lord in a faithful though shadowed way, until at last it will be revealed in total splendor" (103). Dulles calls, then, for both a positive theological appreciation of Catholic history and the renewal of a strong eschatological vision (90–94).

Clearly, Dulles's analysis of catholicity is not the only one that might be invoked profitably, and his concerns are not immediately liturgical. Yet the kind of comprehensive vision of ecclesial catholicity that Dulles sets forth provides an appropriate theological grounding for the agenda of recatholicizing the reformed liturgy.

How does this agenda differ from the others? Unlike the conservative or traditional agendas, the recatholicization of the reform shares with the inculturation agenda the conviction that the reforms of the liturgical books since the Second Vatican Council are fundamentally to be welcomed and embraced, even as they need to be subject to some further development. However, the nature of the direction in which further development ought to proceed is what distinguishes the recatholicization and inculturation agendas from each other. If the inculturation agenda is committed to a substantive adaptation of the revised rites to diverse cultural situations, the recatholicizing agenda is primarily committed to a vital recreation of the ethos that has traditionally imbued Catholic liturgy at its best—an ethos of beauty, majesty, spiritual profundity, and solemnity. In this, the recatholicizing framework is not unsympathetic to the inculturation agenda—even if it does regard the actual achievements of that agenda with considerable reserve—but, in fact, it incorporates the fundamental principles of inculturation set out in the Constitution on the Sacred Liturgy.

The recatholicizing agenda is also open to what it regards as the positive prescriptions of the ongoing agenda of official reform, for instance, better quality translations; yet its primary interest is not with the creation of new texts or translations or with ritual modifications and expanding options.[55] The recatholicizing agenda, unlike the other four, sets no great store on further structural change in Catholic worship at this time—whether in "conservative" or "progressive" directions. This agenda seeks, instead, a period of settling down and intensive pastoral appropriation now that the liturgical books have been thoroughly and systematically revised. In this respect, it embraces a highly conservative view of the dynamics of liturgical change, holding that ritual functions best when it is familiar and predictable.[56] Accordingly, proponents of this agenda tend to regard the various present proposals for further revision as potentially disorienting and destabilizing of the church's public worship and as vitiating "ritual competence" in congregations.

What distinguishes the recatholicizing agenda from the other four fundamentally is that it regards the principal challenge of ongoing liturgical reform as *spiritual* rather than *structural*. The recatholicization agenda stands for a spiritual broadening and deepening of the postconciliar liturgical order set forth in the revised books. It does not regard that order as by any means perfect. It does view it, however, as eminently worthy of reception by the whole church in the postconciliar era and as expressive of spiritual riches in great part unappreciated and untapped. This agenda seeks an intensive rather than extensive renewal of the liturgy, by which is meant a spiritual unfolding of the potentiality of the revised liturgical rites rather than their expansion with new texts, ceremonies, and symbols.[57]

Recatholicization means renewing the spiritual, mystical, and devotional dimensions of the revised rites. It seeks a recovery of the sacred and the numinous in liturgical expression which will act as a corrective to the sterility and rationalism of much modern liturgical experience.[58] This agenda calls for a new attention to the phenomenology of religion and the sacred of the kind represented earlier in this century by such figures as Gerardus van der Leeuw, Rudolf Otto, and

Mircea Eliade, who seem out of fashion among liturgists today.[59] The programmatic elements just described may be subsumed theologically under the category of liturgical pneumatology—a feature of Western liturgy which remains decidedly underdeveloped, despite often expressed intentions in the modern liturgical movement to correct this deficiency.[60]

The aesthetic dimension of worship represents another area in which the catholic expressivity of the liturgy needs considerable attention. As Eastern thinkers often point out, the Christian West tends to regard the aesthetic as extrinsic to the constitution of the liturgy. Thus a new commitment to liturgical aesthetics—by means of which the aesthetic will move from the status of an accidental to a constitutive element of liturgy—remains today a critical need.[61] Encouraging grounds for such a development are found in the considerable interest being accorded the aesthetic in Western theology today, even if surprisingly little attention is paid to the liturgy in the process.

Once noted for its excessive rubricism, Western liturgy of late has become subject to anti-ritual bias, so that there does not exist today an adequate theology of ceremonial in Catholic liturgical life. This deficiency may be corrected by drawing on aesthetic theory, as well as on those strands of ritual studies sympathetic to Catholic sacramentality.[62] In tandem with the correction of this problem is the necessity of recovering a sense of the sacramental objectively of the liturgy, so that liturgical rites are not regarded as human fabrications, but as "God's masterpieces" or the "masterworks of God."[63]

This agenda looks to a renewal of the eschatological orientation in Catholic worship wherein the connection between the heavenly and earthly liturgies is again encountered.[64] One of the most remarkable features of the preconciliar liturgical movement was the resurgence of interest in the eschatological character of Christian worship generated in great part by a new appreciation of the liturgical life of the East. Yet that interest seemed to be diverted soon after the Second Vatican Council as eschatology began to be secularized and politicized and as Catholic life and worship generally began to refocus in the direction of relevance to modern culture.[65]

Related to the eschatological is the renewal of the cosmic sense in the liturgy. Catholic liturgy today notably suffers from a shrunken cosmic consciousness and a shrunken cosmic ritualization. A more adequate cosmic expressivity will serve to draw all of creation, including the saintly and the angelic, into the framework of worship.[66] A renewed cosmic emphasis will help overcome the present tendency of liturgical celebration toward privatization and congregationalist self-referentiality and self-enclosure.

Recatholicization means a renewal of the doxological, praise-filled character of worship capable of rescuing present-day liturgical practice from its excessively pragmatic, didactic and functional conceptions. The fundamental impulses for doxology, I would argue, are found in eschatological and cosmic conceptions. When eschatological and cosmic vision is narrowed or collapses, then the doxological amplitude and expressivity of Christian worship is vitiated. In turn, the lack of doxological vision leads to a failure of Christian imagination and to the radical impoverishment of the whole programmatic fabric of the liturgy.[67]

Practically, the recatholicizing agenda means taking the present rites and working to celebrate them in a much more profound, dignified, and spiritually edifying manner than has generally been the case since the advent of postconciliar revision. It requires a deepening of the liturgical competence of congregations;[68] provision for the training of laity to assume more appropriately the ministries provided them in liturgical celebrations; and, not least, improving the standards of priestly leadership and preaching.

A renewed movement to provide for a more noble character in liturgical music and to restore a Catholic ethos to places of worship by creative contact with the longer traditions of Catholic art and architecture is required by the recatholicization agenda. While the modern movement in art and architecture and ritual-functionalism in music have served to correct some expressive excesses in the past, the time has come to move beyond them and to seek an artistic renaissance of a richer and more imaginative kind than that seen so far in the postconciliar liturgy.

Not least, the recatholicizing agenda implies a new respect for the longer tradition of Catholic liturgical history, including the medieval, baroque, and post-Tridentine eras. Taking the catholicity of the church seriously means overcoming the excessive tendency of modern liturgical scholarship to stake so much on the search for normative historic origins and the corresponding tendency toward a severe bias against almost everything that came after the patristic era. The conviction still obtains among liturgists that little of positive value is to be learned from Catholic liturgical life for most of the second millennium.

However, for a new generation of historians such as Eamon Duffy, liturgical tradition is now less easily dismissed than has been the case for much of the twentieth century.[69]

The recatholicizing agenda operates from a conviction that some important features of the preconciliar liturgical movement were not adequately appreciated in the period of revision after the Second Vatican Council. Thus it seeks to establish contact with neglected strands of the twentieth century liturgical movement associated with figures like Romano Guardini, Louis Bouyer, and Virgil Michel and with the authors of the patristic revival.[70]

While present-day inspiration for the recatholicization agenda comes from diverse sources, the writings of Hans Urs von Balthasar and the theological interests associated with the international *Communio* network are notably important.[71] The liturgical theology, spirituality, and aesthetics of the Christian East, both Catholic and Orthodox, can be expected to play a considerable role. As is evident from this brief sketch, this agenda is well served by liturgical scholars from the Anglican and Protestant traditions. Liturgical organizations sympathetic to the recatholicizing agenda include The Society for Catholic Liturgy formed in 1995.

Evaluative Conclusion

At the beginning of this essay, I declared my preference for the agenda of recatholicizing the reform. This position does not, however, seek simply to invalidate the other agendas. Indeed, my stated preference is founded on my positive judgment of the ability of the fifth agenda to incorporate the strengths of the other four. My final task here is to suggest strengths and weaknesses in the various agendas and to suggest how the strengths may be unified in the agenda of recatholicizing the reform.

What may be said about the agenda of advancing official reform? It can certainly claim strong legitimacy by reference to the Constitution on the Sacred Liturgy and to the postconciliar decisions of ecclesiastical authority in interpreting the Constitution as the liturgical books were being revised. Like most liturgists and sacramental theologians, I believe this agenda deserves strong support in most of its fundamental features. The liturgical books as revised represent overall a heroic achievement. In my opinion, the movement toward the vernacular, the restoration of the chalice to the people, the opening up of liturgical ministries to the laity, and the clarification of the structure of the various sacramental rites were developments of monumental importance. The various principles and achievements of this agenda provide, not least, the fundamental basis for the recatholicizing agenda espoused here.

The official agenda may be criticized, however, for the reasons that it seemed to have proceeded somewhat hastily; promoted a too rapid evolution of the programmatic trajectory of Vatican II; was hampered by an excessively negative reading of the preconciliar liturgy; and was limited by an inordinately verbal and rationalistic understanding of Christian worship. Methodologies informed by mechanistic and functionalist models of ritual, as well as by didacticism in conceptualizations of liturgical participation seem to have been operative to a severe degree after the Council.[72] The progress of this agenda is today no less than in past decades marred by a tendency toward bureaucratic management, so that the leadership of national and international liturgical commissions easily takes on the appearance of a "knowledge class," that is, a class of self-validating technical experts lacking appropriate sensitivity to non-theoretical matters, including popular sentiment on issues of worship.[73] What is not unfairly called "the liturgical establishment" tends to be somewhat authoritarian in outlook and adversarial toward contrary theoretical and practical perspectives on liturgical reform—even of the more reasonable and well-informed kind. This agenda is increasingly the subject of criticism, which it has not, for the most part, taken well, even when such criticism comes from the Holy See. The necessary survival of the program of official reform requires that it proceed more dialogically, self-critically and openly vis-à-vis the other agendas than it has hitherto and that it moderate itself in light of their legitimate aims and ideals.

What of the agenda of restoring the preconciliar? I think it most unlikely and, indeed, very undesirable that the restoration of the preconciliar liturgy could become a major agenda item for future liturgical developments. A return to the preconciliar liturgy would involve intrinsically a rejection of fundamental commitments made by the Second Vatican Council. Liturgical practice is more than a matter of taste or personal spirituality; it embodies a whole set of theological and ecclesiological principles and convictions. For this reason, the present allowance of the Tridentine Mass seems to me legitimate only as a temporary measure. The prescriptions of *Ecclesia Dei* must of necessity give way eventually to the renewing vision of the Second Vatican Council. However, those who seek the celebration of the Missal of 1962 deserve in the meantime more pastoral care, understanding, and respect than local ecclesiastical leaders have been hitherto willing to accord. A more sympathetic and dialogical spirit on the part of bishops and pastors would probably have the affect on many traditionalist Catholic groups of softening resistance to postconciliar changes and of leading them to a more cooperative and receptive outlook on the Second Vatican Council.

Yet, the desire of the restorationist agenda to recover the transcendent character and sacred ethos of the church's worship and to renew an atmosphere of reverence, awe, majesty, and solemnity is to be commended and embraced. Those who advocate a return to the preconciliar liturgy rightly criticize the lack of those features in the practice of the reformed rites. The church's heritage of art, architecture and music, as the Council insisted, must be maintained and developed. The recatholicization agenda shares with the restorationist movement strong common concerns in these areas. The restorationist agenda also highlights the fairly widespread abuses in the liturgical practice of the reformed rites. The degree to which some Catholics have resisted the revised rites and taken recourse to the traditionalist movement because of liturgical abuse merits considerable reflection. Ecclesiastical leaders would do well to redouble efforts to reestablish liturgical discipline and advance more spiritually substantive pastoral practice on the part of those who lead the worship of the church. Otherwise, some of the factors that created the traditionalist movement in the first place will be exacerbated. The preconciliar liturgy—and the restorationist agenda now promoting it—have much to teach the church today, even if the formal aspects of that agenda cannot be substantially embraced.

Regarding the agenda of reforming the reform—at least in its present high profile expressions—I think it unrealistic to imagine that it will have much significant short-term success. In my opinion, the bishops of the English-speaking world are not likely to muster noticeable enthusiasm for the advancement of this agenda, and I cannot imagine that the Holy See would undertake or approve such a program due to its uncertain or risky outcome. Beyond this, some elements of the agenda as outlined by Harrison would be quite unacceptable to even moderately "conservative" liturgical voices—especially the desire to curtail new eucharistic prayers, reduce women's roles in liturgical ministries, and refuse any consideration of adaptation in the area of gender language. This agenda seems too severe in its specific proposals and inadequately appreciative of the revised liturgical order.

An argument can be made in retrospect that greater continuity should have been maintained between the Missal of 1962 (and its 1965 and 1967 revisions) and the distinctly different order of Mass promulgated in 1969. But the rite we now have would be unwisely marginalized in favor of some modification of the Mass as it was before the Council. The creation of yet another rite such as Harrison proposes would, in my opinion, only add to present confusion and instability. Yet, the recovery of some elements from the preconciliar liturgy should not be ruled out in any further modification of the present Mass. The reform of the reform program has some important lessons to teach, especially concerning the dangers of discontinuity in liturgical reform and undue haste in any further round of revisions. As the agenda of reforming the reform matures, it will surely have important contributions to make in discussions about the future of the Roman liturgy. Those who espouse the recatholicization agenda are likely to consider those contributions respectfully. The official and the recatholicization agendas would unwisely refuse to take account of the important warning signaled by the publication and widespread popular reception of Gamber's book.[74]

The inculturation agenda can, as I pointed out, claim legitimacy by reference to articles 37 to 40 of the Constitution on the Sacred Liturgy, and I have no doubt that this program needs to be carried through, especially in relation to non-Western cultures, as well as to the traditional cultures of the West—including, in the United States, Hispanic, Native American, Asian, and African American. As already indicated, this agenda rightly finds support in the present thinking of the Holy See regarding the ongoing evangelization of cultures.

The possibility of new expressions of liturgical catholicity should be explored and advanced. On this project a creative and productive dialogue between the recatholicization and inculturation agendas is possible. Yet, in my opinion, the inculturation agenda has not yet matured, even theoretically. The practical difficulties of carrying out appropriate adaptation of rites, both in Western and non-Western cultures, have already proved daunting. The possibility of the dissolution of the Roman liturgy and the liturgical corruption of the church's worship are very real. Indeed, in my opinion, the most severe problems that exist in the church's liturgical life today, especially in the United States, are the result of an unfortunate practical adaptation of liturgy to American popular culture. These problems include the trivialization of rites and symbols, the ascendency of an entertainment and therapeutic ethos in liturgical celebration, an exaggerated, neo-clericalist style of priestly presidency, and an individualistic and consumeristic spirituality. What Aidan Kavanagh has often spoken of as the *"embourgeoisement"* of the liturgy, that is, its adaptation in the West to liberal middle class concerns, is a matter requiring critical evaluation.[75] The most troublesome challenges facing ongoing liturgical renewal over the next twenty-five years will be, as I envisage them, in the area of inculturation. Accordingly, the greatest of caution is in order as more adequate theologies of the relationship between church and cultures are developed.[76]

The recatholicizing agenda summarized and advocated in this essay has undoubted weaknesses. It could be accused, in turn, of settling in an unprincipled manner for the liturgical books published since the Second Vatican Council; of extrapolating from the new rites a spirituality that they do not possess; and of practicing a simple "politics of moderation" regarding the present configuration of liturgical controversies. On the first point, the recatholicization agenda recognizes that the liturgical books the church now possesses were not easily devised; they carry a massive investment of time, talent, and financial resources; and they are weighted with as providential a character as that properly ascribed to the Second Vatican Council. There is the further related conviction of this agenda group that stability in ritual order and authentic popular ownership of the liturgy are values of the highest importance and they should not be compromised for excessively theoretical reasons. The revised liturgical order is far from perfect; but it was achieved at a high and difficult cost and, thus, merits ongoing respect on the part of the whole church.

Does the recatholicization agenda extrapolate from or impose upon the revised liturgy a spiritual ethos that it does possess? Are the reformed rites capable of bearing the Catholic expressivity I have described? I would answer, yes. This conviction derives from my actual observation and experience as a parish priest. When celebrated with ritual and textual attentiveness, with spiritual profundity, nobility and solemnity, with well-formed ministerial leadership, and with rich musical, artistic, and architectural elaboration, the present liturgy is pastorally most edifying and deeply expressive of Catholic fullness. I would, of course, readily admit that liturgical celebration of the kind I have in mind is not often encountered today and that the liturgy of Catholicism as presently practiced in most parishes does not adequately display the Catholic vision I have described. However, where an impoverished liturgical practice is in operation, it will not be resolved by further structural revisions of the liturgy, but only by the intense spiritual renewal that this essay proposes.

The operation of a "politics of moderation" in this agenda can be readily admitted, if what is in mind is the necessity of the development of a broad consensus regarding liturgical matters and an ecclesial unity inclusive of the legitimate aspirations of the various agendas described in this essay. The agenda of recatholicization has, in my opinion, much to offer in reaching across the divides that presently exist and which require genuine reconciliation before any further reform of the liturgy is wisely undertaken.

---

1. My use of the term *agenda* generally invokes the methodologies of models, paradigms, and typologies that have become a familiar feature of modern theology. An "agenda" may be understood as the *practical* outworking of a *conceptual* model, paradigm or typology.

2. See Avery Dulles, *Models of the Church,* expanded ed. (Garden City, NY: Doubleday, 1987); *Models of Revelation* (Garden City, NY: Doubleday,1985).

3. See, for instance, Frederick R. McManus, ed., *Thirty Years of Liturgical Renewal: Statements of the Bishops' Committee on the Liturgy* (Washington, DC: United States Catholic Conference, 1987).

4. The most useful and comprehensive published source for the official agenda in relation to the Holy See is *Documents on the Liturgy 1963–1979: Conciliar, Papal, and Curial Texts* (Collegeville, MN: The Liturgical Press, 1982).

5. Annibale Bugnini, *The Reform of the Liturgy 1948–1975,* trans. Matthew J. O'Connell (Collegeville, MN: The Liturgical Press, 1990).

6. ___. See the chapter entitled, "Fundamental Principles," in *Reform of the Liturgy* 1948–1975, 39–48; also Kathleen Hughes, "Overview of the Constitution on the Sacred Liturgy," in *The Liturgy Documents: A Parish Resource* (Chicago: Liturgy Training Publications, 1991) 2–6.

7. Beginning with the *motu proprio* on the Sacred Liturgy *(Sacram Liturgiam)* of 25 January 1964, the process of evolution may be traced through the

Instructions on the Proper Implementation of the Constitution on the Sacred Liturgy issued in 1964, 1967, and 1970, as well as through the many specific decrees and official communications of that period. See the chapter entitled, "Implementation of the Constitution on the Sacred Liturgy" in R. Kevin Seasoltz, *New Liturgy, New Laws* (Collegeville, MN: The Liturgical Press, 1980) 26–37.

8. See the commentary on this point in Austin Flannery, ed., *Vatican Council II: The Conciliar and Post Conciliar Documents* (Collegeville, MN: The Liturgical Press, 1975) 39.

9. No. 1; text in *Documents on the Liturgy 1963–1979*, 284. (See n. 4 above.)

10. On the work of ICEL, see John R. Page, "Liturgical Texts in English," in *The New Dictionary of Sacramental Worship*, ed. Peter E. Fink (Collegeville, MN: The Liturgical Press, 1990) 715–21; Frederick R. McManus, "ICEL: The First Years," in Peter C. Finn and James M. Schellman, eds., Shaping English Liturgy: Studies in Honor of Archbishop Denis Hurley (Washington, DC: The Pastoral Press, 1990) 433–59. Noteworthy also are the essays in the latter volume by H. Kathleen Hughes and John R. Page.

11. See, for instance, Adrien Nocent, *A Rereading of the Renewed Liturgy*, trans. Mary M. Misrahi (Collegeville, MN: The Liturgical Press, 1994). See, more generally, Carl A. Last, ed., *Remembering the Future: Vatican II and Tomorrow's Liturgical Agenda* (New York: Paulist Press, 1983).

12. The publications of Michael Davies are the most popular and widely used in English-speaking restorationist circles. See *Liturgical Revolution, Volume I: Cranmer's Godly Order* (Kansas City: Angelus Press, 1976); *Liturgical Revolution, Volume II: Pope John's Council* (New Rochelle, NY: Arlington House, 1977); *Liturgical Revolution, Volume III: Pope Paul's New Mass* (Kansas City: The Angelus Press, 1980); *The New Mass* (Kansas City: Angelus Press, 1985); *The Legal Status of the Tridentine Mass* (Dickinson, TX: Angelus Press, 1992); *The Roman Rite Destroyed* (Kansas City: The Angelus Press, 1992); *Liturgical Shipwreck: 25 Years of the New Mass* (Rockford, IL: Tan Books and Publishers, 1995); *On Communion in the Hand and Similar Frauds* (St. Paul, MN: The Remnant Press, no date).

13. For a "conservative" defense of the Mass of 1969 against its critics, see James Likoudis and Kenneth D. Whitehead, *The Pope, the Council, and the Mass: Answers to Questions the "Traditionalists" Are Asking* (West Hanover, MA: The Christopher Publishing House, 1981).

14. What was known as the "Ottaviani Intervention" against certain proposals for liturgical reform led by Cardinal Alfredo Ottaviani on behalf of Cardinal Antonio Bacci and a group of Roman theologians in 1969 continues to generate in some circles the debate about the "politics" surrounding the promulgation of the Mass of 1969. See *The Ottaviani Intervention: Short Critical Study*

of the New Order of Mass, with a new translation and preface by Anthony Cekada (Rockford, IL: Tan Books, 1992).

15. See Patrick H. Omlor, *Questioning the Validity* (Reno, NV: Athanasius Press, 1969); William Strojie, *The New Mass Invalid Because of Defect of Intention* (Sheridan, OR, no publisher noted, 1972); James Wathen, *The Great Sacrilege* (Rockford, IL: Tan Books, 1971).

16. For an overview of the various groupings within the restorationist category and the history of their development in the United States after the Second Vatican Council, see the essay by William D. Dinges, " 'We Are What You Were:' Roman Catholic Traditionalism in America," in Mary Jo Weaver and R. Scott Appleby, eds., *Being Right: Conservative Catholics in America* (Bloomington, IN: Indiana University Press, 1995) 241–69.

17. Latin Liturgy Association, *Newsletter* 59 (December 1995) 10.

18. ___.

19. ___.

20. ___.

21. Texts in *Origins* 14:19 (24 October 1984) 290; 18:10 (4 August 1988) 149–52.

22. See the essays by Jeffrey Rubin entitled, "Traditional Monastic Revival" and "Louder Than Words," in *Latin Mass Revival: Chronicle of a Catholic Reform* (Fort Collins, CO: Roman Catholic Books, 1996) 47–59; 128–30.

23. See Dinges, " 'We Are What You Were,' " 268, note 74.

24. Raymond E. Brown, *Biblical Reflections on Crises Facing the Church* (New York: Paulist Press, 1975) 24–27.

25. See the reports, "Scholars Meet in France," *Precious Blood Banner,* October 1995, 4; "Liturgy in Critical Focus," *The Tablet,* 16 November 1996, 519.

26. See Dinges, " 'We Are What You Were,' " 242.

27. A 1990 Gallup poll indicated that the percentages of Catholics who, if it were available, would attend the traditional Latin Mass were as follows: 8% always; 17% frequently; 51% occasionally. See *Latin Mass Revival,* 5.

28. It should be noted that Latin Mass groups or organizations are not always in favor of or actively committed to the restoration of the Tridentine Mass. Some groups simply espouse the more frequent use of Latin in the celebration of the 1969 Mass. In this category are the St. Gregory Foundation for Latin Liturgy in the United States and the Association for Latin Liturgy in England.

29. Klaus Gamber, *The Reform of the Roman Liturgy: Its Problems and Background,* trans. Klaus D. Grimm (San Juan Capistrano, CA: Una Voce Press, 1993). See also idem, *The Modern Rite: Collected Essays on the Reform of the*

Liturgy, trans. Henry Taylor (Farnborough, Hants.: St. Michael's Abbey Press, 2002).

30. ___, 3.

31. ___, xii.

32. Public letter of 29 June 1995; emphasis in original.

33. Text from Flannery, *Vatican Council II,* 10. The immediate inspiration for the foundation of Adoremus was the Apostolic Letter of Pope John Paul II, "On the 25th Anniversary of the Constitution on the Sacred Liturgy" (December 4, 1988) which stated: "For the work of translation, as well as for the wider implications of liturgical renewal for whole countries, each Episcopal Conference was required to establish a National Commission and ensure the collaboration of experts in the various sectors of liturgical science and pastoral practice. The time has come to evaluate this Commission, its past activity, both the positive and negative aspects, and the guidelines and the help which it has received from the Episcopal Conference regarding its composition and activity" (no. 20). Text available from Washington, DC: United States Catholic Conference, 1989. See also, "About Adoremus: A Statement of Its Missions, Goals and Principles," *Adoremus Bulletin,* November 1995, 2; the essay entitled, "Adoremus—Society for the Renewal of the Sacred Liturgy," *Voices* [Women for Faith and Family], June 1996, 6; Philip F. Lawler, "A Reform of the Reform?" *The Catholic World Report,* August–September 1996, 40–42.

34. Brian W. Harrison, "What Do We Do Now? Part III: The Gamber Proposal as Long-Term Solution," Adoramus Bulletin, Jan. 1996, 9.1; emphasis in original. The other parts of this essay are "The Crisis in Eucharistic Faith: Implications for Post–Vatican II Reform," *Adoremus Bulletin,* Nov. 1995, 1, 8: "Planning a 'Reform of the Reform,' Part II: Some Inadequate Solutions to the Eucharistic Liturgy Crisis," *Adoremus Bulletin,* Dec.1995, 1, 8. Significantly, the "Reform of the Reform" for which Harrison calls, involves an explicit rejection of the "Traditionalist Proposal," that is, the view that the solution to the present crisis in Catholic worship is simply the restoration of the Mass as it was before the Council ("Planning a Reform of the 'Reform of the Reform,'" 8).

35. ___.

36. Harrison, "What Do We Do Now?" passim. Harrison's proposals regarding the exclusive use of men in lay service in the liturgy is developed at greater length in "*'Fluctuationes Rhythmicae':* The New Feminist Face of the Roman Liturgy," *The Latin Mass,* Fall 1995, 42–49.

37. Aidan Nichols, *Looking at the Liturgy: A Critical View of Its Contemporary Form* (San Francisco: Ignatius Press, 1996). Nichols proposes that the Mass of 1969 be redesignated as a *ritus communis* with multiple purposes, including providing the basis for developing new ritual families in non-Western areas

of the church; serving as a rite for Anglicans and Lutherans wishing to join the church in some corporate manner; and continuing in use "in those parishes and religious communities of the Latin church that do not wish to recover the historical and spiritual patrimony of the Latin rite in a fuller form" (122). See also James Hitchcock, *Recovery of the Sacred: Reforming the Reformed Liturgy* (San Francisco: Ignatius Press, 1995); this is a reprint with a new preface of a work first published in 1974.

38. See Thomas J. Nash, "Adoremus Seeks to Restore a Sense of the Sacred in the Mass," *Lay Witness,* May 1996, 20.

39. In the mission statement of Adoremus, the following question is posed: "Is Adoremus promoting a more careful observance of the liturgical norms approved since the Council?" The answer is, "Yes, but not as our ultimate goal. With Pope John Paul II, we believe that even some of the changes approved since the Council need to be reviewed and measured against a deeper understanding of the Council's teaching" (*Adoremus Bulletin,* November 1995, 2). The same mission statement responds to the question, "Is Adoremus seeking a restoration of the preconciliar liturgy?" as follows: "No. We do not think that a simple return to the preconciliar liturgy will further the reforms legitimately mandated by the Second Vatican Council" (ibid.).

40. On this point, see article 53 of the 1994 Instruction of the Vatican Congregation for Divine Worship and the Discipline of the Sacraments entitled, "Inculturation and the Roman Liturgy," which states: "The first significant measure of inculturation is the translation of liturgical books into the language of the people" (Text in *Origins* 23 [14 April 1994] 745, 747–56). See also Andrew Borello, "The Contextualization of Liturgy and Especially Liturgical Texts: The Tension Between the Universality of the Liturgy and the Specific Situation of the Local Celebrating Community;" Paul Puthanangady, "Cultural Elements in Liturgical Prayers," both in Finn and Schellman, eds., *Shaping English Liturgy,* 301–26; 327–40.

41. Papers related to the conference were published in *Theological Studies* 35 (1974). In that volume, see Walter J. Burghardt, "A Theologian's Challenge to Liturgy," 233–48; Langdon Gilkey, "Symbols, Meaning and Divine Presence," 249–67; James F. White, "Worship and Culture: Mirror or Beacon?" 288–301; John Gallen, "American Liturgy: A Theological Locus," 302–11. See also Mary Collins, "Liturgy in America: The Scottsdale Conference," *Worship* 48 (1974) 66–80.

42. On the broader theological-cultural features of this challenge see M. Francis Mannion, "Evangelization and American Ethnicity," in *Proceedings from the Seventeenth Convention of the Fellowship of Catholic Scholars,* Corpus Christi, TX (1994) 145–92.

43. A comprehensive introduction to this matter is provided in *Liturgy Digest* 1 (1994:2) 78–185. See also *Criteria for the Evaluation of Inclusive Language*

Translations of Scriptural Texts Prepared for Liturgical Use, National Conference of Catholic Bishops (Washington, DC: United States Catholic Conference, 1990); Ronald D. Witherup, *A Liturgist's Guide to Inclusive Language* (Collegeville, MN: The Liturgical Press, 1996); Kathleen Hughes, "Inclusive Language Revisited," Chicago Studies 35 (1996) 115–27; Janet Walton, "Feminism and the Liturgy," in *The New Dictionary of Sacramental Worship,* ed. Fink, 468–73; the essays entitled, "Inclusive Language: A Cultural and Theological Question" and "Naming God in Public Prayer," in Mary Collins, *Worship: Renewal to Practice* (Washington, DC: The Pastoral Press, 1987) 197–214; 215–29.

44. See the various essays and useful bibliography provided in J. Frank Henderson, Kathleen Quinn, and Stephen Larson in *Liturgy, Justice and the Reign of God: Interpreting Vision and Practice* (New York: Paulist Press, 1989); the essays by Elisabeth Schüssler Fiorenza, Enrique Dussel, and Diann Neu in *Can We Always Celebrate the Eucharist?* (*Concilium 152*), ed. Mary Collins and David Power (New York: The Seabury Press, 1982); the essay entitled, "The Liberation Model of Liturgical Theology" in James Empereur, *Worship: Exploring the Sacred,* (Washington, DC: The Pastoral Press, 1987) 97–118. Tissa Balasuriya, *The Eucharist and Human Liberation* (Maryknoll, NY: Orbis Books, 1979) has been particularly influential on the reconstructive role of liberation themes on liturgical practice.

45. Text in Flannery, *Vatican Council II,* 13.

46. ___.

47. ___, 14.

48. ___.

49. See Anscar J. Chupungco: *Cultural Adaptation of the Liturgy* (New York: Paulist Press, 1982); *Liturgies of the Future: The Process and Methods of Inculturation* (New York: Paulist Press, 1989); *Liturgical Inculturation: Sacramentals, Religiosity, and Catechesis* (Collegeville, MN: The Liturgical Press, 1992).

50. See, for example, the volumes produced in the Alternative Futures for Worship series, Bernard J. Lee, general ed. (Collegeville, MN The Liturgical Press, 1987). Noteworthy is the "Introduction to the Series" by Lee in Volume I: *General Introduction,* ed. Regis A. Duffy, 9–28.

51. This agenda title is neither meant to suggest that the other positions are not Catholic, nor to invoke the arguments of some critics that Catholic liturgy has suffered a "Protestantizing" process since the Second Vatican Council. Indeed, some important sources for liturgical recatholicization are, as I shall demonstrate, drawn from Orthodox, Anglican, and Reformed sources.

52. Avery Dulles, *The Catholicity of the Church* (Oxford, Clarendon Press, 1985); see also the essay entitled, "The Meaning of Catholicism: Adventures of an Idea," in idem, *The Reshaping of Catholicism: Current Challenges in the Theology of the Church* (San Francisco: Harper and Row, 1988) 51–74.

53. On this general theme, see Henri De Lubac, *Catholicism: Christ and the Common Destiny of Man,* trans. Lancelot C. Sheppard and Sister Elizabeth Englund (San Francisco: Ignatius Press, 1988; new edition); idem, *The Splendour of the Church,* trans. Michael Mason (Glen Rock, NJ: Paulist Press, 1963); Karl Adam, *The Spirit of Catholicism,* trans. Justin McCann (London: Sheed and Ward, 1934); Ian Ker, Newman and the Fullness of Christianity (Edinburgh: T. and T. Clark, 1993) esp. chapters 6 and 7.

54. For stylistic economy, references here to *The Cathlolicity of the Church* are provided within the text.

55. CREDO: A Society for Catholic Priests Dedicated to Faithful Translation of the Liturgy seeks to foster not only accurate and doctrinally adequate translations but to ensure a language of worship that fosters dignity and beauty in liturgical celebration.

56. For sociologist David Martin, "rite" depends for success on "rote," on a strongly internalized familiarity with the verbal and ritual structures on the part of liturgical participants. See *The Breaking of the Image: A Sociology of Christian Theory and Practice* (Oxford: Basil Blackwell, 1985) esp. 81–102.

57. In an address to the Plenary Assembly of the Congregation for Divine Worship and the Discipline of the Sacraments, Pope John Paul II emphasized the ideal of a *spiritual* renewal of the liturgy: "It was obvious that the spirit of the liturgy could not be restored by means of a mere reform. A true, profound liturgical renewal was necessary. In fact a 'spirit' intrinsically linked with liturgical 'actions' can reside only in the 'human agents' of the liturgy, who are called to 'exercise Christ's priestly office.' However, this does not mean that one should neglect the forms in which Christ's priesthood is expressed and exercised, those 'outward signs' which the liturgy must take into consideration" (Text in Bishops' Committee on the Liturgy *Newsletter* 32 [May 1996] 17–18).

58. If excessive liturgical institutionalism may be inhospitable to the mystical and the spiritual, a spirituality or mysticism detached from the liturgy is equally troublesome. The works of Louis Bouyer are particularly important in integrating the mystical and the sacramental features of Christian life. See *The Christian Mystery: From Pagan Myth to Christian Mysticism,* trans. Illtyd Trethowan (Petersham, MA: St. Bede's Publications, 1990); *Rite and Man: Natural Sacredness and Christian Liturgy,* trans. M. Joseph Costelloe (Notre Dame, IN: University of Notre Dame Press, 1963). Eastern Christianity may be proposed as exemplary on the integration of the mystical and the sacramental. See, for instance, Vladimir Lossky, *The Mystical Theology of the Eastern Church* (Crestwood, NJ: St. Vladimir's Seminary Press, 1976). See also Frans Josef van Beeck, *Catholic Identity After Vatican II: Three Types of Faith in the One Church* (Chicago: Loyola University Press, 1985), esp. chapter 3.

59. Rudolf Otto, *The Idea of the Holy: An Inquiry into the Non-Rational Factor in the Idea of the Divine and Its Relation to the Rational,* trans. John W. Harvey (New York: Oxford University Press, 1923); Gerardus Van der Leeuw, *Religion in Essence and Manifestation,* trans. J. E. Turner (New York: Harper and Row, 1963). Eliade's extensive writings in this area are summarized in the chapter entitled, "The Reality of the Sacred: Mircea Eliade," in Daniel L. Pals, *Seven Theories of Religion* (New York: Oxford University Press, 1996) 158–97.

60. See Patrick Regan, "Pneumatological and Eschatological Aspects of Liturgical Celebration," *Worship* 51 (1977) 332–50; the chapter entitled, "Spirit" in Geoffrey Wainwright, *Doxology: The Praise of God in Worship, Doctrine and Life* (New York: Oxford University Press, 1980) 87–117; Edward Kilmartin, "A Modern Approach to the Word of God and Sacraments of Christ: Perspectives and Principles," in *The Sacraments: God's Love and Mercy Actualized,* ed. Francis A. Eigo (Villanova: The Villanova University Press, 1979) 59–109; *Christian Liturgy: Theology and Practice I: Systematic Theology of Liturgy* (Kansas City, MO: Sheed and Ward, 1988); Aidan Kavanagh, "Liturgy and Ecclesial Consciousness," *Studia Liturgica* 15 (1982–1983) 2–17; Peter C. Sanders, "Pneumatology in the Sacramental Theologies of Geoffrey Wainwright, Jean Corbon and Edward Kilmartin," *Worship* 68 (1994) 332–52.

61. For a valuable introduction to this theme, see the special issue of *Liturgy Digest,* 3 (1996:1) esp. 72ff. See also Don E. Saliers, "Liturgical Aesthetics," in *The New Dictionary of Sacramental Worship,* ed. Fink, 30–39; Nicholas Wolterstorff, *Art in Action: Toward a Christian Aesthetic* (Grand Rapids, MI: Eerdmans, 1980); Frank Burch Brown, *Religious Aesthetics: A Theological Study of Making and Meaning* (Princeton, NJ: Princeton University Press, 1989).

62. See Gordon Jeanes, "Liturgy and Ceremonial," in Paul Bradshaw and Bryan Spinks, eds., *Liturgy in Dialogue: Essays in Memory of Ronald Jasper* (Collegeville, MN: The Liturgical Press, 1993) 9–27; Hugh Hybrew, "Ceremonial," in *The Study of Liturgy,* ed. Cheslyn Jones, Geoffrey Wainwright, Edward Yarnold and Paul Bradshaw (New York: Oxford University Press, 1992; revised edition) 485–93; Richard G. Cippola, "Ceremonial and the Tacit Dimension," *Worship* 47 (1973) 398–404. On the uses of ritual studies in liturgiology, see *Liturgy Digest* 1 (1996:1); Mark Searle, "Ritual," in *The Study of Liturgy* 51–58. On anti-ritual bias, see Margaret Mead, *Twentieth-Century Faith: Hope and Survival* (New York: Harper, 1978) 125–26; Roger Grainger, *The Language of the Rite* (London: Darton, Longman and Todd, 1974) 23–106; Mary Douglas, *Natural Symbols: Explorations in Cosmology* (Middlesex: Penguin Books, 1973) esp. 19–39.

63. See paragraphs 1091, 1116, *Catechism of the Catholic Church.*

64. Recent writings on the eschatological character of worship include Mary M. Schaefer, "Heavenly and Earthly Liturgies: Patristic Prototypes, Medieval Perspectives and a Contemporary Application," *Worship* 70 (1996) 482–505; Jean-Pierre Ruiz, "The Apocalypse of John and Contemporary Roman Catholic

Liturgy," *Worship* 68 (1994) 482–504; Geoffrey Wainwright, "The Church as a Worshiping Community, *Pro Ecclesia* 4 (1993) 56–67. See also Laurence Hull Stookey, *Eucharist: Christ's Feast with the Church* (Nashville, TN: Abington Press, 1993); Don E. Saliers, Worship as *Theology: Foretaste of Divine Glory* (Nashville, TN: Abington Press, 1994).

65. This development may be traced to a tendency to reinterpret the Constitution on the Sacred Liturgy through the hermeneutical structure provided by features of the conciliar Constitution of the Church in the Modern World approved in 1965. For an advocacy of this development, see the chapters entitled, "Two Models of Christian Worship" and "Liturgical Spirituality, Conciliar Foundations," in Shawn Madigan, *Spirituality Rooted in Liturgy* (Washington, DC: The Pastoral Press, 1988) 89–115; 117–37.

66. The eschatological and cosmic dimensions of worship are expressively interrelated in the new Catechism of the Catholic Church. In answer to the question, "Who celebrates the liturgy?" the following answer is given: "These are the ones who take part in the service of the praise of God and the fulfillment of his plan: the heavenly powers, all creation (the four living beings), the servants of the Old and New Covenants (the twenty-four elders), the new People of God (the one hundred and forty-four thousand), especially the martyrs, 'slain for the word of God,' and the all-holy Mother of God (the Woman), the Bride of the Lamb, and finally 'a great multitude which no one could number, from every nation, from all tribes, and peoples and tongues'" (#1138; text in *Catechism of the Catholic Church*, 295). See also Louis Bouyer, *Cosmos: The World and the Glory of God*, trans. Pierre de Fontnouvelle (Petersham, MA: St. Bede's Publications, 1988); Pope John Paul II, Apostolic Letter: "Orientale Lumen," par. 11; (text in *Origins* 25 [May 18, 1995] 7); the chapter entitled, "The Cosmic Setting of Salvation," in Aidan Nichols, *Epiphany: A Theological Introduction to Catholicism* (Collegeville, MN: The Liturgical Press, 1996) 368–90. For Dulles, the trinity is the originating principle of cosmic theology (See *The Catholicity of the Church*, esp. 34–39).

67. Classic works in this area eminently worthy of reconsideration include Josef Pieper, *In Tune with the World: A Theory of Festivity*, trans. Richard and Clara Winston (Chicago: Franciscan Herald Press, 1973); Romano Guardini, *The Spirit of the Liturgy*, trans. Ada Lane (London: Sheed and Ward, 1937) esp. 85–106; Hugo Rahner, *Man at Play or Did You Ever Practice Eutrapelia?*, trans. Brian Battershaw and Edward Quinn (London: Burns and Oates, 1965). See also Wainwright, *Doxology: The Praise of God in Worship, Doctrine and Life;* Daniel W. Hardy and David F. Ford, Jubilate: Theology in Praise (London: Darton, Longman and Todd, 1984); Hughes Oliphant Old, *Themes and Variations for a Christian Doxology* (Grand Rapids, MI: William B. Eerdmans, 1992); Jürgen Moltmann, *Theology and Joy*, trans. Reinhard Ulrich (London: SCM Press, 1973).

68. A classic statement on the ability of the modern person to participate authentically in "the liturgical act" is found in Romano Guardini, "Liturgical Worship and Modern Man," a letter to the 1964 Mainz Liturgical Congress; text in *Doctrine and Life* 14 (September 1964) 426–32.

69. Eamon Duffy, *The Stripping of the Altars: Traditional Religion in England, 1400–1580* (New Haven, CT: Yale University Press, 1992); "Lay Appropriation of the Sacraments in the Later Middle Ages," *New Blackfriars* 77 (1996) 53–68.

70. New editions of classic works from the liturgical movement before the Second Vatican Council are long overdue. Robert A. Krieg points out that the writings of Romano Guardini are today no longer well known; yet he worries about "a risk involved in publishing Guardini's works anew in North America today." The risk is that Guardini could be "misconstrued now to support a neo-conservative or 'restorationist' agenda" in liturgical matters ("North American Catholics' Reception of Romano Guardini's Writings," in *Romano Guardini: Proclaiming the Sacred in a Modern World*, ed. Robert A. Krieg [Chicago: Liturgy Training Publications, 1995] 55). The assumption here is that Guardini and scholars like him would be supportive of the progressive liturgical agenda of the 1990s. Such assumptions defy verification.

71. Balthasar's corpus of explicit writings on liturgy and the sacraments is relatively small. However, according to Gerald O'Collins, the whole character of his theology is one for which prayer and worship form the context (*Retrieving Fundamental Theology: The Three Styles of Contemporary Theology* [Mahwah, NJ: Paulist Press, 1993] 10, passim). The following writings of von Balthasar on liturgical topics are noteworthy: the essay entitled "Liturgy and Awe," in Explorations in Theology II: Spouse of the Word, trans. A. V. Littledale with Alexander Dru (San Francisco: Ignatius Press, 1991) 461–72; the section entitled, "The Eucharistic Cult," in *The Glory of the Lord: A Theological Aesthetics, Volume I: Seeing the Form*, trans. Erasmo Leiva-Merikakis (San Francisco: Ignatius Press, 1982) 571–75; "The Grandeur of the Liturgy," *Communio* 4 (1978) 344–51; the entries entitled, "The Eucharistic Self-Giving of Jesus" and "The Mass as Meal and Sacrifice," in *The von Balthasar Reader*, ed. Medard Kehl and Werner Löser, trans. Robert J. Daly and Fred Lawrence (New York: Crossroad, 1982), 282–85; 285–88; "The Worthiness of the Liturgy," in *New Elucidations*, trans. Sister Mary Theresilde Skerry (San Francisco: Ignatius Press, 1986) 127–40; *Mysterium Paschale: The Mystery of Easter*, trans. Aidan Nichols (Grand Rapids, MI: William B. Eerdmans, 194). See also Mark Miller, "The Sacramental Theology of Hans Urs von Balthasar," *Worship* 64 (1990) 48–66.

72. A useful introduction to the criticisms of liturgical reform by Catholic anthropologists Mary Douglas, Victor Turner, and Kieran Flanagan is provided in Nichols, *Looking at the Liturgy*, chapter 2. See also Aidan Kavanagh,

"Liturgy *(Sacrosanctum Concilium),*" in Adrian Hastings, ed., *Modern Catholicism: Vatican II and After* (New York: Oxford University Press, 1991) 68–73.

73. On the concept of a knowledge class, see Peter Berger, "Ethics and the Present Class Struggle," Worldview, April 1978, 6–11. See also Frederic M. Roberts, Conversations Among Liturgists," *Liturgy Digest* 2 (1995:2) 36–124.

74. For a moderately sympathetic review of Gamber's book by a mainstream liturgical scholar, see Graham W. Woolfenden, "The Problems of Liturgical Change: A Review Article," *Eastern Churches Journal* 2 (1995) 185–192.

75. Aidan Kavanagh, "Liturgical Inculturation: Looking to the Future," *Studia Liturgica* 20 (1990) esp. 102–3. See also Anthony Archer, *The Two Catholic Churches: A Study in Oppression* (London: SCM Press, 1986).

76. The problems of tension between culture and church in Western Christianity are not limited to Roman Catholicism. For Anglican commentary, see Bryan Spinks, "Liturgy and Culture: Is Modern Western Liturgical Revision a Case of Not Seeing the Wood for the Trees?" in Bradshaw and Spinks, eds., *Liturgy in Dialogue: Essays in Memory of Ronald Jasper,* 28–49; W. Jardine Grisbooke, "Liturgical Reform and Liturgical Renewal," *Studia Liturgica* 21 (1991) 136–54; Barry Spurr, *The Word in the Desert: Anglican and Roman Catholic Reactions to Liturgical Reform* (Cambridge: The Lutterworth Press, 1995).

Chapter 10

Rejoice, Heavenly Powers! The Renewal of Liturgical Doxology

This essay examines what many perceive to be a crisis in Christian worship as modernity breaks down in the widespread shift to what is generally named "postmodernity." "Crisis" need not mean doom and gloom, but opportunity, decision, possibility. While I am writing as a Roman Catholic, I expect that the main lines of liturgical crisis extend across the historical liturgical churches; thus my anticipation that the solutions I propose may have some ecumenical applications.

That we have recently entered a new century provides a kind of protocol for considering the crisis of Christian worship in broad terms. In this essay, accordingly, I shall range rather widely, but I hope not too superficially, and suggest three frameworks for the consideration and renewal of the current liturgical situation. The three frameworks are eschatology, cosmology, and doxology.

Each of these is, of course, a separate subject, and each is capable of mustering extensive study and discussion. Few will question, however, the profound connection among the three. Each builds on the other and may be regarded as an elaboration of the other. Furthermore, the order among the three is not arbitrary: I shall suggest that eschatology is the basis for cosmology, and that both of these together provide the basis for the robust and expansive liturgical life that is named "doxology."

My fundamental conviction is that these three interrelated elements of the Christian world order—which were beginning to achieve high relief in the modern liturgical movement (which is roughly contiguous at least at the popular level with the twentieth century)—underwent a reversal in the aftermath of the Second Vatican Council. Accordingly, the reinvigoration of the eschatological and cosmological in theory and in practice is crucial to the renewal not only of liturgical doxology but of Catholicism and indeed the great tradition of Christianity generally with the advent of a new millennium.

In what follows I shall set out the problems in each of the three areas as I perceive them and, then, in a fourth section, suggest some more adequate directions based on untapped resources of the liturgical movement itself.

The Banquet of the Lamb

In the Constitution on the Sacred Liturgy of Vatican II (#8), the eschatological nature of the liturgy is set out in high relief. We read:

> In the earthly liturgy we take part in a foretaste of that heavenly liturgy which is celebrated in the holy city of Jerusalem toward which we journey as pilgrims, where Christ is sitting at the right hand of God, minister of the holy of holies and of the true tabernacle. With all the warriors of the heavenly army we sing a hymn of glory to the Lord; venerating the memory of the saints, we hope for some part and fellowship with them; we eagerly await the Savior, our Lord Jesus Christ, until he, our life, shall appear and we too will appear with him in glory.[1]

The Dogmatic Constitution on the Church of Vatican II (#50) states:

> It is especially in the sacred liturgy that our union with the heavenly church is best realized; in the liturgy, through the sacramental signs, the power of the Holy Spirit acts on us, and with community rejoicing we celebrate together the praise of the divine majesty, when all those of every tribe and tongue and people and nation (cf. Apoc. 5:9) who have been redeemed by the blood of Christ and gathered together into one church glorify, in one common song of praise, the one and triune God. When, then, we celebrate the eucharistic sacrifice we are most closely united to the worship of the heavenly church; when in the fellowship of communion we honor and remember the glorious Mary ever virgin, St. Joseph, the holy apostles and martyrs and all the saints.[2]

The liturgically minded Christian touched by such descriptions may well ask: Where does this conception of the liturgy find practical expression today? Is this the kind of vision that one actually experiences at the average Sunday celebration of the eucharist, not to speak of the other liturgies of the churches? Few will be inclined to answer these questions in a positive manner. So the quandary arises: What has gone wrong? Why was the vision of the liturgical movement and of Vatican II not realized, and how can it be reclaimed?

The problem here is not, of course, new, and some history will be useful. There appears to be general consensus that the eschatological features of Roman Catholicism were at something of a low ebb as the church moved out of its neo-scholastic mold. Eschatology was regarded largely as the discreet study of the last things: death, particular judgment, heaven, hell, and purgatory. In the standard sacramental theology of the pre–Vatican II era, the focus was primarily on what was *present* in the liturgy, but not adequately on what was *yet to come*.

The English Dominican scholar Aidan Nichols is, for instance, critical of this aspect of *Mediator Dei* published by Pope Pius XII in 1947. Reflecting its time, Nichols says, Mediator Dei focused on the rendering *present* of "the most holy being of Jesus to the effective exclusion of any concern for the liturgy as the realized anticipation of the future Parousia of the Lord."[3] But, Nichols writes, the eucharist is not merely the "rendering actual in present time of a *past* reality" but is also "an anticipation of a future to come."[4] Nichols does not hesitate to say that, in most respects, *Mediator Dei* is theologically superior to *Sacrosanctum Concilium*. In its strong eschatological emphasis, however, Nichols finds the Vatican II document far superior.

The focus before Vatican II, we might say, was on the incarnational rather than the eschatological. This emphasis found expression par excellence in the attention given in the standard manuals of Catholic sacramental theology to Christ's eucharistic presence. That Christ is really and truly present in the eucharist is an affirmation that is and of necessity remains firmly implanted in authentic Roman Catholic teaching. But the laudable desire to insist on the reality of that presence, especially after the Council of Trent, was often worked out at the expense of the recognition that the eucharist has an intrinsically and systematically crucial eschatological element. Owen Cummings points out that "in the polemics of eucharistic theology during the Reformation and Catholic Reformation periods, the almost exclusive concerns of theologians were with the two eucharistic doctrines of sacrifice and presence" to the effect that "the eschatological dimension of the Eucharist faded into the background,"[5] even if it never quite disappeared.

This issue has played itself out symbolically in the question of which image of the eucharist is more fundamental: the Last Supper, the Sacrifice of Calvary, the Emmaus meal, or the Banquet of the Lamb Victorious? There is, of course, no theological competition between these images at all, yet there is much to be said for choosing the latter—the Banquet of the Lamb Victorious—as the one that is both more fundamental theologically and more inclusive of the others.

If liturgical eschatology has had a poor presence in Roman Catholicism in recent centuries, this presence was awakened with the liturgical movement's encounter with Eastern Christianity and with the renewal of New Testament and patristic scholarship. The major leaders of the Roman Catholic liturgical renewal (such as Lambert Beauduin, Odo Casel, and Joseph Jungmann) found strong inspiration for a revival of the eschatological in the life of the Eastern churches where it has always had a stronger and more explicit presence. Not surprisingly, the great Russian Orthodox liturgist Alexander Schmemann considered the recovery of eschatological consciousness in the liturgy as one of the principal achievements of the Western liturgical movement.[6]

In the eschatological consciousness of early twentieth-century Western thought, then, there developed a growing awareness that the Christ who is present in the eucharist is also the Christ who stands above and beyond the liturgy, drawing the church forward into the amplitude of eternity. In this vision, the worship of the church is not self-enclosed, complete in itself, as it were, but always has a dimension of reaching forward—of being pulled ahead of itself into the kingdom to come. The dimension of a future glory is the dimension of the *eschaton*, of what is yet to come, even as it is already present in sacrament.[7] To suggest that the eschatological was simply absent in Western Christianity after the patristic period would not, of course, be accurate. The famous hymn attributed to Saint Thomas Aquinas praises the sacred banquet "in which Christ is received as food, the memory of his Passion is renewed, the soul is filled with grace, and a pledge of future glory is given to us." The same theme found strong representation in the Anglican and Methodist traditions.[8] The eucharist is the pledge of *future* glory—a glory not yet fully embraced; the eucharist is the central expression of Christian eschatological hope.

If the reviving eschatological vision appears to have waned since the Second Vatican Council, as I suggest it has, the problem seems to be related largely to the cultural climate of the 1960s and after. In that decade, the eschatological quickly became translated into secular concern, that is, concern with the concrete *now* of the human world. Indeed, it seems as though the strong cultural openness of the Constitution on the Church in the Modern World (*Gaudium* et *spes*) began to provide the new hermeneutic for practical liturgical renewal after Vatican II.[9]

The advent of political and liberation theologies (which did contribute something immeasurably important to postconciliar Catholicism) had a downside: a preoccupation with the present that easily led to the political and social instrumentalization of eschatological themes.[10] Certainly, the relevance of the liturgy to social concerns had always been a strong conviction of the liturgical movement in figures like Prosper Guéranger in France and Virgil Michel in the United States; but the controlling themes therein were of comprehensive cultural transformation in the light of the Gospel.[11] The liturgy, it was fervently hoped, would transform the culture. However, in the late 1960s, the conception of the church and its liturgy as *of service* to culture and society took the upper hand, so that the liturgy began to be instrumentally harnessed to narrow, socially conscious ends.[12] Rather than liturgy transforming culture, the culture set the agenda for liturgical conceptions and practices.

By no means am I playing down the importance of liturgy engaging its social context; nor am I suggesting that the eschatological and the political are opposed. On the contrary, eschatology is inescapably political; but it may not be collapsed into the narrowly political and pragmatic as defined by secular culture.[13] The task of the church is not to remake the human city according to the more progressive insights of the age, but to remake it in the light of the new and eternal Jerusalem, the glorious city of God.[14]

Another factor in the reversal of the emerging eschatological consciousness has been the reductionist Christologies generally subsumed under the "third quest for the historical Jesus." These are decidedly biased against eschatological conceptions of Christ risen and glorified. "Historical quest" Christologies, precisely because of their "low" theological character and their preoccupation with historical data generally, isolate Jesus' itinerant table fellowship practices as the model for liturgy. This, in turn, leads to an emphasis on Jesus' table fellowship as a subversion of societal norms of association, authority, and hierarchy. The eschatology of these conceptions is a radically realized one. Conceptions of Christ in majesty and glory are set in the shadows.

In tandem with this factor, post–Vatican II feminist theology assumed a decidedly negative approach to traditional eschatology, regarding it as oppressive and escapist. Eschatological themes were suspected to be imperialist male politics of domination in liturgical guise. Feminist theology, especially in its radical expressions, has in fact set out to deconstruct Christian eschatological speech.[15]

In summary, eschatological consciousness, so central to New Testament and early Christianity, began to decline—more in the West than the East—soon after the patristic era. It was never, of course, completely absent in the West, but it did lie fallow for quite long periods. With the liturgical, biblical, and patristic movements of the late nineteenth and early twentieth centuries, the theme was recovered and renewed. This development found official approbation at the Second Vatican Council. A decline set in thereafter so that what Cardinal Christoph Schönborn has called "eschatological amnesia" has come to prevail in late modern Christianity.[16] Following Vatican II liturgy began to be increasingly secularized, that is, instrumentalized, then eventually sidelined.

The fundamental problem I wish to identify here, then, may be viewed as a move from eschatology to secularity. The challenge is the renewal of liturgical eschatology, which seeks not escape from the worldly and the secular but their transformation in view of the coming of God's kingdom.

The Praise of All Creation

The second critical dimension of the liturgy that I want to look at here is the cosmic. As I stated already, this dimension builds on the eschatological. Both themes overlap constantly and what may be stated in the context of one may easily be repeated in the other. Cosmology involves the whole created arena of salvation, not only the earthly and the heavenly, but all the unknown regions of God's creativity. The cosmic includes the worlds of angels, principalities and powers, the corporeal, the material, the spiritual, and the energetic.[17] It incorporates the mysterious regions of the heavens and of distant space.

The cosmic element of divine worship was, like the eschatological, fundamental to early Christian consciousness and it has over the centuries generally followed the same career of rise and decline, of loss and recovery as the former. Like the eschatological, cosmology for the most part has remained more explicitly formulated and experienced liturgically in the churches of the East than the West.

The reappearance of cosmic consciousness in the Western tradition during the twentieth-century liturgical movement and its setting therein has been notably captured in a dramatic statement in the *Catechism of the Catholic Church*. To the question, "Who celebrates the liturgy?" the following answer is given:

> "Recapitulated in Christ," these are the ones who take part in the service of the praise of God and the fulfillment of his plan: the heavenly powers, all creation (the four living beings), the servants of the Old and New Covenants (the twenty-four elders), the new people of God (the one hundred and forty-four thousand), especially the martyrs, "slain for the word of God," and the all-holy Mother of God (the Woman), the Bride of the Lamb, and finally "a great multitude which no one could number, from every nation, from all tribes, and peoples and tongues."[18]

In the kingdom of heaven, according to cosmic vision, the world of humankind and angels, of materiality, corporality, history, and human achievement are all drawn up into the praise of God. Salvation embraces not only the individual person, but all that God has made. The liturgy, then, in its cosmic dimension gathers up all creation into itself. But once again, the question arises: Where is this cosmically inclusive sense of the liturgy experienced today? And if in very few places, why is this so? What has gone wrong?

The cosmological theme has its origin in numerous aspects of the biblical tradition: in Genesis, in the Wisdom literature, in Saint Paul, and in the book of Revelation. The Psalms call all creation to praise God. The cosmic dimension of sacramental life was vitally operative in the patristic and early postpatristic periods. Authors like Maximus the Confessor and Pseudo-Dionysius are among the most remarkable and systematized poets of the cosmic.[19] For these authors, all creation and humankind are gathered up in a great cosmic liturgy. In notable figures of the medieval period, like Francis of Assisi, Hildegaard of Bingen, and Mechtild of Magdeburg, the theme found renewed and very imaginative expression.[20] The ancient sense, still vitally operable today in Eastern Christianity of creation and participation in a cosmic liturgy, is well summarized by Orthodox theologian

Paul Evdokimov when he states: "Everything is destined for a liturgical fulfillment."[21] In the "sacramental cosmology" of early Christianity, he writes, "Everything is referred to the Incarnation and everything finds its final goal and destiny in the Lord."[22] Accordingly, "Cosmic matter thus becomes a conductor of grace, a vehicle of the divine energies."[23] He continues: "The rhythms of nature, the flesh of this world, having been enrolled in the sacramental and liturgical action, integrate themselves into sacred history. The sacred space of the Church penetrates cosmic space,"[24] and the Christian liturgy "undertakes the consecration of the whole world."[25] Here the liturgy is not thought of simply as "a copy of the heavenly liturgy but is rather the eruption of the heavenly into history: God descends and sanctifies not only souls but the whole of nature and cosmic spaces."[26] In the same way, "the Church's calendar and the cycle of offerings sanctify and fill with meaning the elements of time and the march of history."[27]

In this vision of things, the eucharist is the consecration of all food; baptism is the consecration of all water. At the heart of this cosmology lay from early times an impressive "cosmic Christology." Christ is not only the shepherd of souls but the first fruits of all creation. He is the center of the cosmos, the one through whom all things were made and in whom all will be recapitulated and redeemed. We find this kind of emphasis very much alive today in the theology and liturgy of Eastern Christianity, but in the West it has had a more mixed career, at least since the end of the Middle Ages.

A process of cosmological disinterest was dramatically opened up by the Protestant Reformation and the hierarchical reorganization of the Christian worldview that accompanied it. Insights developed in the medieval *devotio moderna* were further reinforced in Protestant pietism and formalized philosophically in the Enlightenment "turn to the subject." The cosmic focus of salvation began to be replaced with an anthropological interest. In the fifteenth century, Cardinal Joseph Ratzinger points out, there occurred a loss of "faith in creation."[28] This step, he states, is intrinsic to modernity, which in fact began as a crisis of consciousness.

Dietrich Bonhoeffer described the problem as it unfolded in the Reformation tradition:

> The concept of the natural has fallen into discredit in Protestant ethics . . . this was a disastrous mistake, for its consequence was that the concept of

the natural no longer had a place in Protestant thought. . . . Before the light of grace everything human and natural sank into the night of sin, and now no one dared to consider the relative differences within the human and the natural, for fear that by their so doing grace might be diminished.[29]

Cardinal Avery Dulles regards this lack as a failure in the apprehension of the dimension of ecclesial catholicity, a failure to see salvation in a cosmic setting.[30]

With the Copernican revolution in science came the death of traditional cosmologies.[31] The dimension of the cosmos soon disappeared from Western theology. As transcendence became domesticated, the sacramental life lost its moorings in creation and became interiorized. The sacramental life was no longer viewed as a sanctification of creation, but as nourishment of the individual soul. Despite the efforts of Roman Catholic figures like von Hugel, George Tyrrell, and Karl Adam, and the anti-fideistic stance of Vatican Council I, cosmology found rather wooden expression as the twentieth century dawned.[32]

On the eve of Vatican II, historian of religions Mircea Eliade wrote that modern Western Christianity had long before lost its cosmic power:

> The cosmic liturgy, the mystery of nature's participation in the christological drama, have become inaccessible to Christians living in a modern city. The religious experience is no longer open to the cosmos. In the last analysis, it is a strictly private experience; salvation is a problem that concerns man and his god; at most, man recognizes that he is responsible not only to God but also to history. But in these man-God-history relationships there is no place for the cosmos. From this it would appear that, even for a genuine Christian, the world is no longer felt as the work of God.[33]

The same processes of secularization that caused a collapse of the eschatological inevitably affected cosmology in the post–Vatican II era. Cosmic conceptions were thought to belong to a primitive religious worldview; the assurances of cosmic conceptions of the Christian enterprise gave way to the emerging convictions that only radical subjectivity could be trusted. God was increasingly seen not in terms of universal lordship but as the foundation for the human search for meaning. Cardinal Dulles has suggested that the doctrine of the Trinity is the controlling principle of cosmology.[34] Not surprisingly the advent of radical reconceptions of God led to a loss of trinitarian cosmology. The removal of God from the grand architecture of the universe was accompanied by a growing disinterest in the latter. Today, then, the cosmic sense in culture and in religious consciousness remains fractured, and the psychological and the interior have become the focus of the processes of salvation.[35]

Again, to summarize: The theological and liturgical vision of created reality as God's handiwork and as the material of the world redeemed, so strong in early Christianity, began to wane in the West with the collapse of traditional cosmology during the Reformation, the Enlightenment, and the scientific revolution. Though revived in the liturgical movement, cosmology was not, in fact, adequately underscored even at Vatican II. The central move here, one might say, was from cosmology to anthropology—or, more precisely, to anthropology separated from cosmology. The essence of the problem to be corrected may be described as a move from the cosmological to the psychological. The challenge is the renewal in theory and in practice of the cosmological, not as a rejection of the psychological but as its redemption through an anthropology that unites the cosmic and the psychological.

THE FULLNESS OF GLORY

The collapse of the eschatological into the political and of the cosmological into the psychological generated, in turn, a third problem: the modern crisis in doxology. Prescinding from semantic debates, by doxology I have in mind, "right praise" or "right worship." Doxology means "glory," the knowledge of glory, that which gives glory to God, the celebration of divine glory. Significantly, doxologies have a trinitarian shape: the shape of the relations within the trinitarian life of God, the *perichôrêsis* which invokes the word *choreography,* the dance-like ordered movement of the triune God.[36]

The theme of glory in its biblical and early Christian contexts has been the source of considerable study among major modern theologians in recent decades, most notably Karl Barth, Hans Urs von Balthasar, and Jürgen Moltmann.[37] It has found general expression in explorations of the play of God and of humankind, and in theories of festivity and praise.[38] The fundamental conception is that the end of all things is the glorification, blessing, rejoicing in, contemplation, enjoyment of God.[39] For Augustine, in the kingdom we are finally free for the joy of God and the enjoyment of each other in God, a theme reflected much later in the Westminster Confession of 1647. Though a theology of glory has for the most part remained a notably undeveloped aspect of Western Christianity, the lacuna has begun to be filled by the writings of a whole new generation of theologies of beauty.[40]

The theme of the doxological order of divine and human life remains still largely unknown—and therefore sounds very strange—to modern Christians. Listen, for instance, to how Gregory of Nyssa sets out salvation history under the rubric of dance: "Once," he writes, "there was a time when the whole of rational creation formed a single dancing chorus looking upwards to the one leader of this dance. . . . And the harmony of that motion which was imparted to them by reason of his law found its way into their dancing."[41] Original sin, however, Gregory states, destroyed this dance-like harmony of the spirit, and it will be only at the end of all things that all will again be as it was. Gregory continues: "Our first parents still danced in among the angelic powers. But the beginning of sin made an end of the sweet sounds of this chorus."[42]

Since then man has been deprived of this communion with the angels, and, since the fall, must sweat and most arduously toil to do battle with and conquer the spirit that, thanks to sin, now weighs upon him; but the spoils of victory will be these: that which was lost in his original defeat will once more be his to enjoy, and once again he will take part in the dancing of the divine chorus. . . . And this victory will come and thou shalt be found in the dancing ranks of the angelic spirits.[43]

Among the principal complaints expressed among many Roman Catholics today is that the liturgy has lost its former ethos of glory. The Roman liturgy since Vatican II, it is often said, lacks beauty, awe, majesty, and splendor. Liturgy has become trivial, commonplace, without exuberance, pale, lifeless, and uninspiring. An absence of depth and significance appears to characterize liturgical celebration at the practical level. A sense of cultural weightlessness has set in, so that rites have taken on a superficial and inconsequential quality.[44] The understandable desire to replace the excessive solemnity of the preconciliar era has easily given rise to liturgical triviality since Vatican II.

This problem is no doubt reflected in its own way in the modern experiences of the Reformed churches. Amos Wilder points out, from a Protestant perspective:

The church today has widely lost and all but forgotten the experience of glory which lies at the heart of Christianity. Indeed, in one form or another that experience is a main trait of all religion just because human nature and existence itself derive from inexhaustible energies and cataracts of light and life. That the original plentitude is so widely smothered in the creaturely condition only enforces the special and irreplaceable role of religion in witnessing to it.[45]

Certainly complaints of this kind are not valid (speaking at least from a Roman Catholic perspective) if what is lamented is the demise of the triumphalism that accompanied Roman Catholic worship in certain post-Tridentine expressions. Yet, I believe, the diagnosis is fundamentally correct. The essential problem derives in great part, I believe, from an impoverished eschatological and cosmic consciousness—which works itself out in the impoverishment of the doxological within Christian liturgical life.

It is, of course, important to see that many of these developments were understandable reactions to the excesses of the baroque era, itself in part a reaction to the Reformation's objection to ritual excess in medieval religion. Louis Bouyer's observations of the liturgical ethos of baroque Catholicism are instructive: "The liturgy, as many handbooks of the period actually say, was considered to be 'the etiquette of the great King.'"[46] He continues: "The most obvious features of it were those embodying the external pomp, decorum, and grandeur befitting so majestic a Prince."[47] Accordingly, "In the Presence of the Divine King, a kind of heavenly grand opera could be performed, with all the display of lights, jewels (mostly false), exquisite polyphonic singing and pageantry which commonly accompany a royal reception."[48]

The official liturgical movement in Catholicism—in the person of Pope Pius X—fought the corruption of the liturgy as expressed in the seventeenth and eighteenth centuries in operatic music and whimsical art. It was proper that these excesses should have been cleared away, and it should not be surprising that there occurred a corresponding move toward the ascetic, the clean, and the sober in the liturgical movement leading up to Vatican II.

The seeds of doxological impoverishment were also present in the Catholic Reformation's own approach to liturgy. Given the increasing focus on "matter" and "form" in post-Tridentine theology and the determination (and practical dismissal) of all else as "ceremonial," the latter easily lost its theological moorings. The mechanistic conceptions of liturgy so evident in sacramental theology after Trent led ironically to free reign being given to the ceremonial dimensions of worship. But when theological control over "ceremonies" was abandoned, this area became free to take on a—rather eccentric—life of its own, most notoriously in the baroque period.

A similar anti-doxological "inculturation" of the liturgy was expressed in the increasing settling within Catholic worship of the Enlightenment ideals of rationality, order, and logic, themselves secularized versions of the Reformation mentality.[49] Neutrality toward creation, a fear of human works, and a caution about religion as a human phenomenon coupled with the philosophical convictions of the "age of suspicion" and its "masters," Marx, Nietzsche, and Freud, had deleterious effects on worship.[50] The suspicion that there may be no objective divine partner to the liturgical reach for transcendence increasingly beset modern Christians. That trinitarian thought has been so seriously challenged recently has had immediate consequences for doxological energy. When theologies of God inherited from the past become suspect, the impetus for exuberant worship wanes.

These various strands of influence conspired to provide a cultural background to liturgical renewal in the 1960s and 1970s that embraced sociological behaviorism and mechanism. By behaviorism and mechanism I mean views derived from certain social-scientific schools that liturgical rites operate by a limited and definite set of rational and predictable principles. Liturgical renewal in this model sought to control ambiguous expression and to curtail what seemed excessive or overwrought. The emphasis was on simplicity, clarity, directness of expression, freedom from duplication.[51] What historian Eamon Duffy described as "the stripping of the altars" during the English Reformation has a modern linguistic counterpart in what sociologist David Martin calls "the stripping of the words."[52]

We live in a time, then, when what Doris Donnelly calls spiritual "impediments to praise" are pervasive.[53] Catherine Pickstock has argued that the culture of modernity is intrinsically anti-doxological and that deconstructionist speech, the emerging speech patterns of Western culture, undermines the language of praise. What Pickstock calls the "polis of death" has served a disintegration of the conceptions and practice of praise and glory.[54] In such a climate the attitude of universal affirmation proposed by Joseph Pieper as the fundamental impulse of human festival becomes impossible.[55]

Themes of praise and doxology were certainly recovered in the early liturgical movement and they permeate both the documents of Vatican II and official liturgical thought since then. After the Council, theologians like Karl Rahner, Piet Fransen, and Raymond Vaillancourt produced "celebration" models of sacrament seeking to rescue sacramental theology from narrow theories of efficacy and to restore the biblical spirit of gratuitous praise.[56] But then the celebrative dimensions of worship took off unwittingly in strange directions, largely absorbing the "play" themes of the 1960s and 1970s associated with such figures as Harvey Cox and Sam Keen.[57]

The rather secular and superficial play theory of the 1960s and 1970s had the effect of discrediting and disorienting the emerging biblical and patristic themes of celebration, joy, and festivity in Catholic worship. The essential problem in this development was that conceptions of joy and festivity were abstracted from their paschal moorings, so that the very concept of "celebration" became suspect.[58] What was forgotten in the superficial enthusiasm of those decades is that authentic Christian joy is always forged in the deathly passing over of Christ and that in the biblical tradition, pain is, as Walter Bruggemann points out, "the matrix of praise."[59] Liturgy today, then, finds itself caught between ritual-functionalism—the new version of neo-scholastic mechanism—and the celebrative, self-centered therapeutics of present-day culture, the final stages of doxology corrupted.

In brief, the rich biblical theme of divine glory expanded upon by the early fathers into magnificent conceptions of liturgical praise began to experience wild swings after the patristic era. In the Renaissance and baroque eras, ceremonial was freed to assume eccentric shapes. Hampered by the Enlightenment and its various suspicions, doxological conceptions do not seem capable of finding appropriate practical registers in the culture of modernity. The central move may be described as a transition from the doxological to the pragmatic, with some relief provided by exuberant charismatic pietism. The challenge for today and tomorrow is a renewal of liturgical doxology, which would raise up and redeem the pragmatic and reform human beauty with paschal joy.

Renewing Doxology Today

This essay is not meant as a litany of complaints, but as a prelude to some positive proposals. One should neither exaggerate the problems nor underestimate the extent to which the revised liturgies of the churches today are capable of assuming powerful and transforming expression. They do so in cathedrals, churches and communities throughout the world. The question remains, however: How can the eschatological, the cosmological, and the doxological be more generally restored and renewed in liturgy?

First, the eschatological. At the beginning of a new millennium, the Christian imagination should be grasped anew by the book of Revelation. This interest can serve to bring back into Christian focus the heavenly liturgy as the model for the earthly. Scholars disagree on the extent to which the dramatic portrayals of the New Jerusalem in Revelation reflect the worship life of early Christianity. The model of Revelation does seem, overall, to be deeply liturgical. In this model, the liturgy of heaven and earth are united as the former gathers up the latter.[60] In my view, the importance of this theme cannot be overestimated. Obviously, I cannot here go into much detail. My examples will be mostly from the aesthetic realms of the liturgy, particularly the architectural and the musical—which I think are vastly underestimated as carriers of the themes I am discussing in this essay.

Church architecture is more crucial here than we might think. Traditionally in the West, eschatological themes were carried more in the visual and the representational dimensions of the liturgy than in the verbal.[61] The art of the great cathedrals of the middle ages, for instance, acted to bring into liturgical consciousness the order and hierarchy, the beauty and splendor of heaven. For that very reason, the assault on the visual at the Reformation may have unwittingly brought about a decline in eschatological thought in Western Christendom. As historian Margaret Miles points out, the hierarchical, mediated conception of eschatological redemption set forth in the elaborate visual schemes of medieval ecclesiastical buildings were set aside by the Reformers as "works" standing in the way of free and direct access to God.[62]

Accordingly, the renewal of the eschatological means that Christian places of worship must once again become replicas of the Holy City, the New Jerusalem, the Temple of heaven that is heaven itself. The earthly church building is a sacrament of the city of heaven, and a sign of glorified humanity. This truth requires expression in a dramatic renewal of the iconographic in Christian worship. Orthodox bishop Kallistos Ware has written on the crucial facility of the iconographic in worship:

> The icons which fill the church serve as a point of meeting between heaven and earth. As each local congregation prays Sunday by Sunday, surrounded by the figures of Christ, the angels, and the saints, these visible images remind the faithful unceasingly of the invisible presence of the whole company of heaven at the Liturgy. The faithful can feel that the walls of the church open out upon eternity, and they are helped to realize that their Liturgy on earth is one and the same with the great Liturgy of heaven.[63]

Similarly, a renewal of what Michael Joncas calls the "eschatological" function of liturgical music is also required. Joncas writes:

> Both Jewish and Christian Scriptures image heavenly worship in terms of song performed by angels, creatures, elders and saints in concert. Perhaps the eschatological function of sacred music is most neglected when liturgical music is considered only the self-expression of the worshiping assembly. Through the use of sacred music from many epochs worshipers gain a sense of connection to those who have preceded them in faith as well as the invisible presence of the blessed at their worship. The Preface eschatol expresses it well: " . . . with angels and archangels, with thrones and dominations, and with the whole band of the heavenly armies, we sing a hymn to the glory of God, chanting without end."[64]

More generally, a restoration of faith in heavenly things is crucially necessary to eschatological consciousness, not least a robust faith in the Christ who always stands above and beyond the church and its worshiping assemblies. Carl Braaten has called for the renewal of a "full-orbed Christology" as the key to the renewal of the church today.[65] Similarly, Cardinal Avery Dulles seeks a renewal of a "realist tradition" concerning Christ's headship that has immediate liturgical implications:

> Catholic theology does not yield to the subjectivist view of faith as a freely adopted but arbitrary perspective. Contemporary religious relativism all too casually dissolves the Christ of dogma into a mere cult-object of the Church, so that he is viewed as the product of Christian piety rather than as the source and norm of Christian existence. Catholic realism, on the contrary, concerns itself with Christ because it is convinced that by the very nature of things he demands our attention and reverence. Faith for the Catholic is not a projection of religious needs and desires but a submission to the real.[66]

In turn, the cosmic dimension of Christian liturgy needs dramatic renewal for the future. The theological features of creation are a hallowed part of Christian faith. The fundamental impulses of modern creation theology are, in my view, quite solid and can serve well the renewal of the cosmic in Christian consciousness and in the practice of the liturgy. Karl Rahner's conception of the "Liturgy of the World" and Teilhard de Chardin's "Hymn of the Universe" and "Mass on the World" are spectacular modern conceptions of the cosmic scope of the liturgy.

In his 1995 Apostolic Letter, *Orientale Lumen,* Pope John Paul II offers a stirring vision derived from the East of what he calls "Liturgy for the Whole Man, the Whole Cosmos." The Pope writes:

> In the liturgical experience, Christ the Lord is the light which illumines the way and reveals the transparency of the cosmos, precisely as in Scripture. The events of the past find in Christ their meaning and fullness, and creation is revealed for what it is: a complex whole which finds its perfection, its purpose in the liturgy alone . . . .
>
> Within this framework, liturgical prayer in the East shows a great aptitude for involving the human person in his or her totality: The mystery is sung in the loftiness of its content, but also in the warmth of the sentiments it awakens in the heart of redeemed humanity. In the sacred act, even bodiliness is summoned to praise, and beauty, which in the East is one of the best-loved names expressing the divine harmony and the model of humanity transfigured, appears everywhere: in the shape of the church, in the sounds, the colors, in the lights, in the scents. The lengthy duration of the celebrations, the repeated invocations, everything expresses gradual identification with the mystery celebrated with one's whole person . . . .
>
> Christianity does not reject matter. Rather, bodiliness is considered in all its value in the liturgical act, whereby the human body is disclosed in its inner nature as a temple of the Spirit and is united with the Lord Jesus, who himself took a body for the world's salvation . . . .
>
> To those who seek a truly meaningful relationship with themselves and with the cosmos, so often disfigured by selfishness and greed, the liturgy reveals the way to the harmony of the new man and invites him to respect the eucharistic potential of the created world. That world is destined to be assumed in the eucharist of the Lord, in his passover, present in the sacrifice of the altar.[67]

If liturgical architecture has historically, as I suggested, been a great bearer of the eschatological, it has also played a powerful cosmic role. While there are plenty of examples of excess in this feature of liturgical architecture, especially in the baroque period, the long tradition of portraying the heavens, the sun, moon, and stars, as well as the flowers and fruits of the earth, animals, human labor, and culture underscores theologically the cosmic score of Christian worship. Churches are replicas of the cosmos. Accordingly, what has happened in modern church building, most notably in Roman Catholic circles, in recent decades is of great moment. The modernist movement in architecture, it seems to me, has served to evacuate the cosmic sense in liturgy. The minimalism of liturgical architecture over the past thirty years has visually excluded the world of heavenly hierarchies, of earthly creation and creatures, of the elevated materiality and sonority of art. It is understandable but regrettable that the "visual noise" of baroque Catholic art and architecture has given way to the "visual silence" of many post–Vatican II places of worship. Mainstream liturgical architecture has become, in that sense, deeply gnostic.

In liturgical music, too, there has occurred a loss of the cosmic and a move from what Quentin Faulkner calls "world-centered" to "self-centered" forms.[68] Music in worship is no longer evocative of the great space of the universe but of the small space of the inner self. Not surprisingly, the great Masses and *Te Deums* of Catholic musical history are to many now an embarrassment and have no place in the liturgy. The same could be said of the Reformed traditions: While attentive more to word rather than cosmos, the evangelically robust musical forms that developed in the Reformation traditions have of late given way to musical styles and expressions that are notably pietistic and psychological. To correct these trends, liturgical music in the great tradition must once again become "music for a great space" (to borrow a phrase from composer Richard Proulx), not only the space characteristic of acoustically ambient buildings, but the space of the cosmos, the music of the spheres.[69] The current fascination with the spiritually "spacious" music of John Tavener is worth exploring here.[70] Along with Arvo Pärt and Henryk Gorecki, Tavener has successfully wedded popular taste and sensibility with the more expansive and mystical modalities of liturgical music tradition.

What are the grounds for a renewal of the doxological? The engagement of the liturgy with the eschatological and the cosmic, that is with Christ in glory and the all-embracing vision of heaven, is, as I suggested earlier, the fundamental impulse that generates conceptions and expressions of praise, awe, and majesty in the liturgy. The resources for renewal are, I suggest, to be found in the conception of the world as the manifestation of God's glory. Liturgy is not, as Romano Guardini and Hugo Rahner have pointed out, a useful activity from a pragmatic point of view; it is quite useless.[71] The early church is replete with conceptions of worship that are astonishing in their grandeur and profundity. These are to be found in Augustine, Gregory Nazianzen, Maximus the Confessor, and Pseudo-Dionysius.[72] They are rarely expressed so beautifully as in a great Eastern hymn of Hippolytus addressed to Christ, in which images of dance, music, and festivity are invoked:

O thou leader of the mystic round-dance! O divine Pasch and new feast of all things! O cosmic festal gathering! O joy of the universe, honour, ecstasy, exquisite delight by which dark death is destroyed . . . and the people that were in the depths arise from the dead and announce to all the hosts of heaven: "The thronging choir from earth is coming home."[73]

Liturgy must again become solemn and glorious, profound and ecstatic, serene and exuberant, weighty and festive. The play of heaven needs its earthly counterpart, and the earthly must take on the superabundance of the festival of the heavenly city. Such a vision will serve to restore praise-filled energy, delight, awe, and fascination regarding the divine mystery that is at the heart of the liturgy. Visually powerful liturgical art and architecture have a crucial agency in sustaining and generating the doxological expressivity of the liturgy. These rebound profoundly upon all that occurs within a place of worship so conceived and arranged. Rites and ceremonies take on a glorious, majestic, and awe-inspiring character. Altars, ambos, baptismal fonts, eucharistic tabernacles, and other liturgical furnishings assume a noble and beautiful quality. The ritual space is so configured as to invite, even require, noble and dignified rites and ceremonies.

The language is not that of the everyday, but of the New Jerusalem. The speech of liturgy in doxological mode should be characterized by what Daniel Stevick has called the "tendency to excess":

> The rhetoric of praise tends to multiply phrases and terms. In one of his sermons, Lancelot Andrewes said, "Blessed be God. Yea, blessed and thanked, and praised; Benedictus, Magnificat, Jubilate, and all. All . . ." A lean, economical statement will not do. It cannot convey the sense of wonder, the feeling of overwhelmedness that praise requires. The vocabulary of praise is not unlimited, and intense experience tends to repeat.

Doxological terms follow one another in short, similar clauses: "We praise thee, we bless thee, we worship, thee . . . ."

This stylistic extravagance suggests an act not fully under control. The maker of praise is uncalculating, un-self-regarding, caught up in the reality of the Other, occupied with that Other. For a moment, one is delivered from weighing, planning, arranging. A neatly shaped, understated mode of speech is inadequate. One wishes for "a thousand tongues," one is "lost" in wonder. In praise one is in touch with that which one does not define and hold, but rather that by which one is defined and held. We constantly cite, as we praise, the inadequacy and limitedness of what we can know and express. God's gifts are more than we can number; God's greatness is more than we can grasp.[74]

A new "enchantment" in the liturgy is necessary to counter the attitude of suspicion that modernity has brought to liturgical speech and action. Authentic doxology represents a sphere of spiritual wealth and superfluity even in the midst of direst want. What John Bossy calls the "polyphonic character" of the mysteries must again be performed and the sense of the numinous, the holy, the tremendous, and fascinating given renewed expression.[75] A "sense of plentitude," of an abundance of riches will characterize renewed doxology.[76] The wide range of emotional expressivity that characterized liturgical history, but has more recently been flattened out, needs to be recovered and set free.

THE WAY FORWARD?

A liturgical life equal to the ecstatic call to worship proclaimed yearly in the *Exsultet* of the Easter Vigil provides a most adequate model of a liturgy that can embrace the broad and expansive dynamics of *eschaton, cosmos,* and *doxa:*

> Rejoice, heavenly powers! Sing, choirs of angels!
> Exult, all creation around God's throne!
> Jesus Christ, our King, is risen!
> Sound the trumpet of salvation!
> Rejoice, O earth, in shining splendor,
> radiant in the brightness of your King!
> Christ has conquered! Glory fills you!
> Darkness vanishes for ever!
> Rejoice, O Mother Church! Exult in glory!

> The risen Savior shines upon you!
> Let this place resound with joy,
> echoing the mighty song of all God's people!

---

1. Text in Austin Flannery, OP, gen. ed., *Vatican Council II. Volume I: The Conciliar and Post Conciliar Documents* (Northport, NY: new rev. ed., 1996) 5.

2. ___, 77; see also no. 51.

3. Aidan Nichols, OP, "A Tale of Two Documents: Sacrosanctum Concilium and Mediator Dei," *Antiphon* 5:1 (2000) 24–25.

4. ___, 29. Nichols praises the strength of the eschatological emphasis in the 1994/7 *Catechism of the Catholic Church*, especially in the earlier section of part two which deals with liturgy generally, a section in which the influence of Melkite Catholic theologian Jean Corbon is evident. On this, see Cassian Folsom, "The Holy Spirit and the Church in History," *Homiletic and Pastoral Review* 96:7 (April 1996) 15–23. See also Jean Corbon, *The Wellspring of Worship* (New York: Paulist Press, 1988).

5. Owen F. Cummings, *Coming to Christ: A Study in Christian Eschatology* (Lanham, MD: University Press of America, 1998) 243; see 241ff.

6. See Thomas Fisch, ed., *Liturgy and Tradition: Theological Reflections of Alexander Schmemann* (Crestwood, NY: St. Vladimir's Seminary Press, 1990).

7. For general treatments, see Massey H. Shepherd, Jr., *The Paschal Liturgy and the Apocalypse* (Richmond, VA: John Knox Press, 1960); Pierre Prigent, *Apocalypse et liturgie* (Neuchâtel: Delachaux et Niestlé, 1964); Edouárd Cothenet, *Exégèse et liturgie* (Paris: Editions du Cerf, 1988); idem, "Earthly Liturgy and Heavenly Liturgy according to the Book of Revelation," in Matthew J. O'Connell, ed., *Roles in the Liturgical Assembly: The Twenty-Third Liturgical Conference Saint Serge* (New York: Pueblo Publishing Company, 1981) 115–36; essay entitled, "The Church as Worshipping Community," in Geoffrey Wainwright, *Worship with One Accord: Where Liturgy and Ecumenism Embrace* (New York: Oxford University Press, 1997) 19–33; Mary M. Schaffer, "Heavenly and Earthly Liturgies: Patristic Prototypes, Medieval Perspectives, and a Contemporary Application," *Worship* 70:6 (November, 1996) 482–505; Jean-Pierre Ruiz, "The Apocalypse of John and Contemporary Roman Catholic Liturgy," *Worship* 68: 6 (November 1994) 482–504.

8. See Geoffrey Wainwright, *Eucharist and Eschatology* (New York: Oxford University Press) esp.1–17, 123–54. One of the most prominent Anglican representatives, Jeremy Taylor, speaks of the eucharist as "the antepast of heaven." See Thomas K. Carroll, ed., *Jeremy Taylor: Selected Works* (Mahwah, NJ: Paulist Press, 1990); also Henry R. McAdoo and Kenneth Stevenson, *The Mystery of the Eucharist in the Anglican Tradition* (Norwich: Canterbury Press,

1995) esp. 153ff. John Wesley's *Hymns on the Lord's Supper* (1745) are notable for a high eucharistic eschatology.

9. For an advocacy of this development, see the chapters entitled, "Two Models of Christian Worship" and "Liturgical Spirituality, Conciliar Foundations," in Shawn Madigan, *Spirituality Rooted in Liturgy* (Washington, DC: Pastoral Press, 1988) 89–115, 117–37.

10. See, Cardinal Joseph Ratzinger, *The Church, Ecumenism, and Politics: New Essays in Ecclesiology* (New York: Crossroad, 1988) esp. 143ff.; also Bonaventure Kloppenburg, *The People's Church* (Chicago, IL: Franciscan Herald Press, 1978) esp. 68–72; also the various essays on the liturgy in Edward Schillebeeckx, *God the Future of Man* (London: Sheed and Ward, 1969).

11. Keith F. Pecklers, *The Unread Vision: The Liturgical Movement in the United States of America, 1926–1955* (Collegeville, MN: Liturgical Press, 1998) esp. 81–149.

12. On the strengths and weaknesses of the "servant" model of the church, see the chapter entitled, "The Church as Servant," in Avery Dulles, *Models of the Church* (Garden City, NY: Doubleday, 1974) 82–96; also "Imaging the Church for the 1980s," in *A Church to Believe In: Discipleship and the Dynamics of Freedom* (New York: Crossroad, 1982) 1–18.

13. See Robert E. Webber and Rodney Clapp, *People of the Truth: The Power of the Worshiping Community in the Modern World* (San Francisco: Harper and Row, 1988) esp. 17–83; the essay entitled "Eschatological Politics and Political Eschatology," in Robert W. Jenson, *Essays in Theology of Culture* (Grand Rapids, MI: William B. Eerdmans Publishing Company, 1995) 16–27; Peter L. Berger and Richard Neuhaus, eds., *Against the World, For the World* (New York: Seabury Press, 1976).

14. See M. Francis Mannion, "The Church and the City," *First Things*, no. 100 (February 2000) 31–36; also the chapter entitled, "The City," in Urban T. Holmes III, *Ministry and Imagination* (New York: The Seabury Press, 1976) 13–34.

15. For example, Sallie McFague, *The Body of God: An Ecological Theology* (Minneapolis: Fortress Press, 1993) esp. 197–212; Rosemary Radford Ruether, *Women and Redemption: A Theological History* (Minneapolis: Fortress Press, 1998). For a summary of feminist eschatology, see Cummings, Coming to Christ, 203–206.

16. Christoph Schönborn, *From Death to Life: The Christian Journey* (San Francisco: Ignatius Press, 1995) 14.

17. For a comprehensive introduction to this theme, see the chapter titled, "The Cosmic Setting of Salvation," in Aidan Nichols, *Epiphany: A Theological Introduction to Catholicism* (Collegeville, MN: Liturgical Press, 1996) 368–90. See also Louis Bouyer, *Cosmos: The World and the Glory of God* (Petersham,

MA: St. Bede's Publications, 1988); also the chapter, "The Physical World," in Joseph F. Needy, *The World of the Early Christians* (Collegeville, MN: Liturgical Press, 1977) 47–69. The angelic aspect of creation is generally treated under cosmology, but may be equally regarded in the context of eschatology. See Jean Danielou: *The Angels and Their Mission According to the Fathers of the Church* (Westminster, MD: Christian Classics, 1987); Erik Peterson, *The Angels and the Liturgy* (New York: Herder and Herder, 1964).

18. *Catechism of the Catholic Church,* 1138.

19. While Psuedo-Dionysius has generally held a negative reputation in modern theology and liturgical studies (though there are some signs the tide is turning), studies on Maximus have experienced an impressive expansion recently. See Aidan Nichols, *Byzantine Gospel: Maximus the Confessor in Modern Scholarship* (Edinburgh: T & T Clark, 1994). The classic study on the liturgiology of Maximus remains Hans Urs von Balthasar, *Kosmische Liturgie: Das Weltbild Maximus des Bekenners* (Einsiedeln: Johannes-Verlag, 1961).

20. Aidan Nichols describes St. Francis's "Canticle of Brother Son" as "the greatest Catholic statement of ecological cosmology" (*Epiphany,* 379). This poem is most popularly known through the hymn "All Creatures of Our God and King."

21. Paul Evdokimov, *The Art of the Icon: A Theology of Beauty* (Redondo Beach, CA: Oakwood Publications, 1990) 117.

22. ___.

23. ___, 119.

24. ___.

25. ___, 120.

26. ___.

27. ___.

28. Cardinal Joseph Ratzinger, *"In the Beginning" . . . A Catholic Understanding of the Story of Creation and the Fall* (Grand Rapids, MI: Eerdmans Publishing Company, 1995) 83.

29. Dietrich Bonhoeffer, *Ethics* (London: Collins, 1964) 143–44.

30. See Dulles, *The Catholicity of the Church,* 34ff. The Archbishop of Canterbury's 1947 Report on Catholicity, declares that in Holy Scripture justification has a cosmic configuration and is a renewal of creation: "Hence Luther, in neglecting the doctrine of man as made in God's Image, and in affirming the 'total depravity' of man as the ground of the 'bondage of the will,' was isolating redemption from its proper setting; and this failure to provide a theology of the created order has remained as a permanent characteristic of orthodox Protestantism" (Dulles, *The Catholicity of the Church,* 52ff).

31. For a very readable summary of this development, see George V. Coyne and Alessandro Omizzole, *Wayfarers in the Cosmos: The Human Quest for Meaning* (New York: Crossroad, 2002).

32. Louis Bouyer reminds us that a cosmology of sorts was present in the baroque liturgy—but of a distorted kind. What grasped the baroque imagination was "the literary and aesthetic world of Renaissance neo-paganism" (*Liturgical Piety* [Notre Dame, IN: University of Indiana Press, 1955] 5). This spelled the destruction of the Christian worldview. Bouyer describes the process as follows: "The result was the destruction, so far as daily practice was concerned, of that biblical medium, of that world of types and parables which had always been the natural background of Patristic and medieval tradition. The biblical imagery in which the very Christianity of the Church as expressed in the liturgy, had always been set forth and incarnated, was now displaced by a world of completely pagan figures, entirely foreign to the mentality out of which the rites and words of the liturgy had originally developed" (ibid., 6).

33. Mircea Eliade, *The Sacred and the Profane: The Nature of Religion* (New York: Harvest Books, 1959) 178–79.

34. Dulles, *The Catholicity of the Church*, esp. 34–39.

35. See M. Francis Mannion, "*Liturgy and the Present Crisis of Culture*," in Eleanor Bernstein, ed., Liturgy and Spirituality in Context: Perspectives on Prayer and Culture (Collegeville, MN: Liturgical Press, 1990) 1–26.

36. Catherine Mowry La Cugna is one of the few recent authors on trinitarian theology who has attended to the doxological and perichoretic dimension of this doctrine. See her *God For Us: The Trinity and Christian Life* (San Francisco: Harper, 1991) esp. 270ff. See also the magisterial work by Geoffrey Wainwright, Doxology: The Praise of God in Worship, Doctrine and Life (New York: Oxford University Press, 1980).

37. See Karl Barth, *Church Dogmatics 2/1: The Doctrine of God* (Edinburgh: T & T Clark, 1957) 608–77; Hans Urs von Balthasar, *The Glory of the Lord: A Theological Aesthetics*, 7 vols. (San Francisco: Ignatius Press, 1982–1991), Jürgen Moltmann, *Theology and Joy* (London: SCM Press, 1973), idem, *God in Creation: An Ecological Doctrine of Creation* (London: SCM Press Ltd. 1985). See also Daniel W. Hardy and David F. Ford, *Jubilate: Theology in Praise* (London: Darton, Longman, and Todd, 1984); Hughes Oliphant Old, *Themes and Variations for a Christian Doxology* (Grand Rapids, MI: Eerdmans, 1992).

38. The classic work remains Hugo Rahner, *Man at Play: Or Did You Ever Practice Eutrapelia?* (London: Burns and Oates, 1973). See also Romano Guardini, *The Spirit of the Liturgy* (New York: Herder and Herder, 1998); Harvey Guthrie, *Theology as Thanksgiving: From Israel's Psalms to the Church's Eucharist* (New York: Seabury, 1981); Gerhard Martin, *Fest: The Transformation of Everyday* (Philadelphia: Fortress Press, 1976); Josef Pieper, *In Tune with*

the World: A Theory of Festivity (Chicago: Franciscan Herald Press, 1973). See also Hans-Georg Gadamer, *Truth and Method* (New York: Seabury Press, 1975) esp. 91–119; idem, *The Relevance of the Beautiful and Other Essays* (Cambridge: Cambridge University Press, 1986); Eugene Fink, Le Jeu comme symbole du monde (Paris: Editions de Minuit, 1966); Johan Huizinga, *Homo Ludens: A Study of the Play Element in Culture* (London: Paladin, 1970); Giuseppe Del Re, *Cosmic Dance: Science Discovers the Mysterious Harmony of the Universe* (Philadelphia: Templeton Foundation Press, 2000).

39. See E. L. Mascell, *Grace and Glory* (Denville, NJ: Dimension Books, 1961).

40. For a survey of recent writing, see the special issue of *Liturgy Digest* 3:1 (1996), edited by Nathan Mitchell.

41. *Homiliae in Psalmos* 6 PG 44, 508 bd; English translation from Rahner, Man at Play, 89.

42. ___.

43. ___, 89–90. The theme of art conceived within a theology of fall and redemption has been explored by Cardinal Paul Poupard in "Paradise Lost to Paradise Regained: The Mission of Art"; text in *Antiphon* 4:3 (1999) 35–40.

44. See, for instance, Cardinal Joseph Ratzinger, *The Feast of Faith: Approaches to a Theology of Liturgy* (San Francisco: Ignatius Press, 1986); idem, *A New Song for the Lord: Faith in Christ and Liturgy Today* (New York: Crossroad Publishing Co., 1996); Hans Urs von Balthasar, "The Grandeur of the Liturgy," *Communio* 5:4 (1978) 344–51; idem, "Liturgy and Awe," in *Explorations in Theology II: Spouse of the World* (San Francisco: Ignatius Press, 1991) 461–72; idem, "The Worthiness of the Liturgy," in *New Elucidations* (San Francisco: Ignatius Press, 1986) 127–40; James Hitchcock, *Recovery of the Sacred: Reforming the Reformed Liturgy* (San Francisco: Ignatius Press, 1995); Walter Kasper, "The Council's Vision for a Renewal of the Church," *Communio* 17:4 (Winter 1990) 484–85.

45. Amos Niven Wilder, *Theopoetic: Theology and the Religious Imagination* (Philadelphia: Fortress Press, 1976) 8.

46. Bouyer, *Liturgical Piety*, 4.

47. ___.

48. ___, 7.

49. Waldemar Trapp, *Vorgeschichte und Ursprung der liturgischen Bewegung* (Regensburg: Stenderhoff, 1940. On the question of the influences that went into the making of the liturgical movement there are various opinions. See, for instance, Boniface Luykx, "The Liturgical Movement and the Enlightenment?" Antiphon 3:1 (1998) 23–25; Ernest Skublics, "The Liturgical Movement—A Succession of Models," *Antiphon* 4:1 (1999) 22–25.

50. See William Lloyd Newell, *The Secular Magi: Marx, Freud, and Nietzsche on Religion* (Landham, MD: University Press of America, 1994).

51. Criticisms of these aspects of liturgical reform by social scientists Victor Turner, David Martin, Mary Douglas, and Kieran Flanagen are summarized in Aidan Nichols, *Looking at the Liturgy: A Critical View of its Contemporary Form* (San Francisco: Ignatius Press, 1996) 49–86.

52. Eamon Duffy, *The Stripping of the Altars: Traditional Religion in England, 1400–1580* (New Haven, CT: Yale University Press, 1992); David Martin, "The Stripping of the Words: Conflict Over the Eucharist in the Episcopal Church," in Sarah Beckwith, ed., Catholicism and *Catholicity: Eucharistic Communities in Historical and Contemporary Perspectives* (Oxford: Blackwell Publishers, 1999) 135–49.

53. Doris Donnelly, "Impediments to Praise in the Worshiping Community," *Worship* 66:1 (January 1992) 39–52.

54. Catherine Pickstock, *After Writing: On the Liturgical Consummation of Philosophy* (Oxford: Blackwell Publishers, 1998), passim.

55. Pieper, *In Tune with the World*, passim.

56. See Karl Rahner, "Secular Life and the Sacraments: A Copernican Revolution," *The Tablet* (London) 6 and 13 March 1971, 236–38, 267–68; "How to Receive a Sacrament and Mean It," *Theology Digest* 19:3 (1971) 227–34; "Considerations on the Active Role of the Person in the Sacramental Event," *Theological Investigations* 14 (New York: Seabury, 1976) 161–84; Piet Fransen, "Sacraments as Celebrations," *The Irish Theological Quarterly* 43:3 (1976) 151–70; Raymond Vaillancourt, *Toward a Renewal of Sacramental Theology* (Collegeville: The Liturgical Press, 1979); George Worgul, "Celebrations: Models for Sacraments," *Chicago Studies* 16:3 (Fall 1977) 309–15.

57. Harvey Cox, *The Feast of Fools: A Theological Essay in Festivity* (Cambridge, MA: Harvard University Press, 1969); Sam Keen, *To a Dancing God* (New York: Harper and Row, 1970). See also David Miller, "The Kingdom of Play: Some Old Theological Light from Recent Literature," *Union Seminary Quarterly Review* 25:3 (Spring 1970) 343–60; Robert Neale, *In Praise of Play* (New York: Harper and Row, 1969).

58. On the early liturgical origin of this term, see Benedicta Droste, "*Celebrare*" *in der römischen Liturgiesprache* (Munich: Hueber Verlag, 1963).

59. Walter Bruggemann, *Israel's Praise: Doxology Against Idolatry and Ideology* (Philadelphia: Fortress Press, 1988) esp. 123ff. This theme is also prominent in Karl Rahner, who describes the ascension, for instance, as "the festival of holy pain" of fear and blessing combined ("The Festival of the Future of the World," in *Theological Investigations, Vol. VII: Further Theories of the Spiritual Life* [New York: Herder and Herder, 1971] 181–85).

60. A convergence of thought on this matter is a marked feature of ecumenical eucharistic theologies. See Laurence Hull Stookey, *Eucharist: Christ's Feast with the Church* (Nashville, TN: Abington Press, 1993); Don E. Saliers, *Worship as Theology: Foretaste of Divine Glory* (Nashville, TN: Abington Press, 1994); Arthur A. Just, Jr., *The Ongoing Feast: Table Fellowship and Eschatology at Emmaus* (Collegeville, MN: Liturgical Press, 1993); Geoffrey Wainwright, *Eucharist and Eschatology* (New York: Oxford University Press, 1981) esp. 1–17, 14–154; Scott Hahn, *The Lamb's Supper: The Mass as Heaven on Earth* (New York: Doubleday, 1999).

61. See the essay by C. Clifford Flanigan titled, "The Apocalypse in the Medieval Liturgy," in Richard K. Emmerson and Bernard McGinn, eds., *The Apocalypse in the Middle Ages* (Ithaca, NY: Cornell University Press, 1992) 333–51.

62. Margaret E. Miles, *Image as Insight: Visual Understanding in Western Christianity and Secular Culture* (Boston: Beacon Press, 1985) esp. 195–225.

63. Timothy Ware, *The Orthodox Church* (Middlesex: Penguin Books, 1964) 277–78.

64. J. Michael Joncas, "Re-reading *Musicam Sacram:* Twenty-Five Years of Development in Roman Rite Liturgical Music," *Worship* 66:3 (May 1992) 220. See also the excellent study (both scholarly and inspiring) by Bryan D. Sprinks, The *Sanctus in the Eucharistic Prayer* (Cambridge: Cambridge University Press, 1991) esp. 11–54, 194–206.

65. Carl Braaten and Robert W. Jenson, eds., *Either/Or: The Gospel and Neopaganism* (Grand Rapids, MI: William B. Eerdmans Publishing Company, 1995).

66. Avery Dulles, *The Catholicity of the Church* (Oxford: Clarendon Press, 1985) 87.

67. Pope John Paul II, *Orientale Lumen* (1995). Text in *Origins* 25:1 (18 May 1995) 7.

68. Quentin Faulkner, *Wiser than Despair: The Evolution of Ideas in the Relationship of Music and the Christian Church* (Westport, CT: Greenwood Press, 1996).

69. In my view, the most theologically sophisticated analysis of liturgical music in the contexts I am describing here is found in the writing of Cardinal Joseph Ratzinger. See, M. Francis Mannion, "The 'Musification' of the Word": Cardinal Joseph Ratzinger's Theology of Liturgical Music," *Josephinum Journal of Theology* 5:2 (Summer/Fall 1998) 47–66.

70. Geoffrey Hayden, *John Tavener: Glimpses of Paradise* (London: Indigo, 1995); See John Tavener, *The Music of Silence: A Composer's Testament,* ed., Brian Keeble (London: Faber and Faber, 1999).

71. Rahner, *Man at Play;* Guardini, The Spirit of the Liturgy, esp. 85–106.

72. Hans Urs Von Balthasar states that for Dionysius all theology is an elaboration of the divine mysteries whose primordial expressions are the liturgical songs of heaven. "The 'hymnic' is therefore for Denys a methodology of theological thinking and speaking. . . . Because God is in all things and above all things, being and knowing can only be a festival and a 'dance,' a continuous 'celebration' of the glory that communicates itself and holds sway in all things and above all things, a 'hymn,' a 'song of praise,' which has its own laws must be followed in everything from its basic conception, the choice of point of view, right down to the least form of expression" (*The Glory of the Lord* [San Francisco: Ignatius, 1984]) vol. 2, 160, 172; see also Seely J. Beggiani, "Theology at the Service of Mysticism: Method in Psuedo-Dionysius," *Theological Studies* 57:2 (June 1996), 201–23.

73. Hippolytus, *Homiliae in Pascha* 6, PG 59, 744 df.; translation from Rahner, *Man at Play,* 86.

74. Daniel B. Stevick, "Toward a Phenomenology of Praise," in Malcom C. Burson, ed., *Worship Points the Way: A Celebration of the Life and Work of Massey Hamilton Shepherd, Jr.* (New York: Seabury Press, 1981) 158–59.

75. John Bossy, "The Mass as a Social Institution: 1200–1700," *Past and Present: A Journal of Historical Studies* 100 (August, 1983) 29–61.

76. Though not concerned with Christian liturgy, the notion of divine "phenitude" is explored in an impressive manner in Arthur A. Lovejoy, *The Great Chain of Being: A Study of the History of an Idea* (Cambridge, MA: Harvard University Press, 1964) esp. 99–143.

Acknowledgments

Acknowledgment is gratefully made to these publishers for granting permission to use the following:

"The Masterworks of God." *The Priest* 55:1 (January 1999) 30–40. Copyright © 1999 *Our Sunday Visitor*. Reprinted with permission.

"Penance and Reconciliation: A Systemic Analysis" was first published in *Worship* 60 (1986) 98–118. Copyright © 1986 M. Francis Mannion. Reprinted with permission.

"Stipends and Eucharistic Praxis" was first published in *Living Bread, Saving Cup: Readings on the Eucharist*, ed. Kevin Seasoltz (Collegeville, MN: Liturgical Press, 1982). Reprinted with permission.

"Catholic Worship and the Dynamics of Congregationalism" was first published in *Chicago Studies* 33 (1994:1) 57–66. Reprinted with permission. Copyright © 1994 Civitas Dei Foundation.

"Liturgy and the Present Crisis of Culture" was first published in *Worship* 62 (1988) 98–123, by The Liturgical Press. Copyright © 1988 M. Francis Mannion. Reprinted with permission.

"Sunday in Modern America: A Cultural Perspective" was first published in *Chicago Studies* 20 (1990) 224–35. Copyright © 1990 Civitas Dei Foundation.

"Paradigms in American Catholic Church Music" was first published in *Worship* 70 (1996) 101–28. Copyright © 1996 M. Francis Mannion. Reprinted with permission.

"Toward a New Era in Liturgical Architecture" was first published in *Liturgical Ministry* 6 (Fall 1997) 160–72. Copyright © 1997 by M. Francis Mannion. Reprinted with permission.

"The 'Musification' of the Word: Cardinal Ratzinger's Theology of Liturgical Music" was first published in *Josephinum Journal of Theology* 5:2 (Summer/Fall 1998) 47–66. Reprinted with permission.

From "The Catholicity of the Liturgy: Shaping a New Agenda," in Stratford Caldecott, ed. *Beyond the Prosaic: Rewriting the Liturgical Movement*. Edinburgh: T&T Clark, 1998. Copyright © 1998 and reprinted by permission of The Continuum Publishing Group.

"Rejoice, Heavenly Powers! The Renewal of Liturgical Doxology" was first published in *Pro Ecclesia* Vol. 12, No. 1 (Winter 2003). Reprinted with permission of the publisher.